Rethinking
Social
Welfare

RETHINKING SOCIAL WELFARE

why care for the stranger?

Robert Morris

With the assistance of Sara M. Morris

Longman
New York & London

The Author and the Publisher gratefully acknowledge permission to reprint the following:

Excerpt from "The New Despotism" by Robert Nisbet reprinted from *Commentary,* June 1975, by permission; all rights reserved.

Excerpt from essay by A. Kazin reprinted from *The New York Review of Books.* Copyright © 1981 NYREV, Inc.

Rethinking Social Welfare. Why Care for the Stranger?

Copyright © 1986 by Longman Inc.

Senior Editor: David J. Estrin
Production Editor: Pamela Nelson
Text Design: Gloria Moyer
Production Supervisor: Eduardo Castillo

Library of Congress Cataloging in Publication Data

Morris, Robert, 1910–
    Rethinking social welfare.

    Bibliography: p.
    Includes index.
    1. Public welfare—History.   2. Public welfare—
United States—History.   I. Morris, Sara M.
II. Title.
HV16.M82   1985   361'.9   85-5203
ISBN 0-582-28589-5 (pbk)

Printing 9 8 7 6 5 4 3 2   Year: 94 93 92 91 90 89 88 87 86

CONTENTS

PREFACE

Welfare is a time present, action-oriented expression of human relationships. It is not often that those engaged in helping the less fortunate stop to think about how ideas of caring for others came to take the shape they now have. An interest in this past was ignited by the work of Karl De-Schweinitz who, in his later years, began to assemble the opinions of spokespeople for the poor in ancient times. My interest was antiquarian at first, but in the 1970s it was already apparent that a change in public and political opinion was beginning to surface. This change was expressed in serious questioning about the scope of government responsibility for individual lives but it also opened up new questioning about the balance between generosity to others and about self-regard. This shift began to take on a political expression as other moral and religious issues were argued over in election campaigns. Old liberal ideas about reason, compromise, negotiation and pragmatism came under attack as ideological fervor became more intense. At times during the 1970s and 1980s it appeared that the liberal center was no longer certain of itself and was at risk of disintegrating. Values became as important as technology and practicality. Social welfare issues became identified with this liberal center. As a result, my interest in the past was joined with concern about contemporary values and about the direction which history in the making was taking. The result has been this study, which tries to combine a new look at the long history of ideas about caring for others in Western society with the values that underly today's government responsibility for welfare to fit the temper of the times.

Many efforts to understand the dynamics of modern welfare systems—of the welfare state—concentrate on contemporary events, on the economic and political tides within which current decisions are made (e.g., whether or not to develop a collective effort to remedy any social difficulty). The history of welfare efforts in the Western world suggests that something less transient is also at work, that there exist some deep-rooted beliefs that condition any peoples', any nation's, effort to do justice to the less fortunate, or if not justice, at least to ameliorate the most cruel aspects of the human condition.

The discovery of this substratum, for me, began with the work of Karl DeSchweinitz, who late in his life began to elaborate on the early English Poor Laws by examining the earlier antecedents, especially early Christian

vii

and early Middle Eastern origins. His unfinished manuscript was full of evocative and moving quotations from many spokespeople for the poor over the millenia. In fact, DeSchweinitz's work was originally entitled "Who Speaks for the Poor?" During the early 1950s, those who heard DeSchweinitz speak were moved by hopefulness; in that American era governmental action to realize the hopes of those early advocates was more widely accepted than is true today. I have drawn heavily on the quotations and sources he used, especially in Chapters 6–9.

It is not necessary to assert that the past gives explicit guides to the future. It is only necessary to note that understanding the present is in part a function of understanding how the present came to be, which means understanding its past. This understanding at least can inform the choices to be made as a nation moves into its future.

Such a foundation for social welfare thinking or for professional education has not yet been widely accepted. Social welfare has become a major consideration in modern society, measured by dollars spent, manpower employed, and consequences. However, it is the only major sector of modern society lacking a means with which to understand its own history—in contrast with other sectors of manufacture, of science and technology, of social trends, of politics and of economics, each of which is the subject of intensive historical study and analysis. Some of this gap in the welfare armamentarium is due to the action-oriented base for most welfare activity. There exists a large pool of persons employed by many thousands of social welfare organizations, all struggling to deal with gritty troubles in the daily lives of many people, troubles that the more favored parts of the population do not want to have to think about.

This volume is by no means a definitive history of the ideas of social welfare—of caring for others or of caring for the stranger. It is at best a first effort (by someone who is not a professional historian) to look at the long sweep of ideas about caring for others that have evolved and changed in the history of the Middle Eastern and Western worlds. There have been sporadic efforts in this direction, such as C. F. Loch's *Charity and Social Life* in the late nineteenth century. There have, by contrast, been penetrating studies of the evolution of ideas in specific nation-states, such as the works of Rimlinger, DeSchweinitz, Mencher, Wilensky, Leiby and Lubov. Most of these, however, have dealt with the seventeenth to nineteenth centuries. It was Sara Morris's discovery of Hand's *Charities and Social Aid in Greece and Rome* which opened up for me the rich literature about the classical and medieval periods, and led me back into ancient Hebrew and Egyptian and forward to Medieval and Renaissance sources. The dilemmas that modern America confronts in its welfare programming have their distinct echoes in the efforts of many earlier cultures to find solutions to similar dilemmas. Throughout these recurring efforts, a few concepts and attitudes about caring for others emerged and were elaborated on; they constitute a heritage of values that seem to still influence the thinking of ordinary citizens and the actions of policy makers. These values are a significant part of the liberal tradition. Failure to understand this grounding in thought and emotion seems to lead us into misjudgments about how to proceed today if a centrist position is to be maintained in a world of increasingly doctrinaire extremes. Today's world is not that of the past, but problems of the disadvantaged are not all that different. Only the solutions could conceivably be different, and therein lies the value of knowing the distant, as well as the recent, past.

Whatever the practical utility of this effort will be, I hope that it will reawaken an interest in developing a modest institutional base for historical and analytic effort as a stable and central part of the American welfare system, whatever shape it may take in the future. Past efforts in this direction have not been noticeably successful. Two schools have each maintained an historian as faculty member (James Leiby and Roy Lubov) to study the history of social work. An effort in the 1950s to stimulate professional historians to give more attention to social welfare bore fruit, at least indirectly, in the work of academics like Clark Chambers and David Rothman. Several practicing professionals in welfare, such as Paul Schreiber and Ralph Pumphrey, have maintained avocational activities in welfare history.

Analytic research and "thinking" centers have sprung up, but most are unstable, ill funded and present-time oriented. The Social Welfare History Study Group maintained a loose network of interested parties over many years, but without much institutional or financial support that I am aware of. These initiatives emerged in more affluent times and it may be asking a great deal that more be considered when so much of welfare thinking is under attack. But again, past history suggests that it is in just such times of adversity that much of the study of history has taken place.

The completion of this volume was made possible by many, many colleagues and to list some of them risks overlooking others, but a few must be mentioned. Sara Morris, first of all, for spotting and uncovering valuable written sources and for steady encouragement and criticism. Several faculty members at Brandeis University read historical chapters covering their areas of special competence. Professors Patricia Johnston, Classics; David Wong, Philosophy; David Fischer, William Kapelle and Robert Schneider, all History; Leon Jick, Near Eastern and Judaic Studies; and Rabbi Albert Axelrad. Dr. Krister Stendhal, then of the Theological School at Harvard, was especially helpful and encouraging, as was Clark Chambers at the University of Minnesota. I am especially grateful to Beatrice Saunders and Arnold Gurin who read and provided criticism for the entire manuscript. Their suggestions were invaluable in helping to focus and sharpen the final product. They were a continuous source of encouragement. Appreciation for the original stimulation due Dr. Karl DeSchweinitz and Elizabeth DeSchweinitz has already been made. The Samuel and Lois Silberman Fund contributed generously to help meet the costs of bibliographic search and manuscript preparation. Celia Lees-Low transcribed early drafts with care and intelligence. Of course, the errors of interpretation or fact that are bound to appear are mine alone. Finally, I would express added thanks to the editors at Longman who saw value in the manuscript. The social welfare archives at the University of Minnesota, initiated by Professor Clark Chambers, continues to be a major resource. It holds the DeSchweinitz papers, and a very large collection of other documents bearing on the history of social welfare in America. Its holdings are efficiently organized, and its curator and staff go out of their way to be helpful. The historical section of this volume could not have been completed without their assistance.

Robert Morris
Kirstein Professor of
Social Planning Emeritus
Brandeis University
Waltham, Mass.

Thou shalt not harden thy heart nor shut thy hand from thy needy brother, but thou shalt surely open thy hand unto him . . . sufficient for his need in that which he wanteth.

Deuteronomy 15:7–8

It is the season of kindness, not strict inquiry, of mercy not calculation.

St. John Chrysostom

Two nations between whom there is no discourse and no sympathy . . . the rich and the poor.

Disraeli

PART

I

AMERICAN WELFARE in the 1980s

CARING FOR THE STRANGER

STRANGER

A Major Issue for the Late Twentieth Century

The moral test of a government is how it treats those who are in the dawn of life, the children; those who are in the twilight of life, the elderly; and those who are in the shadow of life, the sick, the needy, and the handicapped.

HUBERT HUMPHREY

It has become commonplace to speak to the great changes which have taken place in American society during the twentieth century, especially since 1940: massive technical and scientific achievement; changed attitudes and behaviors concerning family life, sexual behavior, the role of women; a fast shifting economy in which affluence and depression alternate; changes in the geographic and racial makeup of the population. During these changes many have held to the belief that the future will be better, that individual effort will be rewarded and that the American political system will remain stable.

This American optimism has led citizens to consider the responsibility of government for social welfare as a minor irritation while they go about more serious business. Only occasionally has a great crisis forced their attention to welfare obligations. The Great Depression of the 1930s shook these optimistic beliefs. They were reinstated by the victory in World War II and again eroded by the Recession because of inflation and rising unemployment in the 1970s and 1980s.

The welfare state evolved in the midst of these changes. In the U. S. it took a distinctive shape: it was fueled and maintained by the demands of many interest groups and not by any deeply held sense of social obligation toward the less favored, the poor and the underprivileged. Ronald Reagan's election to office in 1980 brought to prominence again the ques-

3

tions: What is the obligation the more affluent have to the less fortunate? What is the proper role of government in realizing any collective objective? The election of 1980 was less a sharp break with the past than a culmination of a decade-long decline in confidence about social programs. This changed attitude about social welfare may, at first glance, seem minor compared with other developments in politics, economics, science and foreign affairs. However, this attitude when examined more closely represents a change of view about the world the American people want to create for themselves. Welfare becomes a proxy term for values, a lightning rod for differing views about the obligations we owe each other, the virtues of selfishness, the limits of obligation, and political behaviors, which will either unify or further divide a multiethnic population. Though limited in its singularity, social welfare provides a means of addressing certain questions related to human value, and their expression in our society.

The elections of 1980 and 1984 appeared, on the surface, to support an administration whose policies gave priority to a reduction in government and a simultaneous increase in military expenditure. Welfare expenditures have been reduced in relative and absolute terms but the total of federal expenditure has not been reduced—only its rate of growth has been slowed. After twenty-five years in which welfare income transfer payments were used to reduce the proportion of the population living in poverty (from 22 percent in 1959) the numbers began to rise again (from a low of 11 percent to over 15 percent in 1984). A conflict has been joined between the wants or needs of various sectors of society and the willingness of all parties to pay the costs.

In this context discussion about social welfare is more than an argument for or against specific programs, for or against something vaguely identified as the welfare state. The discussion reveals views about the nature of government and of national culture.

The present inquiry will try to answer the question: In a society where 85 percent of the workforce is employed and 85 percent of the population is reasonably secure in its private life, what obligation is owed to the remaining poor 15 percent? In such a society most members rely on their jobs for income, most are at least modestly comfortable in economic terms. Despite persisting anxieties, most citizens are sufficiently comfortable and secure (or expect to become so) to concentrate on satisfying their individual wants and desires; they expect to improve their situations as a matter of course. Because of the belief that the basic economic system will not collapse, many seem to be unaware of the quite different circumstances out of which emerged most of our thinking about social welfare. Those past conditions involved 30 percent of the population who were impoverished in the 1930s; 50–75 percent of the population were poor or dependent on the good will of others in much of the nineteenth century and in the sixteenth century; and 90 percent were dependent on others in some fashion in ancient times.

Does this favorable trend mean that collective obligation to care is now less important? In fact, these issues have greater urgency as a new technical era poses a threat of major economic transformation and consequent change in how we live. Rising unemployment is a probable consequence of great technological and economic change on a worldwide scale. The immediate future may possibly be compared with that of the fifteenth and sixteenth centuries when the emergence of commercial capitalism in Europe led to vast changes in society and to the introduction of Poor Law concepts which have influenced welfare thinking ever since; or to the late nineteenth century when America industrialized. Now, as then, citizens will have to make choices despite pressure to reduce the role of the government.

This formulation should not be oversimplified. For decades American policy has been concerned mainly with economic development, physical infrastructure (roads, water, fire and police protection) and social protection. After World War II the demands of military preparation assumed an equal position in official and popular thinking, largely as a result of the nation's full engagement in world affairs. Popular electoral support is not stable, but for the foreseeable future these four areas for government effort will remain dominant, and among them, social welfare is by no means the most popular in the public view. Public opinion is sharply divided about what constitutes an appropriate military or defense stance for the nation to take, but defense has become a major, not a minor, factor in public thinking because enough citizen groups believe that international political and economic developments require it.

This volume has borrowed the concept of "the stranger" as a way of approaching the subject. The word has both ancient roots and contemporary application. Concern for the condition of the stranger arose very early in both western Judeo-Christian and in Greco-Roman tradition. Today, the recipients of help are likely to be stranger to those who are helping them. The circuitousness of helping by taxation in our urban world makes the helper a stranger to the one being helped. The ancient tradition which lies at the base of any effort to deal with any social problem will influence what we decide to do today when almost all are "strangers in our midst."

Our society is once again questioning how and in what way government should meet human needs. Since the founding of the nation, so vigorous even violent has been the recurring debate about governmental programs that America has long been known as the "reluctant welfare state." The dynamics of urban and industrial life forced our society to adopt a wide range of tax supported programs to alleviate the human disasters which many citizens faced when the more intimate personal

community gave way to large depersonalized and mobile urban conglomerates. More recently this process began to even out the most extreme
disparities in life condition as the gross national product grew along with
an uneven distribution of the benefits of industrialization.

American social programs evolved ad hoc without attention to that
long prior history of social programs in Europe and in the Middle East
and without a clear philosophical or value base understood by all. The
new world frontier made previous history irrelevant. Ad hoc, program-
matic, short-term solutions were considered adequate for each problem
that arose. Beliefs about American Exceptionalism explain much of the
indifference to the history in Europe and the Middle East. However, that
earlier history involved central concepts about the state as a mechanism
in human organization. The social programs captured by the phrase "the
welfare state" are only the accumulated choices sifted out of millennial
struggles with vexing questions about the nature of man's relation to
man.

This work will first explore and outline the evolution of rationales
and justifications for men and women helping each other by informal or
by public/collective ways. If citizens and governments are to find some
reasonable and balanced basis for deciding upon the nature of help given
to those in trouble, then this search into the past is essential to understanding the roots of choice making.

However, more is intended than merely recapturing the past. The
past accounts for a reservoir of popular beliefs which the public draws
upon today when it discusses welfare issues. We will review citizens'
current opinions of welfare as expressed in opinion polls and surveys.
Then the disillusionment of the 1970s and 1980s will be explored with the
factors that have drained support for public activity and led to the crumbling national consensus. Rationales for social programs will be checked
as these emerge in legislative history. Finally, current philosophical and
ethical analysis of public obligation and responsibility will be summarized. History, opinion polls, legislative rationales and philosophical analysis will be drawn together to frame an agenda for welfare advocates
suitable for the last decades of the twentieth century.

SIGNIFICANCE OF WELFARE PROGRAMS IN CURRENT POLITICAL/ECONOMIC DEBATE

Answers to the future of social programs cannot be found in narrow
technical or segmented arguments alone. Social welfare programs are
now implicated in many of the major dilemmas which beset late twentieth century industrialized nations. Welfare, despite its erratic evolution, is a major institution in modern society as well as in government. It

represented 18–20 percent of the gross national product (GNP), directly touches the lives of millions of citizens in all economic classes, and is carried out through thousands of organizations and agencies. It is no longer a peripheral and part-time avocation. Economic, political, psychological and sociocultural concerns invoke welfare solutions and welfare depends on ethical choices made in many other arenas of social life. A broader than usual search for a welfare framework is justified.

The importance of American welfare emerged with the late nineteenth and early twentieth century efforts to engage the national government in relief of major social difficulties. This effort was sufficiently persuasive that both the Democratic party and the progressive wing of the Republican party (the Bull Moose party of Theodore Roosevelt) debated national responsibility in presidential campaigns. The second great step forward occurred in the middle 1930s during the Depression when, after a vigorous national debate, federal responsibility for social needs was finally institutionalized through enactment of the comprehensive Social Security Act of 1935. Following this was a period of approximately 35 years when the range and scope of national responsibility grew exponentially in numbers of programs, numbers of problems addressed, and public expenditure. This period was also characterized by a great increase in national wealth and influence in the world. Beginning in 1970, this great wave of growth slowed and resistance to further growth began to emerge. In this 35-year span an entire generation grew up accustomed to a strong, if uneven, federal presence to deal with social needs. The resistance to this reached a new peak in the election of a Republican administration in 1980 committed to not only a slowing down in growth, but an absolute reversal in the scale of national responsibility for social needs.

The new generation shift shocked those who had come to rely on the preceding welfare pattern, and it exposed the extent to which welfare is embedded in national efforts to accommodate other basic tensions in the American twentieth century. Some of these are summarized below.

Changed Relationships among Income Groups

Much of man's history has consisted of developing ways for people to live together in reasonable security and peace with the freedom to lead their individual lives. These efforts, experiments in a way, have usually been disrupted by violent conflicts between groups, classes and nations, for reasons either of need (exhaustion of resources for food) or greed or ambition. But all such efforts have oscillated between two polar patterns: strict hierarchy, with some usually small classes dominating a usually large and subordinate group, or; relative equality among members of a group or nation state. Whatever the form, each structure has had to define the relationships between its various groups, the rights of each, the obligations each holds to the rest, and access to material resources.

The distribution of power as well as the conditions under which all classes live, determine the stability of each state. Large numbers of deprived and disaffected created instability which was reversed either by force or by some redistribution of goods. In the nineteenth and twentieth centuries this effort to find national, if not worldwide stability, has been expressed in the intellectual and economic confrontation between two main systems of thought—socialism in its various forms and capitalist free enterprise in its equally various forms. Widespread distress and alienation for many persons who demanded some relief accompanied the concentration and elaboration of material power which industrialization made possible. The planned economies of Eastern Europe forcibly redistributed control of economic institutions from one class to another. In capitalist countries this redistribution was expressed in growing social and welfare programs. Through them the state became responsible for directing some national resources to the less advantaged and to other economic interests alike. However, the economic institutions and basic economic decisions remained in private hands.

In this evolution, the welfare state has been one response of commercial and industrial capitalism to social pressures. The welfare state became a third way for groups to organize their relationships with each other, lying between the unfettered class structures of private economic power on one hand and of wholly state controlled economic power on the other. A central characteristic of this third way is the state-planned redistribution of only a part of private economic resources to even out some disparities between all classes and to reduce extreme distress for the least advantaged part of the population. Welfare programs become part of widening concepts of intellectual and economic liberalism which value freedom for all as much as private or state power.

This volume concentrates on the concepts and beliefs which have determined the evolution of social welfare activity which seeks a resolution of the ancient conflict between personal freedom and collective responsibility.

Economic Aspects of Welfare Growth

Social welfare is now a major governmental obligation, expressed in tax dollar expenditure. As a significant factor in the economy, social welfare programs emerged much later in the U.S. than in other western industrial countries and grew rapidly in a short time. Between the enactment of the Social Security Act in 1935 and 1980, public social expenditures not only grew to nearly 20 percent of the gross national product but represented nearly half of all federal government expenditures.

At the same time two other developments occurred. Indirect tax support for upper, middle, and lower-middle-income populations, not the very poor, increased; income tax deductions were generously allowed for home purchase, for interest on loans for consumer purchases, which reduced public revenues. Major industries, especially those with strong labor unions, also began to offer welfare benefits as supplements to wages which average as much as one-third of the total wage bill but which benefit a relatively small part of the population working in major and well-organized industries.

As a result of these and other developments, the earlier popular concepts about welfare were transformed. The wider scope of the welfare enterprise makes it a major factor in the national economy. The beneficiary clientele now includes much of the middle-income as well as the poor population, but through separate tax mechanisms which obscure the distribution of national income and expenditure. The proportion of social expenditures earmarked for the poor declined during the 1970s while the proportion going for non-poor populations increased (Gilbert, 1983). At the same time, auspices became diversified and, while government expenditures dominate the scene, industry and other proprietary and non-profit voluntary groups are major welfare partners. Also the purposes of social programs came to encompass improvement in the quality of life for all as well as relief from serious distress or disability.

Such rapid changes in the welfare infrastructure conflicted as we shall see with conventional and long accepted popular views about the place of welfare in public affairs. This conflict remains part of the reason for reconsidering welfare policies.

Alienation in the Industrial World

For at least 3,000 years men have struggled in different ways to make their relationship with each other more human. The rights and obligations which sum up the claims which human beings have on or between each other have evolved within the framework of a nuclear or extended family, the clan, the tribe, the village, the city-state and finally that of the national state. We have viewed our present arrangements as the result of long and steady improvement. In the western industrial world, the concept of a welfare state has been accepted as a satisfactory way to define the obligations which men and women have for each other—a way to bind all citizens into one state—a way which can be marginally improved without fundamentally revising class relationships.

Mass Society Is Past Testing Beliefs

Individuals and families in the twentieth century more and more live out their private lives in a world shaped by large mass organizations and decisions made in more and more centralized public institutions—actions by national or state government, or by city governments of large metropolitan areas, where it is difficult to trace an individual's influence over events affecting his or her life. At the same time, the institutions of economic activity, through which most people earn their living, are also increasingly large conglomerates; or they are small economic enterprises whose economic viability is determined by far distant corporate or financial institutions.

The complex network of national and international ties binds large and small organizations together in quite uneven economic relationships. The result has been a great increase in the well-being of many citizens, but a measurable proportion of citizens do not make their way in the new complexities and fall to the bottom of or outside the system. In civic life, well-to-do citizens are also alienated from political processes as indicated by the falling proportion of citizens who bother to vote. As will be discussed in Chapter 3, the well-to-do are also divided from each other as they turn to their private and individual interests, giving less attention to community or collective interests.

Welfare reflects the growing alienation of the minority of the population from the majority, as seen in dependency, mental illness, crime, and generally antisocial activity. Welfare is intended to deal with such human problems. Whether it does so at all, or does it well or poorly, depends on whether voters perceive alienation as caused by welfare or see social programs as collective means for reducing alienation which results from social disequilibrium.

This general phenomenon is also connected with persisting dilemmas of race. In the American public perception, it is not yet settled whether the disadvantaged position of several racial and ethnic groups is due to their own shortcomings or to flaws in social arrangements which help them out of mainstream economic and social life.

Racial factors have made more complex and subtle the welding of a unified national society. In the U.S., the major concentration of beneficiaries of social programs is in the large cities (the poorest) or in the suburbs (the middle class). The former include, disproportionately, racial minorities, recent immigrants, the very old and single women or single parent families. Work is either skilled, or unskilled, at near poverty level wages. The ratio of jobs to willing workers seems to have been declining even though the total number of jobs has increased. The number of workers has risen rapidly—women as well as men, and teenagers and the elderly compete in the job pool, and racial prejudices complicate the competition in unfair ways.

In the city centers, where the poor tend to cluster, there are four elements which add up to conditions which degrade such communities and their habitants:

1. Too many of these residents, because of race or poor education, are excluded from the work that is the productive life of the larger community.
2. There is an absence of ordering, reliable and responsive institutions. In the urban ghettos, hospitals disappear, schools are neglected relative to other schools, housing is derelict since incomes are low; sanitation, parks, and recreation facilities are kept at a low standard so that there is little to surround the population with morale-building environments and institutions.
3. The poor usually lack direct access to the political process where decisions affecting them are made.
4. The larger community does not know what to make of deviant and unfamiliar cultures, be they Hispanic, Rastafarian, Carribean, or Asian. Drug cultures which the suburbs tolerate more or less are viewed quite differently in the inner city.

For each of these factors, the question recurs: Is society responsible or are the individuals?

The result is the creation, or the maintenance of what can be called an underclass in American society, many of whose numbers are of minority groups. If this underclass represents some 10 to 15 percent of the population (at least in the largest urban complexes), and if nearly half of all citizens are so removed from the political process as not to vote, then how cohesive can the national society be? Historically, one of the major strengths of any society has been in the way its citizens are bound in some form of social solidarity. This is expressed in a sharing of some minimum values and commitment to political, economic and social structures within which they all live. If this social cohesion begins to unravel, internal divisiveness inevitably undermines national strength and in time the society is so driven by conflict or anomie that it risks decay (Spence, 1981).

These polarizing tendencies separate classes from each other rather than binding them together. "We" who give help through taxes or philanthropy not only do not know, but never even see, the people, "the strangers" to be helped. We cannot know or evaluate them as humans. Those who are now taxed to pay for "helping the strangers" do not see the countless thousands they help and cannot know or understand them. This separation between helper and helped contributed to the crumbling political consensus, speeded by worldwide economic recession. Not only the U.S. but England, Scandinavia and other western states are caught in the shift.

It is in this light that the debate over welfare can no longer be limited to disruption of a particular budget or program. Concluding the debate is delayed by the nature of the alienation issues raised, issues as complex as the nature of man and of human society. The nature of social need in contemporary society has not only changed but has done so faster than our ability to adapt our human response to these changes. The rapid and easy mobility of populations with adequate income has undermined those local social institutions which depend upon stable leadership and following. Those without means are usually left behind in economically depressed areas as those with means move to more attractive areas. At the same time, television has revolutionized the level of expectations for all economic classes. The well-to-do expect to have ready access to the wonders of the material world which are everywhere presented visually. The presentations force the less favored to ask, "Why am I out of that world not entitled to at least some of those goods?" which means "Why can't I get a job which will assure me income to buy them?"

The practical and ethical dilemmas were noted as early as 1920:

> Ethics are not clearly defined. Our estimate of the effect of environment and social conditions have shifted faster than our methods of administering charity. We are all obliged to act in circles of habit based on convictions no longer held. (Addams, 1902, p. 14)

The Changed Economic Profile of an Affluent Society

For those concerned with social programs, or with welfare, the shifting socioeconomic profile of American society introduces a new perspective in world history. Traditional societies have had a pyramidal shape with a relatively few members having substantial means. The broad base consisted of the bulk of the population with limited means and resources. By contrast, the U.S. profile has, in recent decades, taken on a pear-shaped form, with the same small numbers at the top with a large proportion of the base moving up to a middle or lower-middle socioeconomic position. This bulge in the relative size of the middle class, or lower-middle class suggests that for the first time those in most constrained circumstances constitute a relatively small minority of the total population, about 15 percent. The relative well-being of those above the bottom may be insecure, but this very insecurity seems to express itself in a fierce determination to maintain this relative position as against those who are worse off, perhaps out of a fear of dropping back. Its members still expect to improve their lot. This expanded middle class nourishes a conviction that its well-being is a result of individual energy, wisdom and hard work, when in fact the results were due as much to national economic policies and the accidents of living in a vast continent with the vast natural resources to be exploited and developed.

Such attitudes fail to take into account the major change which has overtaken the American economy—the steady growth over twenty years' time of an increasingly long-term unemployed population. The old conviction that there is work for everyone, except for short periods of depression has not yet come to terms with the reality of modern technology and economics which makes the production of so much consumer goods possible with a reduced labor force. New jobs created by new industry do not replace the jobs lost in the old heavy industries. Youth entry into the labor force is delayed more and more, as evidenced by the nearly half of all college age youth who at least enter college. The popularly acceptable level of unemployment was once 3–4 percent, but in 1983 the figure had risen to 7–8 percent. Among minority youth, and especially young mothers with small children, the rate of unemployment runs as high as 50–75 percent and continues for some years for any individual. At the same time older workers displaced by modern technology and factory systems are unable to find replacement work due to age and educational limitations inherent in the education of an earlier generation. The cumulative effect of such trends is to leave a minority of working age adults without full-time work opportunity for long periods of time in an urban world where physical survival depends on earned income. Although the numbers are proportionately small, they pose an unprecedented challenge to deeply ingrained beliefs about helping the able-bodied adult.

It is not yet entirely clear whether the large middle population will act as generously and charitably towards those who have less as did earlier elites who had to fear the reactions of a much larger deprived population. When 80 percent or more of a population is relatively well provided for, it is easier to be generous to others less fortunate when the personal wealth is increasing. But when personal incomes are static or declining, will they be as ready to share what they have so recently acquired? This may become more aggravated as the electronic revolution takes hold. There are indications that the proportion of skilled jobs at high pay may not increase as rapidly as the proportion of semi-skilled or service jobs at low pay. The resulting de-skilling of work can threaten the middle class hopes for its own future. The answer to this question may prove to be the acid test of what the future holds for social programs and for further redistribution of income and the means for well-being.

The Conditions of an Open Labor Market

A basic shift in social and local mores has also revolutionized the labor market and all community life. Women with working husbands also work and their children need new provision. Easy divorce, the increase of women over men, anonymity and easy mobility produce multiple new forms of family life. The single parent family is now commonplace. But where the one parent is a woman, her earnings are uniformly only two-thirds that of similarly skilled men.

Concepts of justice and fairness for minorities have changed. The sacrifices all races made in World War II led to opportunity for higher education for minorities through Veterans' educational benefits. New interpretations of the constitutional provision for equal protection of the law have begun, but only begun, to bring all minorities into the mainstream of society. These interpretations include equalizing rights to work, education, income, etc. The steady inflow of new immigrants, mainly Hispanic, and more recently South East Asian, has increased the size of this minority population who can claim those broadened rights, either for higher wages or for better social protection.

All this adds up to a complex of stresses and strains for which our concept of social provision of welfare has been ill prepared.

Promises and Frustrations of Scientific Optimism

The last quarter of the twentieth century is also fast becoming one of ambiguity and uncertainty for the industrialized western states. Whatever the dangers, hazards and fears of the past two hundred years, they were offset by a strong foundation of confidence that the world can be made better and that the conditions for mankind can and will be improved, however slow and erratic that improvement may be. Intellectual imagination burst the constraints of many static social institutions. Ideas about freedom elevated confidence in the almost unbounded potential for individual creativity. Science and technology promised abundance and even more freedom while industrial methods have created ages of abundance of material goods. If one's horizons are limited to the western industrial nations, many of these promises have been fulfilled for a majority. Certainly the material level of existence for most people has been increased, at least as measured by goods and leisure. There are few remaining constraints on the expression of individual desires. Individuals are free to worship any or no deity, to follow almost any ethic as long as others are not too injured and to follow varied careers. Social and political institutions have proliferated, but few of them make burdensome demands on citizens, other than the one of taxation.

Uncertainties and dangers of war, economic depression, personal violence, loneliness and alienation have until recently been viewed as temporary relapses on an improving path to the future. Setbacks have usually been seen as due to the mistakes of some national leaders or parties that can be avoided next time. They are viewed as problems to be overcome in the same way technical and scientific tools are improved. But this optimism has been increasingly tempered with concern and doubts. One price paid for such improvements is social and economic disruption of old ways of thinking and living. The disruption may last only a generation while new social and economic patterns settle down, but that transitional generation pays a price in human suffering if the changes are rapid and continuous confidence in social order is challenged (Kuznets, 1966; Myrdal, 1962).

Eroding Suspicion about Government

Government and its bureaucracies have played a key role in the belief in growth and progress. But, doubts have increased about the scope of government as it affects individual lives. On one hand citizens depend on government policies in taxation, and commerce to underpin much of private economic activity. Whenever needs emerge which are not well met by private entrepreneurism, the government also acts to provide road construction, water supplies, schools for training workers, police and fire protection for congested urban life, financial incentives for economic development, e.g.: land grants to induce railroads to spread to underdeveloped areas, bailouts for failing industry, education for doctors and social workers, administration of income supports, housing and rehabilitation of the disabled. Most important, for the purposes of this volume, whenever human difficulties arise out of private economic, social, scientific and technical change, government has acted—at least since the middle 1930s. So much so has this become the pattern of the past, that hardly any area of human welfare is free of some governmental intervention, regulation or aid.

At the same time, citizens question the scope or competence of government in daily discussion and in political debates. Underneath the optimism of hope, not much is expected of government, or government is turned to with increasing doubts. Less than half of Americans think that their government can be trusted all or most of the time according to a *New York Times*/CBS poll conducted in 1984 (*New York Times*). Only 40 percent believe that government is run for the benefit of all the people while 49 percent believe that it is "run by a few big interests looking out for themselves."

Cynicism about one agency can lead to a belief that all public agencies are incompetent, that government cannot do well under any circumstances. This in turn produces a lack of confidence in public collective action, which is replaced by a search for some strong authority figure who will "put things right" by force, or reliance on more private organization. Concepts of democratic government are revised.

If government is too big, or too invasive of privacy (through regulation or taxation) or too inefficient or corrupt, then how or why do we entrust even police, fire and sanitation services, or even defense, to government? These questions have already been answered in unexpected ways. In many jurisdictions sanitation is turned over to private companies. As to police, there are already more privately employed police than public police. Basically, the issues appear the same for welfare as they do for sanitation and police. How much responsibility should be assigned to the federal government, and how should it be discharged? If the government only collects taxes and pays private parties to give services, what justifies the tax collection? How much control is suitable over private actions? If it is a belief that equity requires that all be equally served regardless of ability to pay, how far can we press the concept of equity?

What distinguishes welfare from the rest of government are the assumptions about people's obligation to each other. But people often act, privately on selfish terms. What do *I* get out of police or fire protection or support of commerce and industry? In this light, government can be seen as a huge money machine which scoops up money and redistributes it to various groups according to some criterion, usually influence. Each member of society tries to get back as much as possible out of the collective pool.

If welfare is viewed in this light then the question arises about the criteria by which the poor should be given access to that common pool, along with sanitation, farm producers, defense, etc. But welfare is not treated solely in monetary terms, even though it too has become big business, much like wheat, auto, tank and computer production. There *is* a major difference—the relation between investment and the product produced. For welfare, the outcome is made up of human beings, not material things. The "product" is a productive worker, or a law-abiding citizen, or a healthy adult, or a loving parent. And the link between the organization of welfare and the final product cannot easily be traced. Does anything differentiate government's role from that of business or charity?

THE AMERICAN WELFARE STATE: WHAT KIND IS IT?

Social programs are one major instrument which a nation can use to confront the larger problems of social change. Before developing the main theme of this volume, it is useful to clarify what the social program complex in America looks like. Welfare programs usually are taken to mean the sum of those efforts by governments and other organizations to relieve the poverty of distress of a people who are more or less helpless, that is, unable to meet their basic needs by their own labor or by their families. In this sense, public welfare programs are seen by many as modern governments' counterpart of personal charity in the past, a charity encouraged by most religious beliefs and provided for in almost all social organizations.

The American experience with its evolving social programs differs from that of many Western European nations whose experience is often studied as a model for social responsibility. There has seldom been a widely accepted American consensus among citizens of political parties that the *national government* has an overriding obligation to assure the well-being of all citizens through governmental action. In most industrialized nations, the welfare state is a combination of national governmental policy, governmental programs and financing, industrial and corporate, foundation and philanthropic, and family activities undertaken independently of each other or sometimes concerted through national or voluntary planning. But, in many of the Western European countries, especially since the middle or end of the nineteenth century, there evolved a widespread consensus that the protection of people is the first obligation of government although the obligation may be discharged in part through the corporate sector through individuals, insurance, or non-governmental voluntary social agencies.

In the U.S., by contrast, the same combination of organizations and distributed responsibility also exists, but lacking the consensus about the irreducible national responsibility for equity and well-being of all citizens through some form of governmental intervention. Instead, American social programs evolved, especially since the 1930s, as a result of the continuous ad hoc interplay of varying interest groups each pressing claims about the wants and needs of the constituencies, which justify a federal role, at least in financing, to rectify special group inequity or distress. The result has been an efflorescence and proliferation of specific and categorical social programs of almost confusing variety.

The terms *social programs,* or *safety net,* or *social protection* came into use to replace public relief as the variety of publicly funded activities spread beyond the traditional views of helping the widow, the cripple, and the aged and encompassed the mentally ill, those who found it not possible to function adequately in a complex society whether because of personal psychological difficulty or a mental disease. It also spread to include efforts to deal with such diverse deviations as juvenile delinquency and drug and alcohol abuse which were causes for personal, family and social concern. Similarly, training and educating new immigrants to equip them for American life; training youth who have difficulty adapting to an industrial work world; educating and caring for children with developmental disability and handicaps; protecting the health of new mothers and infants by special health and nutrition programs; rehabilitating adults injured or disabled by disease or accident; retraining workers displaced by technological change; and many more all came under the general heading of social welfare. Fundamental to all these was assurance of income security and medical care for the retired, aged or totally disabled.

The concept of a welfare state as different from relief or welfare provided the theoretical underpinnings for such diverse programs and also provided a new intellectual foundation for attacking the dilemmas of public responsibility. An early theoretician, T. H. Marshall, defined social policy (and by inference a welfare state) as the sum of those policies of government which affect actions having a direct impact on the welfare of citizens by providing them with services or income (Marshall, 1965). Another theoretician, H. Wilensky, calls a welfare state one in which government assures the minimum standard for all citizens as regards income, nutrition, health, housing and education, as a matter of right and not charity (Wilensky, 1975). In time the concept also came to mean universal provision of a few social services to the entire population, regardless of income. In some countries the key concept has been enhancing the autonomy of all citizens through health services, day care for children, home care for the disabled, and family allowances to strengthen family income. In such countries, these services are not means tested. The U.S., by contrast, has few universal benefits (excepting retirement), but many specialized, means tested public programs for the poor, plus tax benefits for the better-off.

The American version of a welfare state has taken on a distinctive tri-polar shape, in which only the minor pole is recognized by the general public as being "welfare." That pole comprises a cluster of means-tested programs such as income for the permanently disabled, the blind and the aged; relief for unemployed mothers (and sometimes fathers) with dependent children; and food stamps, medical care or housing supplements for the verified poor. Another pole consists of "earned" benefits such as unemployment insurance, workmen's compensation, veterans benefits, and numerous types of special retirement programs for military, civil service, miners, railway workers, and the more widely available social security retirement program, for other workers. The third pole of the subject, and the one hardly ever treated by the public as a part of the welfare state, consists of benefits which citizens derive from tax privileges such as reductions in taxation for buying a house (mortgage payment reductions) or for borrowing money to buy other goods (interest deduction in tax). Social services, in the second and third poles, are usually provided by a proprietary or by nonprofit marketplace agencies.

These three clusters have one element in common: they exist by action of government to improve the condition of individual citizens directly by goods or services, or by income. In all cases, the financing is provided by government in total or in part, by direct payout, voucher, or remission of taxes which would, if paid, reduce personal income. Another cluster of government activities might well be included, which are regulatory in nature and affect individual life conditions, such as minimum wage laws or environmental or occupational health regulations.

Discussion of the first of these clusters, conventional relief for the poor, arouses the most passion—about the importance of caring for the poor or, conversely, about people who live off the taxes of others. If, however, one uses as a measure of the welfare state the true total of individuals who receive direct, personal benefits or payments or exemptions out of the Federal treasury, the nature of the discussion shifts to one of "who is deserving" and "what is a fair distribution in a democratic society" or "what are the bounds to obligation." Such questions will be discussed in Chapters 4–11. For the present, consider the dimensions of government social welfare using at least three of the four clusters mentioned above.

Conventional relief as welfare accounts for an expenditure of about $177 billion per year through such major programs as Aid to Families and Dependent Children (AFDC), Supplementary Income (SSI) and Food Stamps (Census, 1984). The achievements claimed for these programs include the following: The proportion of families living below the official poverty line dropped from 22 percent in 1959 to 11 percent in 1978. About one-half of this decline can be attributed to income transfer programs. That is, in 1965 when 21 percent of families were in poverty, before transfer payments, 17 percent remained in poverty after transfers. But, in 1976, the posttransfer percentage in poverty had dropped to 11 percent; rising to 15 percent in 1984. However, most income support for those without any resources at all (AFDC eligible families) is set at a level *below* the official poverty level on average (Lampman, 1984, p. 83).

In health care, before Medicaid and Medicare, poor families saw a physician only half as often as did those more wealthy. By 1976, ten years after Medicare and Medicaid were enacted, physician utilization was nearly equalized and hospital utilization was proportionaly higher for the poor. Most of these benefits are targeted to the poor and income determines eligibility, which means that some poor improved access to health care while other working poor lost access (Lewis, 1976, p. 239; Starr, 1982, pp. 372–375; Morris, 1985, pp. 117–118).

The population benefiting from the so-called "earned benefits," those toward which individuals had made some tax contribution, pensions, retirement, unemployment insurance, workmen's compensations, and medical care for the elderly, receive some $230 billion from government sources. This population includes some who are poor to start with, but the majority are not and never were poor. The average income of an aged couple is much less than the average income of all Americans, but it is over twice as high as the poverty level for aged couples. If not affluent, they are on average not in deep distress. To a lesser extent, the same can be said of beneficiaries of workmen's compensation and unemployment insurance (Census, 1984).

In the third cluster, that of tax benefits and remissions, it is difficult to derive comparable numbers without extensive research. It can be estimated that several millions of taxpayers pay less taxes because of tax exemptions and deductions and their "benefit" totals about $256 billion of federal income tax revenue foregone by the federal government (Census, 1984).

The benefits of the latter two forms of welfare state are widespread and difficult to quantify because a direct causal connection cannot be drawn. However, it is not unreasonable to conclude that the life conditions of all these beneficiaries of federal policy live better lives as a result. Retired workers have better lives as their incomes are raised by pensions, even if their nonpension income may leave many of them at near the distress level. Their families also benefit by relief from responsibility for the financial needs of aged parents. The 30 or 40 percent of all medical bills for the aged met by Medicare also relieves pressures on the retired and their families, even though the burden of providing long-term care in cases of severe disability is not relieved.

It is also possible that the increased entry of working class children into college is in part attributable to a general increase in income levels made possible by such programs. In 1920, working class families contributed 2 percent of college entrants while in 1970 they accounted for 55 percent. The comparable percentage for upper-middle class families are 40 percent and 88 percent (Blumberg, 1980).

At a more general level of national income and well-being, income disparities have begun to level off slightly between economic classes, a good or bad result depending on each observer's ideological viewpoint. Between 1953 and 1975, the proportion of families with incomes below $3,000 a year dropped from 10.3 percent to 4.1 percent while those with incomes between $7,000 and $10,000 dropped from 23 percent to 12 percent. In the same period, those with incomes over $25,000 rose from 3.5 percent to 16 percent (Census, 1984). However, between 1947 and 1957, real incomes rose on the average of 20 percent; in the next decade, they rose by 13 percent; then by 3 percent and between 1969 and 1979, they increased by only 1.7 percent. By the 1980s, real income began to fall.

Between 1935 and 1975, the elderly were assured of income security. This permitted them to maintain their own homes, freed their adult children to move and establish their own households. Adult offspring were relieved of simultaneously carrying the financial burden of elderly parents and their growing children with education still ahead of them.

At a macroeconomic level, small shifts took place in the distribution of income. Between 1947 and 1975, the lowest fifth of the population had 3.5 percent of all incomes which in 1975 had risen to 3.9 percent. The highest income fifth had 45.5 percent of all income in 1947, which dropped to 44.5 percent in 1975 (Census: Incomes). Between 1922 and 1956, estimates of wealth, as distinct from incomes, were distributed as follows: in 1922, the top 1 percent of the population had estimated holdings equal to 31.6 percent of the wealth in the nation, and in 1956, this percent had dropped to 26 percent (R. L. Lampman, 1962).

The tax costs behind these shifts are also significant. In 1969, the median income family had $9,277 with taxes of $1,330, resulting in net of $7,947 (in 1969 dollars). By 1979, the median income had risen to $18,469 with taxes of $2,921, resulting in a net of $15,546 (in 1979 dollars). But, if inflation is factored in and incomes are converted to current dollars, the 1979 net income (equivalent to 1969 dollars) becomes only $7,800 (a net loss in income and living standards) (Census).

Despite these programs, the number of persons dependent on public income sources has risen, not declined. Although few social programs were intended to abolish dependency, its continuance and increase has been interpreted by some as a sign of program and policy failure, not of defects in the economy. The social programs were introduced mainly to take care of what was expected to be temporary or limited need and dependency.

In addition to these basic programs, several hundred smaller welfare programs have been established to address smaller scale personal and human troubles: abused or abandoned children, delinquent youth, handicapped children, nutrition lack in infants, children and the aged, rehabilitation of the physically and mentally disabled, transportation for the handicapped, counseling and therapy for the alcoholic, drug addicted and mentally ill, character building and related services for youth, special education for the developmentally disabled, etc. Many, if not most, of these services are financed by taxes. Thousands of independent nonprofit or proprietary service agencies administer these services. The extent and effects of personal welfare services are real in human terms, but cannot be readily quantified.

Medical care inflation has introduced a new component. Public funds now finance organ transplants, renal dialysis, the rescue of seriously damaged newborn infants, and the survival of adults shattered by violent accidents. This new technology and its finance costs many thousands of dollars for each case each year of life, yet is not recognized as part of the welfare state infrastructure.

The American version of a welfare state is not just a matter of numbers. It differs radically from pre-1930 American ideas about caring for others. And, it also conforms both to the conception of a welfare state in which government has extensive responsibility for the personal lives of all its citizens, but it retains much of the character of personal charity so common in the nineteenth century, but now writ large by government, and not personal benevolence.

This duality in American welfare programs under government explains some of the obscurity which surrounds the popular discussion of the subject. Cluster one, the traditional relief programs, are designed very much along lines of charitable effort. They require income testing; they involve agency staff to judge if a person is eligible for help, meaning people deserve the help being offered because they fit into some administrative guidelines which are individually verified. They are intended to address the needs of persons historically considered dependent or helpless and, therefore, deserving of human compassion and relief. Although this is the foundation for such programs as public assistance and supplementary security income, the populations they actually help have changed and now include a mix of traditionally helpless and of able-bodied adults without work or with unavoidable child care problems. The fit between the original intent and current needs of the poor who are often able-bodied is not a good one and confuses efforts to deal with the subject of poverty and dependency.

At the same time, the other clusters of welfare programs serve a generally independent population who believe they have earned their benefits. Their claims are very large and now feed the popular view that welfare is out of control. Such programs do fit into the concept of a welfare state in that they are quite universal (reaching nearly all income classes) and do not depend on personal income testing for eligibility. The cost of these claims make up a large part of what the public sees as welfare, but that same public is also the beneficiary of the programs which are seen as "deserved" and, therefore, of a different kind than welfare programs in the first cluster. The mix of the two as the public looks at expenditures and beneficiaries is ambiguous and confusing, at best. It is this ambiguity in the form of American social programs that may explain the cumulative dissatisfaction which led us to the present shift in national opinion about federal obligation for welfare.

It thus appears that American social welfare programs are extensive and costly; they reach not only the poor but the middle class as well, but under quite different and not easy to grasp circumstances; and the programs, taken in the aggregate, play an important part in other dimensions of national life—its economy and its unity or cohesion. For these reasons, among others, the subject takes on a significance beyond the old views about charity or relief for the poor.

In the next chapter the widening circle of criticisms will be examined, to be followed by a summary of recent trends which lie behind the dissatisfactions and which will in the end determine what social programs will develop into in future decades.

2

THE AMERICAN WELFARE STATE AND ITS CRITICS IN 1980
Right, Left and Center

The welfare state is either on the defensive or has, at best, lost its vigor. Labels such as New Deal, the New Society and the Great Society have become code words for a variety of public policies which increased federal governmental responsibilities to meet an increasing range of human, social, and economic needs. In popular parlance these past policies are regarded as progressive, even radical, while their opponents are identified as conservatives or reactionaries. Debate over policy often revolves around the emotions which these terms arouse. This continuing political challenge, debate, or confrontation, has partly polarized intellectual thought in the U.S. about social responsibility. Alternative views of social and political organization prod the welfare-state critics who object either to the state's overgenerosity or its inadequacy. The criticisms are varied and span the political spectrum from right to left.

To understand the criticisms of social programs, it is necessary to search more widely for the causes of discontent. But first, what are the criticisms?

CRITICS AND THEIR CRITICISMS

Status Security and Insecurity: The Decline of Religion and Hierarchy

The recent unrest about welfare is not limited to views as to the appropriate economic or political structure of society; unrest continually arises over the principles which govern the relationships between people, principles which are rooted in ethical convictions as much as in empirical human needs. Criticisms of this kind are often diffuse, couched in emotion-laden language and juggle ambiguous concepts. Still, such arguments do have emotive power.

For centuries religion and religious controversy provided the framework within which issues of personal relationships were thought out and resolved. But, for decades the impact of religious doctrine and religious principles has been undermined and replaced either by moral principles inherent in scientific inquiry, or by secular political doctrines. Neither of these provides the emotional foundation nor the centuries-long rootedness in human experience which a religious framework for moral behavior once provided. When the once infallible precepts about human behavior were relaxed in favor of freer more exploratory views about the human condition, a great explosion of experimentation resulted. Whereas once everyone had his place, today all "places" or positions in society are expected to be open to all. This disturbs those who are unwilling or unprepared to confront the open society. Some critics emphasize the vacuum which opens up when values, once widely shared, are replaced by constant change and freedom to experiment. To some critics, public responsibility alters the discipline individuals gain from living in a family where one learns acceptable ways of how to survive. They point to the decline in respect for hard work and saving, to the changes in family structure, the increased range of sexual expression, a broader tolerance for consciousness altering drugs. The discipline which comes from being responsible for one's own livelihood is associated with the discipline over all of one's behavior in relation to oneself, one's associates and the stranger. Definitions of what constitutes "right living" become rigid and basically arbitrary, because that very rigidity is believed vital for the self-discipline necessary for "right living" (Murray, 1984).

During the 1980 campaign, Ronald Reagan in major campaign addresses would use such formulations as these:

> Let us make this a new beginning . . . let us make a commitment to teach our children the values and the virtues handed down to us by our families; to have the courage to defend those values and the willingness to sacrifice for them.

> Let us pledge to restore in our time the American spirit of voluntary service, of cooperation, of private community initiative; a spirit that flows like a deep and mighty river through the history of our nation.

> I pledge you a government . . . its ability to act tempered by prudence and its willingness to do good balanced by the knowledge that government is never more dangerous than when our desire to have it help us blinds us to its great power to harm us.

Work and family are at the center of our lives; the foundation of our dignity as a free people. When we deprive people of what they have earned . . . we destroy their dignity and undermine their families. We cannot support our families unless there are jobs and we cannot have jobs unless people have both the money to invest and the faith to invest it. (Reagan, 1980)

In 1984, the Democratic presidential candidate stressed hard work and family and struggle as the core of an American ideal, provided everyone has a fair opportunity to succeed.

In a more intellectual framework, some critics argue that we do not have a way to live compatibly with authority (Freud, 1962), for we no longer accept, as in earlier centuries, class inequality. Since everyone is legally equal, then every difference between groups and individuals becomes a possible case for indictment. But, this conception of equality for all individuals, the elevation of individual rights, has been accompanied by windy generalizations, such as 'The Self' or 'The People', which constitute the new legitimation for complaints about differences in condition. But until the concrete details are worked out about relationships, confusion and unrest grow in a jumble of complaints and discontents. Every difference between classes or in individual condition may become a cause for complaint or disaffection; and every affliction arouses an appeal for justice or entitlement. Concepts of rights and justice are not yet ordered to absorb the confusing cascade of concrete details of complaints (Sennett, 1980).

Is Human Nature Weak or Strong?

Another way of expressing this social concern touches upon views about the essential character of human nature. Do we believe that human beings are inherently good and can only be corrupted or diverted by external circumstances? Or, is human nature flawed and capable of doing great harm unless disciplined by some form of social constraint? This concern is addressed in the question, "Do we feel entirely comfortable with a government capable of developing mechanisms to change the human nature of the citizen?" Do we really want government to change any one of us, even for the better, however that is defined?

Moral passions are more willful than self-seeking passion. Once we make people the objects of elightenment, we go on to make them the objects of pity and then of coercion. (Trilling, cited in Rothman, 1978)

Some critics are deeply distressed that government can try to impose specific remedies for basic aspects of human nature such as sloth, intemperance, size of family, child rearing, and promiscuity. Even if the government did have the capacity to change these basic behaviors in human beings, would we want to see the government change human beings that much? Or, would we rather preserve for all human beings the right to make a choice between good and bad, however that is defined, and endure certain tolerable levels of unemployment, alcoholism, and sexual promiscuity? Do we trust infinite variety in human behavior, or do we want conformity? And, if conformity, within how narrow a compass?

It is ironic, and an example of how difficult it is to classify the underlying nature of our concern about social programs, to realize that the conservative supporters of the 1980 election are themselves divided over what they believe. On the one hand, some argue that government programs undermine the essential strengths of human beings. Other conservatives argue that government intervention in the most controlling fashion is necessary to deal with alcoholism or sexual promiscuity. The argument that the government has too much responsibility and control over the lives of individuals is accompanied, in another compartment of thinking, by the belief that government should exercise more control to assure conformity to one set of standards against another. In this latter view, a family could benefit by having two workers at a nominal wage of $3 an hour rather than one worker earning $6 an hour. Thus, government limitations on women and children at work, minimum wage legislation and protection of trade unions are all seen as bad because they discourage more than one family worker from going to work, and work itself is redeeming; but, government can impose moral standards for behavior.

Libertarian Critique

The libertarian criticism argues that the individual has the right to his or her own earned income; that this is a superior foundation for society to one which the government takes income from one to spend on another's well-being. That kind of taxation is justified only for police and defense, but there is no other right to redistribute income. The post-Depression alliance joined people who were for the government, the poor, and in effect for fair shares including many, who were by temperament more libertarian and individualistic. That alliance is now divided; indeed, many libertarians think they must be antigovernment. Welfare advocates of the old coalition try to persuade libertarians about the importance of money and the redistribution of income so that they can be more discriminating about when government activity is acceptable (Schorr, 1980). Neither libertarians nor their adversaries can agree about the acceptable amount of government intervention.

Invasion of Privacy by Government

Closely related to libertarian views is the criticism that government has simply gotten too big and too intrusive in private lives (Rothman and Glasser, 1978). These critics concentrate on the personal social services more than they do on basic income distribution programs.

One view argues: government rules and regulations are so intrusive to make human freedom and choice intolerable for American citizens in their every day activities. Some of these intrusions affect all of us: the nature of tax legislation and its burdens, regulations about housing standards, home construction, the processing of foods we eat, the uses we can make of our property. The most impassioned criticisms are directed at the ways in which social programs interfere with the freedom of choice of recipients or beneficiaries of social programs. Laws and the courts interfere with the way parents can discipline their children. Parents who are not good housekeepers are criticized. Their children are removed by "officious and investigatory civil servants." Individuals who choose to be completely free from social obligation and who choose the life of begging on the streets are hounded and harassed. The retarded are placed in institutions, because it is assumed they are not capable of learning to take care of themselves in any way. The phrase "persons in need of supervision" has been so widely expanded as a concept that children can easily and legally be removed from parental care. Parents can be considered unworthy, for reasons of poverty, poor housekeeping, alcoholism or other expressions of personal difference and deviance. This criticism does not deny that some social and governmental intervention is necessary for the protection of some persons. It argues that the welfare state has turned over this responsibility so extensively to employees of government that they are now invested with dictatorial decision-making authority. These critics prefer a legal adversarial approach in which the intrusion into the life of a family or an individual must go through the winnowing process of a public court defense.

One critic (Glasser, 1978) suggests that the welfare state's central belief in doing the maximum amount of good through public intervention should be replaced by the doctrine of doing the least harm. Under this substitute doctrine, we would have to evaluate in each case how much harm might be done by a particular public action rather than the amount of good which might result. Society's institutions would be limited in their power over the dependent, including those in nursing homes, in schools, and correctional institutions for the delinquent. This concern with least harm rather than with most good derives from a conviction that Murphy's Law is still operative, "if anything can go wrong, it will." Another version of this doctrine suggests that whenever a social innovation is accepted as a basis for generating large national programs, one must assume that those programs, which achieved so much in their demonstration phase, are later entrusted to their worst enemies for widespread mass implementation. This follows from a recognition that the initiators of social inventions are highly committed and dedicated persons. Once their proposals are translated into mass operation, they are entrusted to clerks and others who have no commitment and only perform a job for their weekly wage.

Flaws of a Risk-Free Society

Another criticism proceeds as follows: Suppose every subgroup in society were guaranteed against risk. The welfare state tries to bring us to this situation. Farmers are insured against variations in crop prices or their bad choice about crops to plant. Older people are insured against any trouble they might have, if they did not save adequately during their youth. Youngsters are insured against any of the ill consequences or neglect of their schooling. What would happen if the safety of all persons were assured for all contingencies regardless of the steps they take to help themselves? The argument runs that we have now insured so many groups of persons against so many risks that virtually the entire population is insured against every possible kind of risk. The result is that no one is left to share the risk and thus there is no way of absorbing the shock of disaster (Wildavsky, 1980).

This insurance against risk is believed to reduce an individual's incentive or desire to take steps to improve his or her situation. Not only do entrepreneurs avoid risks to increase the national wealth which might increase the well-being of all persons, but individuals will resist the risk of moving or starting over in a new job when an old good paying one disappears. The caution introduced into the behavior of citizens is believed to lead, in the end, to a slowing down and a calcification of social and economic structure so that society itself becomes stagnant and decadent (Wildavsky, 1980). These critics do not say that the welfare state insures against all risks. However, they do argue that the psychological and underlying moral attitudes make it difficult for citizens to experiment, to grow, and to take risks. As a result, we do not learn because learning is believed by them to come from taking chances and learning from mistakes.

Such essential moral or social-psychological questionings have their economic connections as well. Some critics argue that a society in which risks can be taken and, in fact, are encouraged produces a net increase in economic capacity through greater productivity, greater imagination and invention. Increasing the national wealth benefits most people.

This utilitarian belief argues that the absence of risk-taking leads to economic stagnation and to an ultimate decline in the well-being of most people. These arguments are advanced at the most macrosocial level, and do not address the moral question of what happens to the losers in such an idealized risk-taking society.

Other critics of overprotection argue that it makes people careless, not cautious. They believe that overconfidence in protection leads to: neglect of one's health, careless auto driving, sloppiness and neglect of work—all because the consequences are covered by protection through social programs without personal cost.

Proliferation of Special Interests: A Social Pork Barrel

Another social criticism points out how an open democratic society encourages the proliferation of an uncontrolled variety of special interests and interest groups. Each group views the government as a kind of social "pork barrel" from which each is entitled to draw some part of the general wealth. Since this is viewed as a never-ending and constantly growing demand, everyone eventually turns to government for subsidy for some defensible purpose. The aggregation of these special demands upon the wealth of the nation becomes so all-consuming that little or nothing is left for investment necessary for the production of goods. Taxation becomes so onerous that all surplus income goes to feed government debt, incurred to carry public burdens. Little is left to regenerate the economy.

Erosion of Local Community Ties

Another line of social criticism argues that the welfare state leads to the decay of a sense of community and of social cohesion. Political critics of both the Right and the Left seem to agree about this decay of community, but they differ sharply about the explanations. Conservative critics argue that the welfare state has produced an undesirable reliance upon the federal government's solutions to human problems. They argue that many of these problems could be better handled through some more communally organized, voluntary action.

Radical critics argue that the structure of the economy and the persistence of a large impoverished population left by that structure produce impotent populations structurally incapable of communal organization. The affluent members of society have abandoned their concern for the less advantaged. For them, some superordinate authority within the government is necessary to revitalize the foundations of communal cohesiveness. Conservative critics counter by arguing that public bureaucracies leave decisions with bureaucrats rather than with citizens voluntarily acting in their civic capacities. Radical critics often agree, but reply that distribution of civic responsibility is unfair because only those with economic means can participate either in public decision making or in voluntary organization. If the very poor and disadvantaged are to ever assume their proper participatory role, some rectification of the imbalance is necessary.

Such critics further argue that the welfare state has created a structure of services which either maintains a docile poor population or undermines the remaining strengths of the poor and disadvantaged by taking all responsibility for their lives away from them and placing them in the hands of a bureaucracy. Although they differ about the means, both ends of the spectrum agree that the welfare state has failed in not serving human needs. The conservatives believe that personal responsibility for one's well-being is sufficient. The progressive critics argue that the disadvantaged require compensation to offset the unfair economic influence from which the affluent benefit (Nisbet, 1975; Jordan, 1973; Cloward, 1982; Galper, 1975; Murray, 1984).

Critics point out that many of the intermediate institutions which served as a check between a highly centralized authority and the life of individuals have been weakened in the welfare state. With agencies and bureaucrats designed to protect "the people from their exploiters," centralized bureaucracy's power over human lives is increased. It transfers that power from the individual or the intermediate institutions and associations which once protected their freedom. De Tocqueville quotes Rousseau in arguing "it is especially dangerous to enslave men in the minor details of life. For my part, I should be inclined to think freedom less necessary in the great things than in the little ones if it were possible to be secure of the one without the other" (1980).

Revolutionary Consequences of Equality: And the Loss of Self-Respect

Conservative critics speak of nineteenth and twentieth centuries' vision of equality as a revolutionary force behind the growth of centralized organizations and bureaucracies:

> For once the idea of equality becomes uppermost it can become insatiable in its demands. It is possible to conceive of human beings conceding that they have enough freedom or justice in a social order; it is not possible to imagine them ever declaring they have enough equality . . . in this respect, it resembles some of the religious ideals or passions which offer by virtue of the impossibility of ever giving them adequate representation in

the actual world almost unlimited potentialities for continuous on-slaught against institutions. Affluence is a fertile ground for the spread of equalitarian philosophy where the pains of affluence manifestly in-clude in our age the pain of guilt over the existence of any or all in-equalities. (Nisbet, 1975, p. 34)

In this view, earlier constitutional assurances of equal opportunity have been reinterpreted in the twentieth century into a government guarantee of equal conditions, equal results, or equal opportunity, which is consid-ered debilitating to human vigor. The search for equality in all forms through government had led to the opposite result. One discovers how centralized government directly invades the lives of almost all indi-viduals. This leads to dependence and disobedience (Sennet, 1980).

Freud wrote:

> . . . there is no longer any way to live compatibly with authority. The coherent utilizations depended on a universal respect for inequality and we have lost forever that kind of innocence. We are all legally as good as one another now and every difference is an indictment. (Freud, 1962, chap. 3)

Here, the progressives or radicals and the conservatives certainly differ. They disagree about the desirability of equality in its most literal sense, and they disagree about the responsibility of government to assure that such equality is brought about. The welfare state becomes implicated because, while it does not articulate absolute equality for all citizens, it reduces the disparity between the unprivileged and the privileged classes. The welfare state, except for modest programs of income redistribution, has not yet gained political control of all economic institutions, but it has proceeded through the manipulation of institutions such as schools and social programs which intrude in the daily life of all. These programs were designed to provide greater equality of opportunity through better access to a few primary social goods such as income or education, but, in fact, they fuel the demand for equality not only in opportunity but in all life conditions.

To critics, the underprivileged and disadvantaged have lost the basic foundations for their own self-respect. Public programs that might have helped to restore respect offered neither equality nor inequality but only an enormous political bureaucracy. The unintended consequence is to replace freedom of development and the potential of elaborating volun-tary and intermediate associations with centralized bureaucracy. To make people's condition equal when there is inequality in the human capacity seems futile. Given the immense range of aptitudes, desires, aspirations, strengths and motivations, any effort to secure equality across that range ends up redistributing inequality (Nisbet, 1975).

War and the Welfare State

For critics of both extremes, the national welfare state affected the distribution of income, property, education and working conditions, all as an adjunct of a war economy and a warlike state. Many opponents of military action also object to enlarged government welfare. Students of the two world wars conclude that the need, at least in Europe, to mobilize total populations for war made it necessary to justify wartime sacrifices by promising a better life and more welfare programs for all. They point to the association between these two wars and the great explosion of welfare state programs in several countries, especially England, after World War II. To such critics the programs and the wars which encouraged their growth were unwise and unncessary. We find ourselves unexpectedly living in a world of military police and bureaucratic power that cannot help but have a corrosive effect upon liberties which are vital to any free society.

From the point of view of a tactician of political power, personal liberty diminishes central power. Those in power use welfare to soften the impact of political power by creating the illusion of individual freedom in a society grown subtly more centralized and collectivized. This is treated, by critics, as destructive of the diversity of allegiance, the autonomy of enterprise in all spheres and the spirit of spontaneous association that any genuinely free civilization requires.

CONSERVATIVE AND RADICAL ECONOMIC CRITICISMS

The economic criticism of the welfare state is less complex and better defined than the social and moral criticism. The sharpest radical criticism points to the ways in which maldistribution of economic resources distorts distribution of free behavior. Economic differences means that the affluent have more freedom than those with little wealth. Public welfare actions are one means for altering this balance; because the gross disparities in both personal and economic freedom have persisted for a long time, redistribution within a private resource society is impossible.

Conservative economic argument runs as follows: Welfare programs undermine the federal government's budget and the gross national product by depleting the health of the economy itself through diversion of resources from "productive" to "unproductive" purposes. Since all welfare programs depend upon an economic base which can yield the funds to support them, the growth of the welfare state is in the end self-defeating for its own purposes. The undermining of the economic vigor of a society means less money is available to do the good things which the welfare state promises. Also, there is less to provide the minimum acceptable standards of living for all persons regardless of their social need.

The general upward trend in productivity has obscured this argument. Each year there has been an adequate social increment sufficient to permit distribution rewards to those who are *economically active* and at the same time to provide for social needs of those who are not economically active. When this increment declines, as in times of economic stagnation, the crisis of welfare becomes clear since resources are clearly limited.

This economic argument is blunted by the absence of economic evidence that investment in welfare programs is a direct cause of an economic decline. Other uncontrolled and unpredictable factors explain the rise and fall of the economy. In West Germany, Sweden, Norway and France the economic slowdown up to 1983 was less and the welfare investment was much higher than in the U.S. Nonetheless, some critics trace an association between the slowing down of the economy and the rise in the proportion of the national product and the budget devoted to welfare.

More radical and Marxist-oriented critics elaborate their criticism with certain a priori assumptions. They begin with the belief that the control of economic resources is fundamentally at the root of most difficulty when those resources are in the hands of a private and privileged few. They argue that most social programs have been designed to maintain a docile, controlled and impoverished labor pool to assure willing workers at low wages for whatever jobs are available and thus depress wages. Social programs are seen as essentially oppressive and coercive rather than helpful. Rehabilitation programs, for example, are likely to be coercive because their objective is to restore that individual to his role as low income worker in an economy profiting others. The labor pool requirements of a controlling economy and a middle class (dominating the staffing of the organization) determine the structure of social programs. Professional judgment about what it is best to do in a given situation of distress is used instead of the judgment of the poor who are considered unable to make good judgments themselves. Such critics believe that all individuals, including the most poor and disadvantaged, have vast reservoirs of potential strength which has been beaten down by the pressures of an exploiting economy. What the poor need more than anything else is a set of programs which builds upon this latent and potential strength to create their own remedies (Pemberton, 1983; Judge, 1983).

In Marxist analysis, relief and welfare programs emerge because certain classes are dispossessed by others, and the latter become a threat to the former. Welfare is not intended for the benefit of society or for those who are dispossessed but rather to placate them and to protect the dispossessors (Pemberton, 1983; LeGrand, 1982).

While the political Right and Left disagree on many things, they both turn to economic argument, but for different reasons, to support their cases. Conservatives argue that money spent for welfare is unproductive. It gives the money to individuals who cannot be trusted to spend it wisely, who do not save—and, therefore, do not add to the volume of economic resources to increase economic vigor. Money taken away from the affluent could be better spent to maintain economic activity. By contrast, the political progressives or liberals argue that without social programs, between 15 and 20 percent of the population would not have the means with which to purchase the goods produced by the economy, therefore, the economy would be in even worse shape than it is now. But, the Left will argue that more money needs to be spent in direct social benefits in order to stimulate the economy.

Although there are many theories that social programs are either a drag or a stimulus in economic terms (Blumberg, 1980), there is no widespread consensus.

Taxes and Economic Decisions: Dislike of Taxes

Much of the economic argument remains at the level of debate among experts. However, in one respect the economic issues are understandable to almost all citizens and are a powerful stimulus to dissatisfaction with social programs: the level of taxation levied upon individuals, part of which is attributable to the growth in social programs. Whereas in the 1930s most citizens paid relatively small sums in income tax and in local property taxes, today it has been estimated that individuals with the most modest incomes may be paying as much as 20 or 30 percent of all of their earned income in taxation directly or indirectly, which means that percentage of earnings is not available for private expenditures. The issue becomes serious when the benefit these individual taxpayers receive from social programs does not seem to warrant so large a diminution in personal disposable income. An accumulation of local property taxes, income taxes, social security taxation (12 percent of the entire wage bill), excise taxes and sales taxes compose the highest figures for taxation.

Another way of estimating the tax burden is to estimate the total of the gross national product which has to be cycled via taxation through government budgets as part of the circulation in the economy. In some Western European countries, this figure reaches 50 percent.

This information is not only publicized in the media, but is felt in

TABLE 2.1   Percentage of GNP in Selected Countries
Cycled Through Government Budgets[1]

Norway	54.9%
Holland	53.1
Sweden	52.2
Denmark	50.4
W. Germany	41.9
France	41.2
Britain	40.8
Canada	37.7
U.S.A.	32.5
Japan	22.4

[1]Wilson, "The Swedish Dream Grows Tired," quoting in turn *Current Economic Trends*, p. 290. Dec. 1977. *New Society*, Dec. 6, 1979, p. 544.

each weekly paycheck, and it becomes clear to ordinary citizens that they have entered a world in which their contribution to benevolence and philanthropy—for themselves or for others—bears very little relation to what is actually happening to them. In the past, religious discipline called for tithing or the exhortation to give at least 10 percent of one's income in helping others charitably. It is not important to argue whether or not this 10 percent figure was widely realized; for twentieth century workers to confront the fact that they give anywhere from a fifth to a third of personal income to government is a shock. It is not easy to separate what goes to welfare and what maintains government. For them, the presumed gratifications of private charity which came from private tithing or giving are no longer possible, since taxed personal income is taken away before they have a chance to use it and it is expended on objects and persons unknown to them and for causes which may be far removed from the interests of many of them.

In a democratic society, it is assumed that all taxpayers have approved social programs towards which their incomes are now used, but it is quite different to confront the reality of the personal burden imposed in part by this accumulation of social programs. It is too easy to separate one's behavior into compartments and to call upon human generosity to support social programs on the assumption that somehow "somebody else will be paying" when, in fact, everyone must be paying. The costs become painfully clear, and an enormous strain is placed upon one's convictions about what it is to care for the stranger in the modern welfare state.

Dislike of Bureaucracies and Inefficiency

Another economic criticism is based on the imputed inefficiency of public programs. All sides of the political spectrum probably agree in their skepticism about public bureaucracy and its inefficiency. One group of critics argues that trying to transfer money from the rich to the poor through national social mechanisms is similar to trying to carry water in leaky buckets. First, the social programs distort the incentive which individuals have to work, save and innovate. Then, social programs also involve a large administrative apparatus not only to deliver the benefits but to insure that there is compliance in meeting the cost and carrying out the regulations of the transfer programs. These administrative costs are often estimated to run as high as 30 percent of all federally appropriated funds consumed in intermediary levels of administration before the ultimate beneficiary sees any of the intended benefits. The critics also argue that despite social programs the number of persons in society who are economically dependent upon these programs has increased in the past 40 years rather than declining in proportional terms. It was first believed that Social Security would make means-tested relief programs unnecessary in time. In reality, the number of beneficiaries of both social insurance and of relief have increased. The persons receiving income benefits or income transfers now represent a percent of a larger population in 1980 than in 1940. To many critics this evolution is sufficient evidence in itself that the social programs have failed, and are economically inefficient. They are seen as organizationally deficient. Even more, this is taken as evidence that the administration of social programs, as well as their policies, are part of the problem for they create a pauperized class by removing incentives to independence—making it easier for individuals to depend upon public benefits rather than take care of themselves. This is allegedly seen in the tendency for husbands and fathers to leave their children, and the tendency for parents to separate and remarry while the needs of their children are in part at least taken care of by public programs.

This multifaceted attack on bureaucracy usually overlooks the historical fact that the evolution of bureaucracy took place for two reasons. Large-scale organization which accompanied the industrial revolution and its associated urbanization required some formal mechanism to mediate exchange and relationships among various groups and parties. Equally important, bureaucracy was long seen as an essential corrective to the abuses of private charity. It was seen as a neutral, more fair and objective way to handle the diverse needs of a complex society according to law and rights, rather than by personal whim and bias. Despite this justification for the emergence of a welfare bureaucracy, the criticisms have power and weight which cannot be ignored.

Another bureaucratic flaw is found in the technical requirements of large-scale, formal organization for welfare which militates against the welfare or well-being of the needy and recipient populations. Staffs are forced in the end to consider not so much what is good for their clients, but what is good for the agency. Ends and means become confused and many would say that such organizations serve administrations and staff more than they help clients. Examples abound in the way in which hospital admissions and discharges are organized, the way in which nursing homes are managed, the way in which child protective agencies function, and the way in which relief agencies manage to dispense their financial supplements. Employees thus become co-opted into defending their agencies as instruments of control for existing distribution of power rather than acting as free professionals employed to look after the interests of their recipients regardless of the consequences for the agency.

Class Inequity under Welfare Programs

The political Left differs from other social critics in that it concentrates on the inequity embedded in disparities in income under current welfare arrangements. Economic status differentials, although slightly improved until 1978, have since returned to the earlier long-term trend of a widening between those who have and those who have not. This inequity is considered so much a drag on the economy by lowered ability to buy goods that this alone justifies more growth in economic terms. This trend has presumably accelerated with the change in national policies forecast by the 1980 national elections. The Internal Revenue Service, in an analysis of income tax returns filed in 1978, noted that in that year there were 2,041 persons with yearly incomes of one million dollars or more and that this number had more than doubled since 1983, while the total number of tax returns had only increased by 11 percent. In percentage terms, the number of persons earning $1 million a year in income increased much more rapidly than did the total number of persons paying taxes. This very wealthy class did not pay taxes at all on more than 25 percent of their incomes, compared with an overall national average of 13 percent. Such inequities loom larger to one school of criticism than to another, which justifies the inequity as necessary for general economic vigor.

DIFFERING POLITICAL BELIEFS ABOUT A WELFARE STATE

Aside from social, economic and psychological concerns there are equally powerful criticisms rooted in the differing beliefs which people have about the nature of the political order which is best suited to human needs. The most vigorous criticism is based on the belief that that government is best which governs least (Nisbet, 1975). In this view, the well-being of any social order lies in a set of political institutions which provide the greatest opportunity for growth, expression and strength of a great variety of private and voluntary associations. Only in this way can a society continue to grow through the vigor of many of its component parts. To believe that the infinite richness of human nature and of the human potential for social organization can somehow be contained, planned and controlled by a national government with a set of national programs is seen as a manifest impossibility. While there is no conclusive evidence that any one political order is in itself accountable for the vigor of society and while disagreement with this viewpoint has been argued, there is little disagreement, at least in the U.S., that too much government is undesirable. But what is too much?

Perhaps the best that can be said about the political critiques is that groups and individuals hold strong beliefs and have strong convictions, not necessarily supported by objective evidence about the most desirable scope of government.

It is likely that, in the U.S. at least, the prevailing belief calls for a flexible, indefinable, and constantly shifting balance between suspicion of too much concentration of power in any one organ of government and a dependence on government whenever the society is threatened. The ambiguity about where to draw the line is found in the historical and political debate whether the U.S. at its inception was seen by the founding fathers as a confederation of independent states or as a national entity created by all the colonials to serve their collective needs (Will, 1979).

Just where a population settles at any one moment in time between the extremes of freedom and control, the person and collectivity and freedom and justice will change, but it is clear that a significant change is in the making because of the vague, widely diffused unhappiness with the current balance between government and the individual which took shape between 1935 and 1980 (McLoughlin, 1978). What the judgment about the change in that balance will be, cannot yet be clearly foretold.

Whatever the outcome, it is clear that the judgment about the political structure has to balance a population's hope that government will both protect individuals' private rights and also assure that those rights are in fact achieved. Just how those rights are to be defined, how broad they are to be and how much state authority will be invested to bring them about is the arena for political debate.

One practical and more manageable dimension of the political argument is administrative in nature. It has to do with the public perception about the size and competence of political bureaucracies. No program in the welfare state is conceivable without a structure of agencies and organizations with manpower paid for by public funds. These organizations include governmental agencies working under a civil service or under a patronage system, or nonprofit or proprietary agencies living primarily on public subsidy. There is widespread belief that tax dollars should not be used too generously to support a large staff of persons devoted to doing the public business, although efficiency in doing the public business is also desired. True, some major social programs such as the Social Security system which process paper by standardized criteria require a large manpower pool and are generally conceded to be efficient and satisfactory, but other programs such as public welfare departments which give help on a more individualized and discretionary basis are generally considered inefficient. Studies in England report that administrative costs of social insurance run about 1½ percent, but those for cash relief run about 10 percent (Dilnot, Kay and Morris, 1984). What the critics try to evaluate is whether the political cost of maintaining a bureaucracy is commensurate with the gains produced for either individuals or society.

An ironic dilemma needs to be confronted in evaluating the criticisms. Most large public programs are properly accused of being impersonal, tripped up in red tape, confusing and not especially responsive to human need. On the other hand, public reluctance to provide sufficient funds for the staffing of these programs makes it inevitable that most programs have underpaid staffs which are constantly turning over. Agencies rely more and more upon mechanical means to process essentially human problems rather than relying on individual discretion. They rely upon rules and regulations to control the decisions of ill-trained individuals, all of which adds up to a lack of responsiveness, personnel overload, and "burn-out," confusing and bureaucratic, red tape.

Political Failure to Reconcile Large Claims and Limited Resources

A further criticism, political as much as economic, is directed at the difficulty open democratic societies have in resolving conflicting demands from claimants which vastly exceed available resources. This opens a vast area of economic and political debate but the concern has one simple expression: how to begin programs which benefit only part of a class at first even if the aim is to benefit the entire class over time. This activates impatience with action which takes a long time to mature and also suspicion that promises for the future cannot be trusted. This immediately introduces a limitation on the willingness of a welfare society to take on correction of great inequities quickly when very large expenditures are involved. Recent examples are not difficult to find. New York City's Planning Department chose one neighborhood in each of its five boroughs to augment federal financing to make physical improvements in those communities. The sums involved were some $243 million of federal grants for the purpose. A great variety of neighborhood groups protested the entire process, arguing that such funds should be distributed among all neighborhoods and that pilot and demonstration neighborhoods should not be selected even if the sums distributed more widely would be insignificant. That this tendency is not limited to the U.S. is testified to by a similar experience in Rome where city government tried to improve one of the numerous new but impoverished neighborhoods surrounding the city. It was unable to act because neither the Rome nor the Italian government had the economic means to improve all neighborhoods simultaneously and political suspicion frustrated the choice of any one neighborhood with which to make a step forward.

New Class Power in the Welfare State

The dissatisfaction with political doctrines and the bureaucracy, which both liberals and conservatives sometimes share, is carried to a philosophical and intellectual extreme by dissident Marxist critics from Communist countries. They have argued that a new class has emerged in industrialized, planned societies, a class which is made up largely of intellectuals and bureaucrats in positions of public responsibility. In their view, it is sound and constructive to have distinct political and economic powers with the legitimacy of power in each sphere reached separately. In the economic sphere the central factor is a belief in the rationality of the market, in the laws of supply and demand which ensure an acceptable supply of resources. In the political sphere the same is achieved through political competition in a multiparty system. However, these critics argue that in redistributive societies (i.e., Communist or planned), the economic and political spheres are merged and legitimacy is arrived at differently. Intellectuals have gained a monopoly of decision over what is rational for society and how resources are to be allocated. In these societies intellectuals concern themselves with securing approval for their power by establishing that they are the sole custodians of the best and most equitable means of redistributing resources (Konrad and Szelenyi, 1984).

This argument echoes the criticism and the defense advanced in the U.S. by those called "technocrats" in the late 1930s and early 1940s (Bingham, 1935). The confidence placed in the hands of scientists of the past and in the hands of computer specialists and electronic data processing experts in the current era suggest that something very persistent has arisen in all industrialized societies however organized. The fact of reliance upon a class of competent technicians or intellectuals for information management in western free market nations is matched by the emergence of combined political and economic power in the hands of the same kind of intellectual bureaucratic class in eastern planned societies. The trend and the concern seem to be worldwide.

A related political criticism is found in regional rivalries among the states. Whereas national programs are intended to even out regional differences, regional loyalties lead many to argue that their (if not the national) good will be served if there is less federal action. Officials in oil rich states such as Texas complain that "their" oil is being unfairly taxed to benefit northern poor. And, the 1981 White House Conference on Aging reported significant differences between Sunbelt, Midwestern and Northern states about: the extent of federal programming for the elderly, social security and taxation (APHA). Regional differences and interests seem to be cracking, if slightly, the national consensus even about that bedrock of social programming—the Social Security program. It is being replaced by claims of some regions that their wants have a greater claim on resource allocation decisions than does the consensus about a national need.

IS DISCONTENT A PRELUDE TO ANOTHER "GREAT AWAKENING"?

If we compare the American social welfare programs in their practical aspects and the economic, political and moral reactions to them, we may be justified in thinking that welfare issues may represent more than a passing budget crisis. An accumulation of distinct and separate dissatisfactions among many elements in modern society coalesced to bring about a major change in a national election. The dissatisfactions range across a dissonant variety of special interests: differing views about race relations, sexual morality, the fate of old yet basic industries, the nature of family freedom, changing access to employment, inequitable distribution of reward in relation to effort, etc.

It is reasonable to view 1980 as a significant turning point—possibly a prelude to the kind of "great awakening" which has described previous shifts in American social thought (McLoughlin, 1978). The concept of *a great awakening* implies that there are periods in a nation's history when unplanned changes, insecurities, threats to persons and tradition, accumulatively produce an unrest which leads to major political changes. This unrest breaks traditions and leads to changes in political structure, social organization and policies. In McLoughlin's analysis, past awakenings have first produced a conservative tide looking to the past. This was soon followed by social reform looking to the future. In this light, the 1980 recession in welfare support may presage a new approach. But, what shape will it take?

Undoubtedly, between the 1930s and the late 1960s the nation's political and economic policies were based on a sense of confidence about the future. A great depression had been survived; a great world war had been won. Despite temporary recessions, the economy grew, scientific and new technology advanced. More tolerance in social behavior created a more open, flexible society. But, by the late 1960s and early 1970s tensions and contradictions increased so that the optimism of the previous decades seemed unreal. Expectations of growing affluence were not being realized sufficiently. Although a skilled working class and middle class population were doing well, the economic transformation in industry was undermining the economic viability of major industries and reducing opportunities for the less-skilled workers. Increasing numbers of minority citizens felt excluded from the rewards for their efforts or excluded from the opportunity of securing adequate rewards. Skilled workers, as well as the middle class, were not able to realize as much benefit from their work as they felt entitled to. At the same time, the costs in taxation to support government and social programs were making it increasingly difficult for the employed workers, the middle class, to enjoy the freedom of choice in spending their income as they desired.

Although we are mainly concerned here with the position of social programs, these broader undercurrents need to be kept in mind. For it is these very undercurrents which remind us that we are not simply experiencing a confrontation between a political Right or Left, progressive or conservative, the outcome of which depends upon the amount of political acumen with which one party or the other assembles its resources in support of its ideological views. The loss of self-confidence in the future and the emergence of an age of anxiety illustrate some of the problems. The conceptual framework which designers of social programs use are being so thoroughly challenged that the framework itself may have to be altered.

If we examine the concrete substance of criticisms which have been advanced, we soon discover that there are underlying questions asked by persons regardless of party. Thoughtful people may differ substantially about methods, but their basic concerns cut directly into the views all have about the nature of their society.

As we read the writings, the political manifestos of all parties and critics, a few themes begin to suggest that an awakening may be in the making. A few recurring themes or objectives are:

personal freedom
equitable distribution of rewards
social justice
respect for differences

importance of mutual aid and cooperative effort
care for the vulnerable and the helpless

When partisan debate finds such recurrent general ends hard to realize, differences emerge about how to proceed practically:

- The scope of government: to what extent is government responsible for equality in life as well as for creating certain acceptable conditions for life?
- What limitations on private and individual effort are tolerable and socially productive?
- What are the outcomes desired by each partisan faction?
- How much control should be entrusted to government? Should this control be focused over the well-to-do, the rich corporations? Or, on the deviant and the poor?

Answers to such questions will shape the foundations of social programs in the 1980s and the 1990s. The answers will be found in better understanding of the two forces: the pressures for change in the late twentieth century, which will be discussed next; and the resistance to change, which can be found in the long history of man's attempt to deal with the needy, which produced the belief with which most citizens still approach these issues.

SUMMARY

Major criticisms of present day welfare programs are moral, economic, social, psychological and political in nature.

These divergent streams of criticisms of the welfare state seem to have, despite their inconsistencies, converged in the last quarter of the twentieth century into a wider river of discontent, either with welfare organization as now arranged or with the very concept itself.

3

THE FUTURE CHALLENGES THE PAST
Some Underlying Social Forces

Democracy makes the individual turn in on himself.

ALEXIS DE TOCQUEVILLE

The criticisms reviewed in the preceding chapter are diverse and are best treated as symptoms of an unsatisfactory state of affairs. They can also be viewed as expressions of various ideological positions on the nature of people in their organized societies. However, if our interpretation is correct, this spate of dissatisfaction, leading to demands for change in our welfare arrangements, is more likely to reflect deeper tendencies in the late twentieth century for which the pattern of welfare developed in earlier years is not adequate. What follows is a summary of three major trends which underlie the current dissatisfactions, trends which call for a rethinking of the basic premises on which governmental programs are built. This approach is useful for, without it, the debates about the future of public responsibility promise to be a continuous repetition of ideological positions leading to stalemate rather than resolution. The trends are: the changing nature of dependency; changing attitudes about obligation to self or to others; and the unexpected consequences of democratization of welfare. In the face of these tendencies, the advocates of public responsibility and their opponents both rely on inherited views about collective obligation to relieve the needy, but do so with a clouded understanding of what that inheritance really is.

In a real sense, the protagonists of opposing views argue past each other. The conservative nature of inherited conceptions about collective obligation to the distressed will be considered in Chapters 4–10. The new conditions, which propel change, will be considered next. The two: tradition and change, oppose each other, creating a tension which, it is predicted, will crack the mold of current welfare state thinking and open the way to a new pattern for government responsibility.

Much of the stalemate in argument over policy derives from perceptions which each party has about the wishes of the general public or electorate. As will be discussed at length in later chapters, these perceptions are in error as to the facts of citizen viewpoints. The opponents of federal responsibility look backward to an ideal of personal and family responsibility in which government has little to do, a viewpoint which is completely at variance with the early American use of local government to deal with problems of dependency. It is also at variance with the public views which persist today, as revealed in opinion polls and in election results, supporting public responsibility, but in rather clearly defined areas.

By contrast, the advocates of welfare expansion believe that citizens need only be informed clearly that some difficulty or need exists and they will turn at once to government for remedy. Or, if they do not believe that, they undertake to educate voters about such growing needs and about the necessity for governmental action. Again, as will emerge in later chapters, this view of public values badly overstates the potential. There is a long history of popular support for government action, but in sharply circumscribed areas of need, and for sharply limited purposes.

For such reasons, the policy arguments in the political arena do not really touch the deepest sources of popular support. This makes it all the more difficult for the arguments to address in practical terms the new conditions of social need or dependency which now confront the American system of welfare.

This discussion becomes especially sharp when we see that it takes place alongside another argument in the context of a larger political arena, this time the worldwide confrontation between socialist and capitalist modes of organizing national societies. In many parts of the world, it has become conventional to believe that socialism is the most effective way to resolve deep-seated human troubles. This has stimulated those committed to more open, capitalist forms of organization to consider how state power in a market economy can be redesigned to address persisting human difficulties. The antisocialist approach is not altogether unified, but a significant section does believe in the uses of government as a part of the political confrontation more than it believes in a hands-off laissez-faire approach. The pragmatic attempt to find some reasonable way for dealing with the new conditions pressing on old welfare ideas is thus caught in an ideological argument about the political forms of governance.

Changing Nature of Dependency: Able-Bodied Dependency

Public and advocacy views about the scope of public obligation are slowly being made irrelevant by the changing scope and nature of dependency in the modern world. The helpless are now joined by the able-bodied for whom there is no work. The controversial issue of dependency is complicated by the fact that three now dependent able-bodied groups have emerged in historically unprecedented numbers. The able-bodied elderly, a new phenomenon produced in part by the very science which we expect to abolish need; the young, often teenage unmarried mothers with small children; and minority youth, usually male, are a product of a freer and self-regarding society which also has an open and mobile economy. These groups present dilemmas not hitherto confronted by modern industrial nations.

The arguments, pro and con, about unemployment often confuse issues of economic dependency and lack of opportunity for paid work. Opponents of welfare argue that some people are "naturally" dependent on others and are therefore out of work. Supporters of social programs argue that lack of jobs makes poor people dependent. This way of framing the issue misses a crucial point, that there are long-term and short-term cycles to work opportunity. In the long view of history, each major change in the mode of production has produced more goods and more work for growing populations. But, in the short run, a large part of the working population is displaced and suffers greatly during a generation or more, until the new economic pattern settles down.

In the late twentieth century, at least for the U.S. and Western Europe, technical changes transformed heavy industry societies into "post-industrial" or new technology and service economies. Economic development in underdeveloped areas and world trade and finance shifted heavy production of steel or textile and clothing manufacture to new parts of the world. In the resulting shift, technology creates fewer jobs than it abolishes at least in the short run, and only some of those new jobs require advanced education. Some youth without educational aspirations are committed to long periods of unemployment or sporadic work at low pay without hope for improvement. Racial minorities have disastrous unemployment rates. Middle-aged adults are made redundant by new technology and many will never find work. The aged, once considered weak and helpless, are now much more physically fit, alert and active (at least until their eighties for most), and they too want to have some useful role in society. Unfortunately, our basic social security laws are premised on a different view of the aged—as worn out and rather helpless.

Economists argue that each major economic transformation takes care of these unpleasant facts by creating more jobs over time and by more wealth creation which can be shared. History gives some support to this long view. In the late nineteenth and early twentieth centuries, America's economy was transformed by an industrial revolution of mass production with heavy industry—autos, steel, chemicals, railroads. In 50 years America became not only a dominant world economic power; its population grew; it absorbed millions of immigrants; and by World War I provided work for most of this increase (Kuznets, 1966). What is easily overlooked is the widespread unemployment, depressions, and hunger which laboring people had to live through before the promised "prosperity" was realized for more than a few in the middle class. For over a generation, farmers moved to cities, poverty was widespread, urban riots were frequent in the major cities, and militant labor unions fought to organize workers. The period was one of turmoil and unrest. Only after World War I did the new economy stabilize, for a time, so that the promise of new jobs was realized. This promise was lost in the 1930s depression and retrieved in the post-World War II era (Hofstadter, 1955; Schlesinger, 1960; Pease, 1962).

A very similar cycle arose in England in the fourteenth, fifteenth and sixteenth centuries when new forms of national organization, new trade patterns, world exploration, and exchange of industrial skills led to a major labor upheaval. Traditional farm lands were enclosed to encourage sheep raising and wool production for textiles. Farm workers were displaced as agricultural productivity shifted from local use to manufacture to serve a new urban and world market. Then, new markets created new jobs over time. But, in the transition a succession of wars, and exploration in the new world displaced a large part of the once rural population. They became wandering beggars looking for work. Their existence, and the chaos of a new labor market led in time to the Elizabethan Poor Laws which became the foundation for later American efforts to cope with similar upheavals (Thompson, 1968; Rimlinger, 1971).

So, economic historians are right to point to long-term trends in the industrialized world which do not support a pessimistic view. What they slide over is what economists call transitional unemployment which comes from technological change. This is sufficiently longterm to destroy the lives of those "transitionally" displaced from their traditional work. In the western industrialized world, and especially in the U.S., industrial changes have transformed both workplace and culture. Population has increased, the total number of jobs has increased, women, as well as men, have been absorbed in new opportunities, and the volume of material goods has increased so that standards of living have been raised for all, creating a large middle class and improving the base level of life for even the poorest, although not necessarily in an equitable manner (Kuznets, 1966).

These results are used to argue that new technology will, *in time*, improve everyone's condition. What is usually overlooked by this optimistic assessment is the extent of time involved. In the past, the great bursts of industrial energy were accompanied by a time lag of perhaps a generation before the benefits began to reach most people. In that transitional generation, a generation of human beings suffered hunger, poverty and loss of role as old ways of life were displaced by the new, and old ways of work disappeared. True, *in time,* more people found new jobs and were better off than before in a material sense, but in that time, human wastage was enormous and inhuman. The writings of nineteenth century England and early twentieth century America are full of descriptions of the human losses, which were the fall-out of the progress (Booth, 1970; Bremner, 1956, Riis, 1970).

The late twentieth century seems to be entering another cycle of massive economic change, with heavy industry playing a less basic role in the U.S., and becoming a major growth factor in underdeveloped countries. In its place, information systems, electronic technology, services and finance grow. The displacement of workers and transformation of work opportunity seems to be as great as that experienced in the nineteenth century in the U.S. and in the sixteenth century in England.

Whatever the long-range benefits prove to be, the short-term problems are clear. High technology is now creating new jobs, but not yet fast enough to replace jobs lost in the auto and steel industries. The new jobs are also not located in parts of the country where unemployment is greatest. Most of the jobs are routine, low paying, and require little skill or education. Research summarized at the Aspen Institute found ". . . industrialists are confident that *eventually* new technology will . . . create more jobs than it destroys." But, "eventually" may mean a decade or a generation (*Economist* 24 March 1984; Aspen Institute).

In the 1960s, there were 2½ unemployed workers for every job vacancy reported. In the 1970s, there were 4 unemployed for each reported vacancy (Abraham, 1982). During 1982, about one half of all unemployment was "chronic," a figure which combines the total of discouraged workers who have given up hope of ever finding work and the long-term unemployed (Sherraden, 1983).

These phenomena are spread throughout the western industrial world. The Organization for Economic Cooperation and Development reported that unemployment as a percent of the workforce rose steadily in France, England, West Germany and Italy between 1979 and 1983 and forecast a continued rise in 1984. To make the trend more ominous, the trend toward long-term unemployment, defined to be 12 months or more, is rising in European industrialized nations. The proportion of all unemployed who are out of work over 12 months is projected to reach 45 percent in France, 40 percent in England and 30 percent in West Germany (*Economist,* June 9, 1984). Rising productivity (due to new technology) explains the forecast. At the same time, the proportion of part-time workers in the workforce increased almost everywhere. In the U.S., the rate ranged from 13.9 percent to 14.4 percent between 1973 and 1981. This trend is often interpreted as disguised un- or underemployment; alternatively, it is interpreted as a sign of a new lifestyle. The latter interpretation is supported by studies in Canada and the U.S., but these indicate that 25 percent and 32 percent of part-time workers respectively want full-time employment (Economist, 9 June 1984 and 16 June 1984). There are more optimistic viewpoints but a closer look at even the optimists leaves some reason for concern. One analysis concludes that if real growth at 3.5 percent a year (the rate during 1952–72) can be sustained up to 1995, then unemployment may drop to 4.5 percent. The drop will result in large part because the growth in total labor force is assumed to decline–meaning fewer new workers over the next ten years (Silk, 1984).

Such evidence has led many thoughtful economic analysts to conclude that recent optimism about the abolition of poverty through growth is hardly justified. The notion that increased investment in machines is the best way to ensure economic growth is possibly outmoded. The idea that prosperity may be better served by employing human beings even if the machine can do the same job is coming into fashion again. The European Commission has ominously concluded that, for the mature economies of Europe heavy capital spending in the past decade has produced a poor return, in part because real wages have risen rapidly ahead of technical progress (*Wall Street Journal,* November 19, 1984).

It is increasingly clear that the tempo of change has accelerated, but that this human loss has not been appreciably reduced. If we look at unemployment figures in the U.S. in recent decades, the social problem of unemployment seems to have taken on a more complex form. We now have at least four groups of able-bodied unemployed, each with its unique character which calls for its own solutions. There are workers in their middle years whose workplace has disappeared in the face of international competition or technology, e.g., steel, auto and rail workers. When they are in their middle years, their unemployment may last a short time, or it may last for many years. The outcome depends in whether there exist reasonable ways for them to learn new skills, reasonable ways for them to move (or be moved) to parts of the country where new jobs have been created, and whether new jobs have been created fast enough to absorb them as well as young workers newly entering the labor force. For a significant part of this group, unemployment stretches into retirement. Most difficult of all, for most who do find work, or fail to in time, the result is downward mobility–their next economic status is likely to be lower than the one they formerly occupied, meaning declassing and reduction in standard of living.

The next group is made up of new labor force entrants, young people and mainly those belonging to minorities whose educational opportunities have been hampered by remaining racial prejudice. For many young people, special training helps, but, for many, long years of total or erratic unemployment is the likely outcome. Many of them, no one knows for sure how many, never enter the official labor force. They "drop out," are the permanently discouraged who may enter either an underground economy of sorts and eke out a living, or they enter a life of crime or dependence. Chronic unemployment for minorities has increased twice as fast as for other populations (Sherraden, 1983; Bane and Ellwood, 1982).

A third group is made up of single parents with small children. They can and usually want to work, but family responsibilities require changes in workplace hours and conditions for them to carry the double load of job and family. Changes in workplace, or supports such as child day care, are at so primitive a level that many single parents cannot carry out both responsibilities. They end up on AFDC and remain economically dependent until their children are old enough to look after themselves. But by that time, age and lack of work experience or education place the mothers at a gross disadvantage in the workplace. This population mostly of young mothers, often teenaged, have replaced the conventional widow for whom AFDC was originally designed.

Finally, there is the large reservoir of older workers who retire under present industrial and public policy incentives, although they have, on average, 10 or 15 years of active, vigorous life ahead. Many of these retired persons want to do something productive and useful, although not necessarily at full time. As labor shortages crop up for certain tasks, they are a prime unused labor resource, especially as the proportion of minor children and retired adults becomes a larger and larger part of the total population, leaving a relatively smaller middle-adult workforce to perform all the tasks of modern society.

The evidence about able-bodied dependency is unclear and difficult to assess in simplistic terms. What does emerge clearly is a phenomenon of sizable persisting dependency or unemployment among able-bodied citizens of all ages. Two firm and one speculative bits of evidence support this conclusion. Recent studies of people in poverty, mainly a population of AFDC mothers, reveals that about 60 percent of those who are in poverty at any one time are likely to remain in that state for eight years or more (Bane and Ellwood, 1982). While many on AFDC do turn over rapidly and leave welfare, a larger percent take so much longer, for reasons noted above, that their life chances are irretrievably marked for the worse. While about two-thirds leave welfare because they earn more or are reconciled with their husbands, 40 percent of this two-thirds soon return to welfare again. Another 14 percent leave only when their children have grown up.

Another bit of evidence is hard to ignore. In the past ten years, debate in the U.S. has come to treat an unemployment rate of between 6–

7 percent as acceptable—almost "normal"—whereas the previous decade's figure was 3–4 percent. Such averages conceal gross regional and ethnic disparities and exclude those who are discouraged or who only find sporadic part-time work year to year. The creeping rate of accepted unemployment may become ominous. Many unemployed are not captured by statistics on unemployment. In 1982, the Chairman of the Council of Economic Advisors reported that the unemployment rate in a time of full unemployment is 7 percent (Feldstein, 1982).

To this new category of clearly needy, the able-bodied for whom there is no work for long periods of time, must be added an increase in the volume of conventionally accepted dependency. Our medical science makes it possible for large numbers of permanently disabled infants to survive into adult life with their severe handicaps. An estimated 6–19 percent of newborn infants with low birth weights or respiratory trouble will have life-long neurological damage (Morris, 1976; Newacheck, 1984). Their numbers have doubled in 25 years. A hundred thousand youths with spinal cord injury sustained in war, by sport, automobile or work accidents, can now live for decades with full or partial paralysis.

At the other end of the age spectrum, the proportion of those over 65 years of age has increased to 12 percent in 1984 and is projected to rise to 15 percent or even 20 percent in future decades. In some states (Florida) and many small towns, the proportion is already 20 percent. The aged over 75 years are the fastest growing sector of the population. They are the ones who face severe disablement and debilitation. Twenty percent of them will have no close surviving relatives. Taken together, this population forces new attention to the ancient tradition of responsibility for the aged. The able-bodied over 65 have capacities, little role to play in society and are supported by a younger generation. Those over 75 need amounts of medical, nursing and personal care far in excess of that envisaged in the past. The intergenerational obligations have reached a level unknown in past eras (Colvez and Blanchet, 1981; Rice and Feldman, 1983).

For our society to cope with such a phenomenon, we still fall back on either of two formulae: either the individuals are at fault in not finding a way out of their dilemmas alone and independently; or, we expect that technology will produce new jobs and higher incomes fast enough to absorb this population in a relatively short period of time. The clues we have, viewed over several years' time, indicate that neither approach is suitable. A new approach to the complexity of modern day dependency of the able-bodied willing to work is called for.

The growth in number of people without work contains an anomaly, the impending shortage of workers for many of the basic tasks of welfare which involve care for the physically or mentally handicapped. The traditional pool of such caretakers has shrunk as women enter the primary labor market and are freed from household drudgery, and as the network of young adults and relatives also shrinks with lower birth rates. The permanent tasks which social support services entail are often unpleasant and unrewarding: looking after the demented, the incontinent, the paralyzed, or children with severe functional disorders. Although pay for skilled professionals in the personal care fields has risen, the unskilled nonprofessionals—on whom fall many of the burdens of actually looking after this population in the home or institutions—remains to a large extent underpaid. At the same time the otherwise unemployed are usually unskilled and not sought after by social agencies responsible for caring for helpless people, especially when the agencies lack the financial resources to provide training or wages attractive to those who make up the permanent unemployed pool.

There has not yet evolved any framework for reducing this contradiction by linking the unemployed pool and the manpower requirements for personal care at the less than professional level. If it is not addressed, some unpalatable consequences can be foreseen: a great increase in wages for low skill work in welfare; or a return to massive institutional care for the helpless without any improvement in labor skill for caretaking; or simple neglect of a most helpless population. It is unlikely that the situation can be relieved by blaming the unemployed for not filling positions which are physically demanding, which are viewed by most people as servile and degrading, which are poorly paid, and which are located in organizations reluctant to welcome untrained personnel. There is an opportunity to develop new ways to link these two aspects of welfare: unemployment and welfare manpower requirements. Although the reservoir of ideas for government initiative in work (considered in Chapter 13) is a starting point, it is not in itself sufficient for the task.

This analysis excludes those who drop out of society's vision and disappear into a limbo of unemployment, who no longer try to make their way against the obstacles which contemporary society and its economy place in their way. They are not counted as part of the labor force; they are not counted any longer as unemployed. Many of these show up in crude estimates about an underground economy where people survive somehow, by barter, cash exchange without records, or crime.

Since 1980 it has become popular to argue that unemployment is caused in large part by the economic drag of badly planned welfare programs, in other words, that the welfare state produces unemployment. A recent analysis finds that all social benefits (including those accruing to the middle class) may account for at most a 6 percent reduction in hours worked by persons in the labor force. While this reduction may reduce GNP by about 4 percent there are offsetting social benefits which need to be considered, some of which result in redirecting resources to education or health. Even more interesting is the argument that, as people are economically better off, at any level there is a natural desire to enjoy the fruits of their higher income by having more leisure time (Lampman, 1984, p. 141). The implications of this argument about the link between work and welfare are explored further in Chapter 13.

Changed Attitudes about Self and Community

While these changes have been taking place, public attitudes about obligation have diminished. Resistance to taxation is pervasive in the middle class, as well as among the wealthy who, together, make up 80–85 percent of our population. Less well known is a decade-long increase in skepticism about government's ability to do everything well and an even deeper dissatisfaction about the way our welfare system is working, a dissatisfaction which is shared by all parts of the political spectrum, including the poor themselves.

More disturbing than this is the continuing growth in self-regarding opinion which leaves less and less room for concern about others, especially strangers (Lasch, 1978; Fishkin, 1982; Hochschild, 1981; Cook, 1979). We have come to expect that each individual is entitled to realize his or her own potential to the utmost, but obligation to help others has not been a major criterion of citizenship, of morality, or of behavior—especially when helping a stranger reduces the means for one's personal improvement. The force of obligation, once rooted in primary institutions such as the family and the neighborhood, has been attenuated. No institution regularly teaches concern for others as a major criterion of character: not church, nor schools, nor family. And if they try to, their authority is not strong. Individual freedom is enhanced, not group obligation. Individuals move easily so that neighborhood roots are not put down deeply and community cooperation is diminished. Individuals have personal associations which arise out of work or hobby, both of which are means to personal satisfaction, and not a basis for social sharing.

The economic profile of the population supports this self-regarding tendency. Fifteen percent of a nation's population is very poor and, by world standards or standards of the past, the condition of most of this 15 percent is not desperate (Lampman, 1984; Bawden, 1984). The 80 percent in a middle or lower-middle class position have reasonable comfort, but are insecure in their hold on this comfort. How much generosity is it reasonable to count on when this less than secure majority in the middle receives appeals for the poor who are able-bodied, who are seldom seen, and who are sometimes of a different race and culture?

This self-regarding tendency has been building for at least a hundred years, aided by the power of Freud's work which turns the thoughts of so many of us to that inner world of self which he opened up. Most of us are freer than were our forebears, but it is doubtful that we are more caring about strangers.

The Self-Regarding Society

The doctrine of *utilitarianism* has come to be used in the search for balance between freedom for self-realization and collective concern for the general well-being (what produces the most good for the most people). Since it is difficult to define the general good the closest approximation becomes the sum of individual activities, each directed at satisfying individual desires. Theoretically, this definition avoids individual actions that injure others through government, moral conviction, ethical standards or social pressure. But, as the institutions of religion and philosophy have declined in significance as far as daily life is concerned, so has the social pressure of face-to-face community life. In their place the twentieth century has produced elaborate and complex structures of government, but it is just such government power which is viewed with skepticism. Therein lies the contradiction. Government is used to underwrite emancipation of the oppressed, to liberate disadvantaged groups, to expand civil rights at the same time that the burden of caring for others through government has come under the sharpest attack.

We have come to rely on the driving force of the individual and special group interest to construct public organization for the common good, and at the same time we fear that government destroys or limits individual freedom and growth. Nevertheless, lacking any general principles for sharing, we rely on the joint effort of like-minded persons with special interests to be pursued. Steel and auto manufacturers, utility companies, wheat, cotton or tobacco farmers, auto and garment workers are now joined by groups politically concerned with such single issues as abortion, women's rights or school prayer. Instead of fertilizing the democratic political process, the opposite may have occurred. The more special interest groups become active, the more citizens withdraw from general public issues. They vote less; they withdraw to the protection of private insurance; to private pursuits of family, neighborhood, or to pleasure seeking. An extreme seems to have been reached in which joint effort for one cause comes to mean escape from collective responsibility for the larger society in which all must live, e.g.: the opposition to taxes while expecting service benefits; the evasion of regulations; the call to replace a national social security system for private insurance; the preference for private health insurance in place of national health insurance; and the growth of private police, sanitation and security forces which now exceed the public police forces.

These tendencies have been exacerbated by growing polarization in the society, in which the once dominating middle or lower-middle and working population is being squeezed into two groups, growing farther and farther from each other. If one uses the median household income for 1983 ($26,105) as a base and include in the middle class all who are between 75 percent and 125 percent of that median, then the middle declined to 23.2 percent of all American households, a drop from 28.7 percent in 1967. Forty percent of those leaving dropped down in economic terms and 60 percent rose higher. At one end, those in poverty rose from 11.1 percent in 1973 to 15.2 percent in 1983; and the proportion of upper income families rose from 36.3 percent of the population in 1967 to 39.3 percent in 1983 (Thurow, 1984). The results are increased self-interest due either to anxiety about the future or to confidence about further self-improvement.

These trends have been building certainly since 1970, with roots planted well before then. The 1980 and 1984 elections revealed the extent of drift in public opinion, and in public debate away from government, but with an absence of serious public discourse about joint activity and toward private efforts. One large-scale study in England, a bastion welfare state, found 65 percent of informants favoring some public protection *but* with freedom for individuals to contract out to buy their services privately, 44 percent favored people paying more for their health care (Judge, 1983).

The balance between authority and freedom, the individual and the group, is hardly a technical, numerate issue; it forces attention to philosophy, values, and ethics which become the secular forum for probing questions once settled by religious doctrine. Superficial assertions about prized values in social welfare do not do justice to the more basic questions, such as:

1. What is an acceptable balance between our individual and our social wants? How will we reconcile the desire of each of us to be free to act in ways which please us alone, while at the same time, we depend on others for so much of our existence—nourishment, shelter, love.
2. What is our view about the nature of humans? Are men and women altruistic, or greedy or some mix of both? Can social organization be improved on? In effect, is man's condition and man himself, perfectible? By natural processes or by joint action?
3. What is the nature of rights which people claim for themselves? And what are the corresponding obligations? Does the balance of rights and obligations differ among those who are members of a kinship family and between those who are strangers to each other?

Such questions are embedded in the welfare debate, although the answers determine the nature of a culture, the character of all human relationships and organizations, not just the fate of a welfare program.

In the U.S., the argument in favor of social responsibility has been weaker than in other western nations. It often has been argued that Marx and Freud, along with Darwin, have shaped twentieth century thought. I may be straining to suggest that Marx, stripped of his later Leninist and

Communist Party incrustations, represents the search for collective social responsibility; while Freud represents the search for private, personal, and perhaps selfish gratification. In the U.S. at least, it is the latter who captured the popular imagination and unwittingly laid one foundation for the resistance to public and social responsibility in favor of individualistic approaches.

If this interpretation is approximately right, it explains the recent turn of events in which the foundations of national public responsibility for human needs is challenged at its core by individualism as much as by the new conservatism. The ancient conflict between altruism and selfishness is now being played out on a large political stage. Welfare programs are at the center of the drama.

There is an opposing view about the generosity of ordinary citizens: that they are more generous in their behavior than in the past. As affluence spread, so grew willingness to contribute to philanthropic causes, as well as voting for increased taxation to support so many social programs. The evidence pointing to choice between the two views is ambiguous at best. Opinion surveys have not elicited any clear preference in the trade-off between more services and more or less taxation. Most surveys find respondents supporting specific welfare programs but opposing welfare in general (Cook, 1979; Schiltz, 1970; Miller, 1977; Jaffee, 1977). They are about equally divided between those who support more welfare and those who want to cut it to a bare minimum. While it is true that 1980–83 efforts to slightly reduce Social Security benefits were bitterly contested and defeated, at least temporarily, these benefit more in the middle class than those in deep poverty. At the same time, tax cutting has continued to be widely popular. There is little shared consensus about a core of public responsibility for welfare. As for philanthropy, much the largest share of giving is for religious or educational institutions, not for welfare.

Democratizing Welfare: Unexpected Consequences

One explanation for this ambiguity in public attitudes may be found in the special form which modern social welfare has taken: tax funds are used to help both the poor or disadvantaged *and* the middle classes, one through direct benefits, the other through tax concessions. This leads us to probe the consequences of this democratization of welfare for civic concern for the poor. If this has, in fact, occurred, then the foundation for philanthropy in human relations may have also been transformed. Philanthropy has been, historically (at least after the Greek period), an act of generosity flowing from those who have means to those who have little. Its premises and motivations were voluntary and personal, based on an individual sense of obligation, rooted in fear or guilt or a conception of human decency. Democratization has converted a personal sense of obligation in the giver to a claimable right held by the recipient. But, it has also resulted in a system which builds up social benefits (the sharing of the national collective wealth via legislation and taxation) through satisfying the wants of more and more interest groups. Not only the poor but the middle and upper economic classes also benefit from special treatment by foregone consumption taxes (i.e., taxes foregone for borrowing to buy houses, automobiles, to pay for education), and special treatment of income and costs of corporations and industries.

At the height of the war on poverty, 1965–1968, the Office of Economic Opportunity received about $6 billion or about 1 percent of the national budget. In 1961, spending for the non-poor came to 30.1 percent and in 1976 it rose to 54 percent (due to Social Security and Medicare benefits which are not mainly for the poor). In 1983, AFDC, a major welfare program, cost $8.2 billion while forgiven taxes for home mortgage interest came to $19.6 for those with incomes over $30,000; and capital gains benefits (intended to stimulate the economy) came to $28 billion (Harrington, 1984; LeGrand, 1982).

It may not be stretching a conclusion too far to suggest that the modern welfare state, as evolved in the U.S. at least, is fueled and maintained by the demands of many interest groups rather than by a deeply held sense of obligation toward the poor and underprivileged. If any of this speculation proves valid, then the foundations for the future welfare state may be quite different from the past, which combined a long history of philanthropic concepts of obligation with newer ideas about rights and expectations of all citizens. Democratizing in this sense also meant equalizing access to social welfare for all, not for the poor. The unexpected consequence may be that the old sense of civic obligation to others— especially a minority—is now competing with a more self-regarding concern for one's self and one's group.

Two 1984 analyses support this conclusion. Lampman (1984, p. 122) found that 56 percent of cash and in-kind benefits go to female-headed families with minor children, the disabled, and the aged who constitute 25 percent of the population. All others received 44 percent of benefits, mainly in the form of health and education benefits. Most of these latter benefits are not conditioned by earnings, they are universal benefits, whereas most of the benefits received by the aged, disabled and mothers with children are earnings-conditioned, that is, means-tested in some way. In a similar vein, Bawden (1984, p. 39) divided social programs between those available to everyone and those available only to low income persons. He found that between 1965 and 1984 expenditures for programs available to all averaged 80 percent of all expenditures, and were of course distributed without regard to economic need. In the same period about 20 percent of all expenditures were assigned to programs for low income individuals.

The popular assumption that growth in welfare or governmental expenditures has been due to a "welfare dependent" population is not well founded. In fact the total number of beneficiaries under Aid to Families and Dependent Children, Supplementary Security Income and General Assistance (the traditional relief categories) increased only slightly above the growth in population between 1970 and 1981, or at a rate of 13.2 percent against an 11.5 percent increase in population (Bawden, 1984, p. 77).

Some further evidence to support this interpretation is found in aggregate data derived from the U.S. Census, especially if these data are viewed in a broader perspective than is usual for welfare analysis. Consider gross data on the total numbers of persons directly dependent for income on the federal budget, but without regard for customary designations of welfare beneficiary; and then match these with data about distribution of federal funds through *all* payments to individuals.

This summary is incomplete in many ways but the basic trends are probably accurate. If we were to add the AFDC and SSI population (10,742,000 in 1960 and 23,152,000 in 1980), the total number of persons dependent on public taxes directly for income grew from 5.9 percent in 1960 of the total population to 10 percent in 1980. If one excludes these categories and limits the total to military and civilian employees and institutionalized persons such as prisoners, etc., the proportion of the

TABLE 3.1   Persons dependent on Government Tax Payments
in 1960 and 1980[1]

	1960		*1980*	
Total U.S. population	179,323,000		226,505,000	
Military: on Active Duty	2,476,000		2,051,000	
Direct civilian				
Employees	1,047,000		960,000	
Retirees	256,000		1,360,000	
In federal prisons	212,193		314,272	
In state prisons	—		791,000	(1979)
In other institutions	1,887,000		2,172,000	
Children in care	73,000		48,000	
In nursing homes	491,000	(1963)	1,240,000	(1978)
Institutions for retarded	158,700		148,195	
Juveniles in custody	76,576		73,958	
Parolees	155,100	(1974)	301,000	(1979)
Total "institutional dependents"	4,873,311		7,908,425	
Percent of total U.S. population	2.7%		3.4%	

SOURCE: *Derived from Statistical Abstract of the U.S. 1981, Tables 29, 598, 330, 326, 183, 187, 173.*

TABLE 3.2 Public Cash Income Maintenance Payments in 1960–1979

Total	1960 $25.9 Billion		1979 $193.2 Billion	
	Dollars	*%*	*Dollars*	*%*
OASDI	11.1 billion	43 %	104 billion	53.8%
Public Employees	2.6 "	10.1%	34.3 "	17.8%
Veterans Benefits	3.4 "	13.1%	10.6 "	5.6%
Public Assistance	3.3 "	13.0%	12.4 "	6.4%
SSI	—		7.2 "	3.7%
Unemployment Insurance	3.0 "	11.7%	9.9 "	5.2%
Temporary Disability	.4 "	1.6%	1.0 "	.6%
Workmen's Compensation	.9 "	3.5%	8.5 "	4.5%
R. R. Retirement	.9 "	3.5%	4.4 "	2.3%

SOURCE: *Statistical Abstract of the U.S., 1981, Table 524.*

population so supported has risen from 2.7 percent to 3.4 percent. Our record of public generosity is substantial, but note the not insignificant increase in military retirees from 5 to 17 percent, and in nursing home residents, from 10 to 15 percent of the institutionally dependent population. If such data were enlarged to incorporate all beneficiaries of social insurance retirement, then the proportion of middle class or nonpoverty recipients would increase even more.

If we turn to the distribution of funds among these recipient groups, the shift to favor the more secure in the population becomes more clear-cut.

The trend in federal payments to individuals favors public employees, the retired (not all of whom are poor), and the work injured. Public assistance beneficiaries (AFDC and SSI), veterans not drawing military benefits, and the temporarily unemployed have reduced their share of the total. The proportion of such payments going to social security, federal employee and military retirees has risen from 50 percent to 63 percent.

The Social Security Act is often selected as a target for reduction on the grounds that it is mainly a "middle class" program. It would be more accurate to charge that it is a truly universal program, the most equitable in the American system. Still, it is true that it reaches a significant minority who are not poor. Twenty-one percent of its beneficiaries have household incomes over $20,000 a year, of which, on average $5,300 may be attributed to social security payments. At the same time 43 percent of elderly households have incomes under $10,000 and 2.2 million live at the poverty margin. As a universal program it reaches many with low incomes, and a sizable minority who are not poor.

This distribution of welfare benefits is also found in England where the highest socioeconomic group absorbs 40 percent more of national health services than do lower income groups; 50 percent of education expenditure and 100 percent more of housing benefits (LeGrand, 1982).

Consequences

This broader view of what welfare means in a modern state was first pointed out by Richard Titmuss, but public and citizen understanding has not yet caught up and public action is commonly taken on the basis of older beliefs about what the term *welfare* means. It is possible that much of the difficulty in coping with modern allocations in a welfare state derive from this split between understanding and the reality of political choices.

In effect, we have democratized our political behaviors without a comparable change in our accepted conceptions about the scope of welfare. The inherited roots of caring for others were embedded in ideas about charity, from those who have the means to those who lack them. The premises were voluntary, personal, rooted in a sense of obligation or guilt or fear. But, democratization has not only converted personal obligation into claimable rights, it has produced a system which shares national income among more and more interest groups through spreading the scope of social benefits. The poor, as well as the middle classes, all benefit from special treatment, but the latter more than the former. This sense of income sharing is maintained by the competing demands of many interest groups, each seeking their own preferment, not by a sense of obligation to others. The civic sense of obligation to the poor now competes with self-regard for each person and his or her group. When the poor and worst off are so small a minority, their power to make claims is reduced.

The consequences for a future welfare strategy are profound. If we concentrate on the neediest, we must rely on some concepts of obligation the strong have for them, rebuilding a sense of obligation. Such obligation could be cast in terms of charity or in terms of equity and equal rights, but either stance must be so formed as to secure the acquiescence, in the end, of a now dominating majority. If, instead, we concentrate on creating a new society, democratizing of benefit to all citizens, we face the conflicts of innumerable interest groups and lack principles with which to protect a weak or small minority. Habermass and Schumpeter have suggested, each in his own way, that governments may have difficulty sustaining the enlarged expectations that democracy imports into a market economy (Taylor-Gooby, 1983).

These tendencies seem to shatter the paradigms we have used up to now to deal with those in trouble. In creating a new paradigm, encouragement may be found in a theory of great awakenings in American history, first in 1730–1760, then in 1800–1830, and third in 1890–1920 (McLoughlin, 1978). In each of these three periods, a generalized sense of unease produced a return to older religious beliefs and then a surge forward with new ideas more suited for the times. In the 1890–1920 period, the surge ahead joined religious faith and primitive socialist ideas in a social gospel movement, and the Progressive Era. But, how we will now refashion our structure for social caring is still problematic.

The solutions we find for the future will depend on the meaning we give to philanthropy, to concern for others, and to the welfare state concept. Do these terms mean, in an open democratic system, wide acceptance that most of us must give to help others, not only voluntarily but through compulsory philanthropy which public, tax financed programs require? Or, do they now mean the competition of various specialized interests each jostling for a share of social welfare? If the former, old concepts of obligation may have to be reinterpreted and reaccepted in modern society. If the latter, what will protect the helpless in the competition?

If the foregoing line of reasoning proves valid, then the shaping of welfare state programs in the near term future will be quite different from the past efforts to press forward on all fronts. The state to come may be different, but we lack firm or, more important, widely acceptable, concepts with which to proceed in constructing that future. The thrust of these remarks is to emphasize the extent to which welfare advocates face a task of conceptualizing before they will be ready to move on to political action to secure enactment of specific legislation. The concept building will involve attention to basic moral dilemmas, to stubbornly held popular ideas, as well as to abstract ideological formulation. The future will probably not be as selfish as the enemies of a welfare state propose, nor as expansive as the advocates would like.

It is humbling to recall from our history that the one period when a state combined public and private resources to assure minimum existance for *all* citizens was the classical period of Greece and Rome when most were poor. Conditions of life and public expectations and adequacy of provision are much different now, but the central principle of universal state responsibility, at least for food for the poor, was well established 2,000 years ago, and then lost until recent times.

The last chapter sets forth an alternative agenda which tries to wed new conditions to our historical past so that a new national consensus can be formed.

But, before we can jump to the future, it is necessary to study the foundations for popular and commonly held views which permeate the day-to-day thinking of most citizens and policymakers. The next chapters trace these foundations and their contemporary expression in public opinion.

PART

II

THE EVOLUTION of CARING CONCEPTS

THE EARLY RECORD
Middle East and Biblical Foundations

> *Thou shalt not harden thy heart nor shut thy*
> *hand from thy needy brothers but shall surely*
> *open thy hand unto him.*
>
> *DEUTERONOMY 15:7–8*

The preceding chapters have laid out in broad terms the uncertainties which confront the welfare state as critics from all parts of the political spectrum have probed its weaknesses. We turn to the history of man's evolving methods for dealing with human distress as one way to better understand the present and to anticipate the future. This history is offered as the intergenerationally transmitted reservoir of beliefs which today governs ordinary citizens' reaction to various welfare proposals. We inevitably turn to the Bible and to its ancient Middle Eastern antecedents.

The Bible, especially the Hebrew Bible, is not only a religious text, it also constitutes a rich written record of the evolution of ethical thought upon which the major streams of contemporary altruistic behavior are based. The biblical stories summarize a record which has been constantly refined, sifted and reorganized over several millennia. The current canonical form took shape perhaps 500 or 600 years before the common era and was reinterpreted, elaborated, and refined over the next several years.

This history was shaped within the Middle East and eastern Mediterranean ranging over what is now Iran, Iraq, Turkey, Syria, Israel, Jordan, Egypt and Greece. This region contributed to the early Hebrew history and also to the intellectual foundations of the modern world. The people who produced the Jewish scriptures were not only shaped in this environment, but they were themselves an amalgam over centuries of differing tribal and clan groupings which finally coalesced into what became known as The Twelve Tribes of Israel. They brought with them echoes of their diverse origins which in turn were finally shaped into an accepted body of ethical, historical and symbolic writing.

65

The Example of Earliest Egyptian Values: Negative Virtues

Similar evolution was taking place in Assyrian, Mesopotamian and Chinese societies with each taking a different form. Egyptian sources are used here to illustrate a much wider history. The Egyptian culture, the most ancient with a substantial written record, developed a set of ethical concepts which contributed to subsequent developments. An early Egyptian inscription reads:

> But justice lasts forever and goes down into the necropolis with him who renders it. When he is buried and joined to the earth his name is not wiped out on earth but he is remembered for goodness. That is a principle of the divine order. (Pritchard, 1955, p. 4).

There is also an early form of what later came to be known as the Golden Rule, "Do to the doer in order to cause him to do (for thee)" (Pritchard, 1955, p. 409). One can interpret such surviving statements as implying that the motives for "goodness," however that was then defined, were a personal concern about one's afterlife, or a way to insure acceptable treatment by others in this life. But since most of these statements refer to the behavior of a ruler, a Pharaoh, in his relations with subordinates or inferiors, they may have been efforts to temper the exercise of power in an authoritarian class structured society. However interpreted, that society articulated limits on purely selfish, willful, behavior, and had accepted concepts about obligations which people owe each other.

Such inscriptions usually refer to the obligations of great or of powerful individuals to render justice on the basis of need, not on the exchange of favors. High officials and rulers could command with authority, but they were expected to be moved by rules of justic and mercy. This combination of power and benevolence was first personified in the person of the king but ideals governing his rule were expected to be observed by other powerful persons. Benevolent or just behavior appears to be a beneficence granted by a superior to a subordinate or inferior. There is no suggestion of right held by the subordinate. Whatever goodness or justice meant, it was embedded in dependency of the weak upon the strong.

Some of this dependency with generosity is captured in a variety of proverbs and precepts compiled by the Vizier or advisor of the Egyptian Pharaoh, King Eizzi, around 2450 B.C.E.

> Let not thy heart be puffed up because of thy knowledge; be not confident because thou art a wise man. Take counsel with the ignorant as well as the wise.

> If thou art a leader commanding the affairs of the multitude seek out for thyself every beneficial deed until it may be that thy own affairs are without wrong. Justice is great and its appropriateness is lasting.

The Vizier Ptah-Hotep advised his son:

> If thou art one to whom petition is made be calm as thou listeneth to the petitioner's speech. Do not rebuff him before he has swept out his body or before he has said that for which he came. A petitioner likes attention to his words better than the fulfilling of that for which he came.

> If thou art one of those sitting at the table of one greater than thyself take what he may give when it is set before thy nose. Thou shouldst gaze at what is before thee. Do not pierce him with many stares for such an aggression against him is an abomination. Let thy face be cast down until he addresses thee and thou should speak only when he addresses thee, laugh after he laughs and it will be very pleasing to his heart and what thou mayest do will be pleasing to his heart. (Pritchard, 1955, p. 4)

Just what was meant by good or just behavior is explained, in part by what have been called "negative confessions." Papyri gathered under the title "Book of the Dead" contain a variety of such "confessions" which suggest behaviors to be avoided by the deceased because this should assure a good life after death. Many of these negative confessions are injunctions not to injure another person rather than being assertions to do a positive good for others. For example:

> I have not done violence to a poor man; or I have not made anyone sick or weak.

> I have not taken milk from the mouths of children. (Pritchard, 1955, p. 4)

A significant part of the ethic of that time may have been the avoidance of injury to others, a concept which persists millennia later in conservative political views about the proper limits for government.

However, there are also hints that the concept of goodness and justice included generosity or altruism beyond the avoidance of doing evil and the maintenance of a status structure. As early as 2600 B.C.E. some maxims were inscribed for a nobleman of the 27th century B.C.E.,

> I gave bread to all the hungry of (his domain); I clothed him who was naked there. (Breasted, 1934, p. 123)

And for another nobleman of the 26th century B.C.E.

> I gave bread to the hungry, clothed the naked, I ferried him who had no boat. (Breasted, 1934, p. 123)

Such statements are preserved in writings buried with the deceased and would appear to be evidence carried by the deceased into the next world as proof that he had lived what the religion of the time considered to be an appropriate life.

Thus far the lay reader of these epitaphs would be justified in concluding that the motivation for justice and goodness lay in a basic selfishness—assuring a safe afterlife or selfish security in this life. But, in Egypt as elsewhere, ruling structure and religious beliefs outline the structure of other human relationships.

For thousands of years the social, political and economic organization which men created was shaped by belief in the relationship between men and some superordinate power, or superior gods. Secular and religious life were not separate. Men saw themselves acted on by powerful superordinate powers which might be exalted, pleased, placated but never controlled. Secular power was tangible, but an unpredictable nature was omnipresent. Great men and small were subject to the demands of a religious conception about this relationship.

In Egypt Pharaohs were not just selected worldly agents of the gods, they were gods on earth who were expected to be guided by certain concepts of doing rightness or justice, being true. As a result, many terms such as "maat" refer to unselfish or just behavior, a rightness which is both created by, inherited and passed down from king to king. The orderly stability of the state depended on expected behavior which also consolidated the status quo (Breasted, 1934, p. 123; J. A. Wilson, 1951, p. 48).

From the earliest record, men evolved ideas about not injuring others, about justice in relationships between weak and strong, about unselfish acts performed because they seemed just. It was incidentally true that such moral and ethical precepts, however narrowly they were defined, also served the interests of individuals, and of powerful institutions.

Development in the Jewish Scriptures

The Hebrew Testament elaborates its ethical concepts, discusses them more fully and transmitted them more fully than is true for other early societies. For the first time the obligation to a stranger is enunciated as well as the obligation to members of the immediate family, tribe, or clan. The poor are not only mentioned but their characteristics and their requirements elaborated upon. The reasons supporting a particular behavior towards the disadvantaged were elaborated in a subtle and complex formulation, which outlined not only man's relationship to a deity but man's relationship to his fellow man and to his social order.

Throughout this history it is possible to trace a continuing tension between the unfairness, the brutality and the injustices encountered in the real world on the one hand and the attempts to introduce and to impose more civilizing, humane ideals upon peoples and leaders struggling in an imperfect world. A moral code evolved about behavior in relation to real life conditions. Calls to behave with justice or goodness—

vague abstractions—are interspersed with examples of what constitutes goodness in specific situations.

The evolution of a moral code was neither direct nor steady. Tribes and clans and antagonistic groups, not yet nations, were in continual conflict with each other. The Hebrew experience was a centuries-long attempt to mold, to maintain, and to preserve a collective identity in which tribal practices, forms of governance and religious practices were constantly invaded by practices from other groups as well as by the physical threats of welfare and struggle for secure territory. The written record alternates between violence, warfare or selfishness and generosity, friendship, charity and humane concern for others. Different behaviors are in continuous contention.

Despite these difficulties, it is possible to trace the growth of precepts about human relationships, and about relationships between the weak and the strong which resonate so well with contemporary concerns about human welfare that they can be treated as antecedents. This is not to argue for any direct, lineal evolution of ideas. Rather certain concepts were articulated which add to the sum of man's meandering efforts to define and soften the pattern of humane interaction.

It is not clear whether biblical ethical concepts were enforced by peer social pressure with religious exhortation or by enforceable civil actions. The earliest Middle Eastern world was a mix of rural and agricultural populations and relatively small (by present day standards) urban centers. For hundreds of years people's associations and relationships were governed by their membership in tribes, and by bonds of kinship. Life was lived out in relatively small face-to-face communities although ethnically diverse tribal members may have lived together. Government was carried out at different times by religious leaders or judges or kings who were men, not gods as in Egypt.

Although life was built upon a religious foundation, people in their daily lives wavered between the perceived or taught wishes of a superordinate deity and the harsh demands of daily existence. There was alternating belief, backsliding and repentance as to particular religious forms, but a belief in or a fear of supernatural power persisted. Sometimes men believed they could discern a rational pattern to the wishes of a deity. Natural hazards of existence, the disasters of social relationship were seen to be linked to an individual or a nation's conformity to the wishes of such a deity. This belief could equally be drawn on to justify a priestly class of leaders or to impose civilizing and socializing rules of behavior to maintain stable social and political organizations. Whether the ethical writings of the period represent efforts to create a social order, or to humanize man's relations with his fellowman, or to impose a religious theological basis for man's relationship to a deity, or a combination of the three, is less important than is the nature of the concepts which emerged.

The closeness of small community life implied above cannot be interpreted to suggest equality among all members. Differences emerged early. Some were strong leaders, some were more powerful or more wealthy than others. In the emerging class structure, however, the persistence of the past cannot be overlooked. In both ancient Israel and in later ancient Greece, special status and regard was attached to the founding fathers whose arrival and lives were dimly retained by an oral tradition out of the very ancient past. In both peoples, concepts of virtue and valor were attributed to these fathers of the nation and their descendants. This attribution was used to legitimize certain ways of behavior to each other. Some in Israel held positions of special influence which took the form of priesthood in the Temple. This attachment to the past may have been due to various considerations. Early settlers or their survivors may have become more wealthy than later arrivals—simply by virtue of having been on the scene first. Similarly, they would then be able to pass the accumulation of wealth and, therefore, of influence on to their descendants. Or the desire to preserve the historical continuity of the nation may have been powerful; or worship of ancestors may have been part of the culture. Whatever the reason, the hold of the past over the present was very strong, major changes took place slowly within the society, and the past was a powerful legitimizer for concepts about behavior between individuals and groups. Despite this slowness, revolutionary changes in thought developed and took hold. These are briefly summed up, not as a simple evolution but as a complex of ideas which were given enduring place in a written record.

The Obligation to Perform Acts of Positive Good

Perhaps the most revolutionary concept, for our purposes, was the assertion that individuals have a positive obligation to perform acts of helping or doing good for others. It must remain a matter of speculation whether in prehistoric societies, people developed a pattern of helping each other because they sensed the need to do so to preserve the small family or tribe from decimation, as a simple matter of small group survival, or whether such caring impulses are imprinted in the human species through genetic selection, as the sociobiologists suggest (Wilson, 1975) or through divine creation. But sometime around 800 B.C.E. it was possible to reduce an oral tradition to written form in which one persistent theme was the injunction to help the helpless. The following excerpts from various sections, and thus various time periods, illustrate the point:

> If there be among you a needy man, one of thy brethren, in thy land thou shalt not harden thy heart nor shut thy hand from the needy brother; but thou shalt surely open thy hand unto him. (Deut. 15:7–8)

> Thou shalt not oppress a hired servant that is poor and needy whether he be thy brother or the strangers that are in thy land within thy gates. (Deut. 24:14)

> When thou reapest thy harvest in the field, hast forgot a sheath in the field thou shalt not go back to fetch it; it shall be for the stranger, for the fatherless and for the widow; when thou beatest thine olive tree thou shalt not go over the boughs again; it shall be for the stranger, for the fatherless and for the widow. When thou gatherest the grapes of thy vineyard thou shalt not glean it after thee; it shall be for the stranger, the fatherless, and the widow. (Lev. 19:9–10)

The strength of injunction to care in a positive active way for the most helpless—the widow and orphan—is underlined in Exod. 22:20–23:

> Ye shall not afflict any widow or fatherless child. If thou afflict them in any wise . . . my wrath shall wax hot and I will kill you with thy sword. . . .

With so violent a punishment for injuring the widow and orphan, God himself promises to punish the transgressor directly. This is perhaps the only place in the Jewish scriptures where God threatens to punish directly; in the case of all other violations of the law punishment is through indirect means.

The antiquity of concern for a stranger, albeit an individual not a group, is shown in Exod. 24:12–25 in the story of Abraham, the patriarch of Israel's servant who is sent to Abraham's homeland to secure a wife for his son Isaac. The servant chooses Rebecca as wife because, in her behavior to the servant, a stranger, she displays thoughtfulness and caring to ease his thirst and to assure him a night's lodging.

But an even more general and far-reaching concept about concern for the poor is found in the story about the destruction of Sodom and Gomorrah as retold in Ezek. 16:49–50. Sin is not only individual abomination, but collective when a whole community is affluent and well-fed but neglects its poor:

> Behold, this was the iniquity of thy sister Sodom: pride, fulness of bread and careless ease was in her; neither did she strengthen the hand of the poor and the needy.

By another reading:

> [See, this was the guilt of your sister Sodom: pride, surfeit of food and prosperous ease . . . she did not aid the poor and needy.]

The obligation to care for others was differentiated from the Egyptian concept of justice which seemed to mean avoidance of injury to another. In the Jewish scripture, helping others is a positive obligation to act, not a negative one to refrain from injuring. Isa. 1:17 urges, "learn to do well, seek justice, relieve the oppressed, judge the fatherless and plead for the widow" which may suggest that caring for others is a powerful enough concept to stand by itself and to be followed for its own value. However, elsewhere it is asserted that the mere fact of giving alms is in itself an act of justice, an idea elaborated in the interpretations of later centuries so that the Hebrew word 'Tsedakah' literally means not charity but justice—do justice, not do charity. In Prov. 21:3 it is said that alms-giving is greater than all sacrifices of the temples, for giving alms means doing justice; it is more acceptable to God than making sacrifices. Without legalism, just relationships between human beings involves sharing so that the helpless are not deprived nor is the stranger.

Perhaps more important than such verbal distinctions are the acts which constitute helping. They are not merely the giving of alms, or the sharing of the produce of one's farming (by not gathering the gleanings) but include physically helping the blind and the crippled. This elaboration can be traced in various guides about how to help others. Thus in Isa. 58:6–8:

> Is this not the fast that I have chosen? To loose the fetters of wickedness. To undo the bands of the yoke, and to let the oppressed go free and that ye break every yoke? Is it not to deal thy bread to the hungry and that thou bring the poor that are cast out into thy house? When thou seest the naked that thou cover him? Then shall thy light break forth as the morning and thy healing shall spring forth speedily and thy right-eousness shall go before thee.

Such exhortations or assertions do not suggest a society in which laws of state enforce the obligation to care for the helpless; but their reduction to the fundamental literature of that society suggests a powerful chain of normative or norm forming values and aims. The behavior of individuals is influenced by a religious structure, by the peer pressures of face-to-face communities, and by reiteration, not by civil laws.

Care for the Stranger

Ethical thought developed beyond concern for one's immediate kinfolk or for the members of the small group making up a tribe or clan, bound together by ties of kinship and living together. The obligation to show concern extended to the stranger in the group to whom was owed the same obligation as was owed to a member of the family.

Understanding earliest ideas about the place of the stranger is complicated by the concept of *stranger* in ancient times. In the earliest biblical period the basic form of social organization was probably the extended family (Ben Dor, 1982). But the extended family was, at first, tied to land which had to provide support for all.

A recent study (Ben Dor, 1982) suggests that because "the sojourner, orphan and widow" became "strangers" to their own kinship group due to economic and cultural pressures which threatened its survival, patriarchal societies depended on family possession of enough land to support all its members. Constant subdivision of land among male sons reduced holdings below a survival level which meant that some sons received no land and had to leave to find work elsewhere. Daughters who married outside the kin group became "strangers" in that they were no longer part of a close group attached to "its" land. The ties of kinship oscillated between dispossession (for survival) and caring. A body of ethical principles evolved out of alternative reactions to group members who were treated as "weaker" in terms of group survival. Decisions were taken concerning each other's rights and obligations. The departing members might be living in the same community, geographically nearby their own family, but they were strangers in the new extended family they entered. It is possible that injunctions about caring for the stranger were ways of inculcating a sense of obligation to these dispossessed or relocated. In this way some family obligation to its kin remained but was modified by recognition of their new status.

Such ideas of obligation were also extended to other strangers, meaning non-kin individuals, who found themselves in a host area. Strange groups or tribes were often viewed with suspicion and hostility, but obligation was imposed to treat strangers in need. This was a major advance in human relationships. In the history of the flight from Egypt it is said, "There shall be one law for you and for the stranger who dwells among you." That which is done for the majority is sanctioned for "outsiders". Later post-biblical explanation of this evolution was that Jews, historically, were slaves and strangers in the land of Egypt. Once they left and re-established themselves in their own land and homes, they were continuously enjoined by the annual celebration of exodus (in the Passover ceremony) to remember that they once were slaves and strangers in an alien land. In thankfulness for their deliverance, they were obligated to avoid repeating that experience for others. Later suggestions such as this are made:

> In a city where the are both Jews and Gentiles and collectors of alms collect both from Jews and the Gentiles; they feed the poor of both, visit the sick of both, bury both, comfort the mourners whether Jews or Gentiles, and they restore the lost goods of both for the sake of peace. (Montefiore, 1960, p. 424)

Such appeals are often repeated, and the concept of caring for the stranger is included whenever reference is made to the obligation to care for any disabled or helpless person. The bonds of personal identification between human beings were present: strangers were individuals who were known, could be seen face to face and could be evaluated by the helper. Whatever underlying impulse leads to caring for others—compassion or self-protection—that impulse was sustained by human interaction. It was a caring relationship quite different from that called for in an urban, impersonal society of the twentieth century.

The origins of giving to or helping the helpless are obscure. One interpretation assumes that the practice derived from ancient views about sacrifices men made to the gods to appease a supernatural force. They can also be viewed as attempts to stimulate whatever charitable instincts the gods might have to confer material benefits on the earthbound worshipper. They can also be seen as altruistic gestures to provide sustenance to the gods through ritual temple gifts; the pagan world often considered gods as dependent upon material sustenance given by men (Sarna, 1966, p. 158).

In the earliest form, giving sacrifices or gifts to the gods was an example of "I give that you may give," a self-serving act. Somehow the urge to satisfy a deity was transmuted into a charge to give to helpless humans as a way of pleasing the gods, and this finally became a secular injunction although with religious sanction to care for others. In later post-biblical elaboration, the injunction became infused with belief that loving care for others was a way to approach God in reciprocal loving manner. Whatever the evolution, the concept of helping the helpless was well established by 800 B.C.E.

The Methods of Helping Others: Individualization

Almsgiving or helping others was surrounded by many clues and details governing the behavior between giver and receiver of help. Some of the language, in aphorisms and tales, has a modern ring if one risks anthropomorphic translation of ancient terms into modern usage. But an important limitation must be introduced. Although the general concept of the helpless or the poor is used repeatedly, the examples given to illustrate the general term are almost always those of the widow, the orphan, the crippled or the victim of some natural disaster. With one exception to be noted later, the remission of debt and bondage, differences in status and well-being are assumed to be a natural state of the world; this is not a time when comfort or affluence for all could be thought of as a possibility. While belief in helping victims of circumstances over which they have no personal control was widespread, there was little consideration of equal sharing of goods.

Individualization was early introduced into thinking about care. Post-biblical commentators who analyzed the meaning of each word of the Bible noted that Ps. 41:1 "happy is he who *considers* the poor," not "happy is he who *gives* to the poor." This is taken to mean that, in fulfilling the commandment to help the poor the giver must take into account their human need, the reasons for their circumstances of need, and their past condition.

In Deut. 15:7–8:

> If there be among you a needy man, one of thy brethren, thou shall not harden thy heart not shut thy hand from thy needy brother; but thou shalt surely open thy hand unto him and thou shalt surely lend him sufficient for his need in that which he wanteth (i.e. lacks).

The emphasis is upon "need," the need of one who lacks specific things.

Elaboration of the meaning of such terms as "consider" and "need" became especially rich in post-biblical and Rabbinic times. There are anticipations for contemporary views about welfare programs designed to meet the circumstances and requirements of an individual recipient. In later commentary, examples are often given about how the giver must consider the social status of the needy person. If a needy individual, who was formerly well-to-do or of high status, is now the victim of disaster he should be given help according to his former status including, if necessary, a horse and a slave or worker to help him with it. There is no suggestion of equalization for all.

An even stronger condition for helping others is the maintenance and building up of self-respect. Instructions about *how* charity is to be given and *how* care is to be extended are as important as the injunction to look after the needy itself. The texts and their later interpretations command men to treat those who are less fortunate in terms which will preserve and sustain their dignity, make it possible for them to maintain themselves with respect in their community and enhance the prospect for their resuming an independent way of life.

The most widely quoted injunctions about charity have to do with the means by which it is administered. A hierarchy of value is established. At the lowest level there is some honor to him who gives charitably to another under conditions in which the receiver knows who the giver is and the help is given directly. However, the highest honor is reserved for the donor who helps another in such a way that the receiver (who is unknown to the donor) neither knows who is giving the help nor that in fact it is given in charity.

Is it unreasonable to suggest that the injunctions to leave the gleanings of the field or of the orchards behind and not to take everything in the harvest implies that the poor are able to come and take what they need from these leavings without being demeaned to have to beg from another directly. An ancient rabbi is quoted as urging that "He who gives money to the poor publicly, it had been better that he had given nothing than that he had given him and put him to shame (see P. Hag. 5A in

Montefiore). The principle of preserving the self-respect of the beneficiary is pervasive. Some Rabbinic leaders used to wrap their alms in a fold trailed over their shoulders so that when they went to visit, the poor could help themselves secretly without his knowing who was helping himself to this "poorbox."

But always the best form of relief was considered to be in the form of a loan, even if later it becomes necessary to convert the loan into a gift because the recipient is unable to repay it.

> He who gives alms a blessing is upon him; he who lends is yet better and he who gives a poor man money to trade with and become a partner with him at half profit is better than either. (Montefiore, 1960, p. 425).

One of the highest forms of philanthropy was that in which the donor provides capital to the needy person to help him undertake or re-enter a useful enterprise (Montefiore, 1960). When direct alms are given that donor is more worthy who says to the needy person "I am loaning you this, not giving it to you. I'm loaning it to you without interest even if there is no certainty that the loan can be repaid." For a wealthy person to take a poor person in as a partner was considered the best of all charity and the one to be most richly rewarded in God's eyes.

Obligations of the Poor: Work and Self-Respect, Independence

Lessons about caring for others were given with full appreciation of the variety in man's character and temperament. Each person's obligation to work for his own well-being and condition was as important as the obliga-tion to help those in distress. The reiteration of the few categories of need for which charity or helping is enjoined: widows, orphans, crippled, vic-tims of disaster—implies that others were considered more or less re-sponsible for their own lives. Poor individuals were expected to regain their independence; the poor were expected to work if possible before relying upon the alms of others. For example:

> Hire yourself out to work which is strange to you rather than become dependent upon others. (Montefiore, 1960, p. 409)

> When thou needest the labor of thy hands, happy shalt thou be and that shall be well with thee. (Ps. 128:2)

A Rabbinical interpretation of Gen. 21:24 and Job I.10 is:

> From this passage we learn that the merit of labor avails where the merit of ancestry cannot. Learn then that a man should not say "I will eat and drink and enjoy good and I will not burden myself for heaven will look after me." Therefore it says, "his handiwork hast thou blessed." It is

incumbent upon a man to toil and work with his hands and then God sends his blessing. (Montefiore, 1960, p. 443)

And about Gen. 2:15;

Great is work for even Adam did not taste anything til he had worked for it is said God put him in the garden to work and keep it.

Intimations of Freedom: Equality and Equal Opportunity

These earliest injunctions and later teachings were not limited to charity and work or to the conditions under which one person helps another. Although there are no comprehensive logical statements of all the cumulative wisdom and conviction about generosity or caring, the Old Testament, and its subsequent interpretations are a mosaic of aphorisms, commandments and stories which accumulated over centuries in response to many explicit and practical human conditions, needs, and aspirations. But, for example, there exist clues about concepts of equality of opportunity:

At the end of every seven years thou shalt make a release. And this is the manner of the release: every creditor shall release that which he has lent unto his neighbor: he shall not exact it of his neighbor and his brother . . . . Howbeit (if) there shall be no needy among you—for the Lord will surely bless you in the land which the Lord thy God giveth thee for inheritance to possess it—even only thou diligently harken unto the voice of the Lord thy God to observe, to do all this commandment which I command thee this day . . . . (But) if there be among you a needy man one of thy brethren, within any of thy gates in the land. . . thou shall not harden thy heart nor shut thy hand from thy needy brother, but thou shall surely open thy hand unto him and shall surely lend him sufficient for his needs in that which he wanteth. . . . For the poor shall never cease out of the land: therefore I command thee saying, "though shalt surely open thy hand unto thy poor and needy brother in thy land" (Deut. 15:1–11)

"If thy brother be sold unto thee he shall serve thee 6 years; and in the seventh year thou shalt let him go free from thee. And when thou lettest him go free from thee thou shalt not let him go empty; thou shalt furnish him liberally out of thy flock, out of thy threshing floor and out of thy winepress; that wherewith the Lord thy God has blessed thee thou shalt give unto him." (Deut. 15:12)

These seem to be the seeds of primitive socialist thought within a religious framework. In this early period all that man has, including his very life, is viewed as a gift from God to be held in trust and to be retained only if the injunctions of God are observed. Periodically we shall be relieved of burdens which fate, condition or human error have imposed—so that a fresh start can be made. While it is accepted that there *may* always be poor *generically, any individual* is to be helped in ways which will reduce the likelihood of this dependency. When slaves, indentured servants or by extension employees are dismissed they are not to be dismissed empty-handed. Instead, such individuals are to carry with them sufficient means with which to make their own life based on the assumption that their periods of employment, servitude or bondage contributed to the creation of the wealth which the employer accumulated during the period of this servitude.

Interdependence of Rich and Poor

Despite the clarity of the concepts just summarized, there also exist in this early history other comments and assertions which are open to various interpretations. These may represent contradictions in the human condition which remain unresolved to the present. Must there always be some who are poor? There is little to clear up whether it was believed that the poor would always be with us, later becoming the justification of a status quo distribution of power and means. What is clear is that in those earliest of times, the rich and poor could not ignore each other and still be considered to live morally or in conformity with the wishes of God. Both rich and poor existed, were bound together, and owed something to each other.

The Rationales for Caring for Others

The main tenets about caring for others evolved in the biblical period but the motivation for their acceptance remains unclear. A sociological reconstruction could infer that earliest leaders and philosophers sought to define the characteristics of a civilized order in which human beings could live with some security and stability in a world less than benign. Religion and its institutions had at least a latent function to give a structure for concepts essential for group survival. The structure educated average members of the community about behavior requisite for a stable and fruitful existence. Fear, the threat of retribution by an all-powerful deity, was used at first. The biblical history posits a compact between God and His people, with injunctions about behavior which could not be lightly ignored. Whatever originally led to the inclusion of charitable acts between human beings, failure to act appropriately explained disasters which befell individuals or the group. Thus, Isa. 1:17 exhorts "learn to do well, seek justice, relieve the oppressed, judge the fatherless and plead for the widow." But his exhortation is also accompanied by the accusation that the nation has become sinful and its people laden with iniquity. Originally, this meant worship of pagan gods and abandonment of ritual observance. Only much later were other behaviors given religious sanction. As a result, the country has become desolate, the cities are burned with fire and strangers devour it. The people are appealed to change their evil ways through the word of God who says:

> Let us reason together. For your sins be scarlet they shall be as white as snow if ye be willing and obedient but if ye refuse and rebell ye shall be devoured with the sword.

These commandments were transmuted into concepts of justice. Still later they were interpreted to mean expressions of love and loving kindness between human beings, the foundation for a community of love which binds all men together through the acts of helping each other. Such loving relationships were still seen as the earthy expression, between humans, of the relationship which men reasoned should exist between God and mankind. Fear was replaced by love as the impelling justification for this giving and caring relationship between those who are better-off and those who are in trouble. The perfectibility of mankind is expressed in the degree to which concern for others is infused by love, not pity or fear or insurance in an afterlife.

To the post-biblical Rabbis, alms giving is greater than all sacrifices of the temple because giving alms means doing justice and is more acceptable to God than making sacrifices. Alms giving is considered to be increasingly perfect in human behavior according to the amount of love that is shown in it. Simeon the Just said:

> Upon three things the world is based: upon the Torah, upon the Temple service, and upon doing of loving deeds. The world of the beginning was created only by love. (Montefiore, 1960, p. 430)

The biblical basis for such interpretation appears, for example, in Prov. 21:3:

> Loving deeds are greater than alms giving. (Hos. 21.3, 10:12)

The caring acts which individuals perform for each other are earthbound expressions of the loving relationships which exists (or can exist) between God and man. Temporal loving deeds serve as advocates between men and their God. Almsgiving is great not because it saves the individual from the threat of retribution, but because it brings closer the day of ultimate redemption and human perfection, whether in this world or in some future world.

In the twelfth century, the scholar Moses Ben Maimon known as Maimonides codified more than a thousand years of Hebraic tradition, rooted in the original biblical period interpretations.[1] Psalms 119 and 108,

---

[1] The following section draws on the Introduction of the *Code of Maimonides* by Isador Twersky (New Haven: Yale University Press, 1980).

which read "Accept I beseech thee the free will offerings of my mouth Oh Lord and teach me thine commandments," are interpreted to mean that there are self-imposed obligations rooted in personal and nonlegally enforceable behavior. These parallel the formal commandments which lack a formal structure for enforcement. He postulated a congruence between each individual's creative and spontaneous gestures and duties imposed with God's fixed laws.

The seventh book of the Maimonidean Code deals with philanthropy, gifts to the needy and the nurturing of a deep-seated altruism. It is concerned with "instilling pity or compassion for the weak and the wretched, giving strength in various ways to the poor and inciting us not to inflict the hearts of the individuals who are in a weak position" (Twersky, 1980, p. 266).

The cumulative 613 commandments or ordinances which are scattered throughout the Old Testament and in subsequent commentaries were ordered by Maimonides into a pattern in which three purposes were identified:

1. To establish a civilized society based on the principles of social utility and justice.
2. To develop the ethical personality, based on principles of good and love of fellow man.
3. To reach intellectual perfection through knowledge and experience of God.

In Maimonidean retrospect it is argued that human nature is almost immutable, but not completely so. Human nature is not easily changed. Love and charity do not come easily, without effort. The transition from polytheistic idolatory to a belief in the transcendence of a single God was a foundation for the evolution of other beliefs about human relationships.

At an early stage giving was insufficient; it was expected to show sensitivity, sympathy and graciousness. An objectively benevolent act could be vitiated by rudeness: "Did I not weep for him who was in trouble, was not my soul grieved for the poor?" (Job 30:25) is interpreted to mean that whoever gives charity to a poor man ill-manneredly and with downcast looks has lost all the merit of his actions, even if he should give a thousand gold pieces. Giving should be with grace, with joy and sympathy for the poor, otherwise sharing with others becomes a hedonistic indulgence, not a religious performance.

SUMMARY

It is possible to "stitch together" from these disparate injunctions, summary statements, words of the Old Testament and their interpretations a coherent early structure for helping others.

1. All who are needy including strangers are the appropriate objects of caring. Members of one's group who are widows, orphans, the sick and aged, along with the stranger, represent the core of the needy—those who became so by virtue of conditions beyond their control.

2. The cohesiveness of a face-to-face community depends upon the maintenance of supportive relationships among all the members and so the methods of alms giving are designed to encourage independence, self-respect and dignity.

3. Work to help oneself is an obligation on all.

4. The differences in economic and social status require that the variant needs of individuals be taken into account including the level of present need as defined by past status.

5. The value of caring depends upon its execution in loving kindness rather than as an unpleasant duty. We are obligated to be concerned with others.

6. Whatever fate or nature gives to each one, that material wealth is still only possible due to God's beneficence; none of us is sole owner of his good fortune. Our relationship with this ultimate source requires that we share our surplus with others less fortunate. Whatever wealth one has is partly due to and owed to those who worked for us.

　　　　Such concepts represent one foundation of contemporary thinking. The ancient society changed as economic, political, social and military conditions changed, as invasions and dominance by other powers emerged. Towards the end of the pre-Christian era, the nation had many elements of corruption and decay. Vigorous attempts were made by dissident groups to restore ethical principles, to revive the ideals of loving devotion to God. By the time of Hillel the Elder (37–4 B.C.E.), the Essenes, the Hasidim and many other groups were seeking to restore an ethical foundation to their life while under Greek or Roman rule. Some stressed mercy or loving kindness, others social justice and still others argued for a sharp distinction in the world between good and evil. Hillel recognized that most people were neither wholly bad nor wholly good but represented some mix of the two. The balance of good or evil could be modified by an appeal to a morality outside of individual material interests. He sought to revive concepts enunciated in the Psalms about the poor and the especially beloved of God, concepts with which more prosperous and influential groups associated with the Herodian Court were not especially sympathetic. In this period Hillel's statement remains a moving testament to the value and place of altruism in human affairs: "If I am not for myself, who will be for me? But if I am for myself alone, what am I? And if not now, when?"

　　　　After first century turbulence in the Middle East (successive rebellions against Rome), we next consider a different basis for care in a different society—ancient Greece.

5

ALTRUISM IN THE GREEK AND ROMAN WORLD
Concepts of Reciprocity[1]

> *Why should the worthy be in want when you have wealth?*
>
> *HORACE*

The Emergence of Secular Concepts about Altruism in Polytheistic Societies

The monotheistic and religious ideas which were briefly summarized in the preceding chapter became one foundation of Western thought. Two different strands in the ancient world were added to what became the moral basis for Western approaches to philanthropy. One of these strands is the evolution of Catholic Christian thinking, taking off from Hebrew scriptures. The second strand is that represented by the concepts, philosophies and practices of ancient Greece and Rome.

GREEK ORIGINS AND DEVELOPMENTS

Greek society shared several elements in common with those of the ancient Middle East but differed in other material ways. The Greek society was also tribal in origin. Identification with early progenitors played an important part in shaping the class structure and the types of citizenship rights which evolved. The society was small scale, a face-to-face one in which social pressures were important. The early foundations for philanthropic thinking emerged around 700–800 B.C.E., when the Greek society valued the self-maintaining units of that society—the family and the phratry or clan and brotherhood. Religious beliefs were polytheistic.

---

[1] Much of the following discussions about concepts of philanthropy and rationales for caring for the stranger are drawn from A.R. Hands, *Charities and Social Aid in Greece and Rome*, Thames & Hudson: London, 1968, and works cited.

The borderline between the gods and man was blurred. In mythology gods sometimes visited humans directly and even lived with them. By some theories of the time, about the third century B.C.E. (Dill, 1905) the gods were once great kings and warriors who were deified for their good deeds. Intellectually much attention was given to the development of philosophy and science not necessarily rooted in religious belief: medicine, logic, philosophy and mathematics flourished. While there was a significant agricultural hinterland, with some religious centers such as Delphi and Delos, the Greek culture was organized mainly in relatively small city states rather than around one major city-state. Each housed a core of religious worship with many small dependencies and an agricultural hinterland.

Although many contemporary concepts about democracy have their origin in early Greek philosophy, Greek society was "democratic" only as regards a relatively small percentage of the population in any city state. By 300 B.C.E. out of an estimated population of 500,000 in Attica, 40 percent would be slaves, 12 percent full citizens of the *polis,* and the rest in other statuses—resident foreigners, artisans or freemen without full citizenship rights. Control was held by relatively small elite groups which, at first, traced real or imagined descent from tribal forebears; it was a wealthy independent class whose members did not need to work. The broad base of the population was either slave or artisan; in Greek thinking a poor man was any man who had to work with his hands, even though he was independent in an economic sense and frequently owned a small number of slaves himself. The man who was not 'poor' was the man who did not need to work with his hands.

Most of the record upon which present understanding is based is a record of the intellectual elite, the philosophers and the upper class, their letters, their plays, and the surviving records of city-state official actions. Except through this intermediary record, little is known of how the great bulk of the population treated each other in their more humble daily affairs. Practically, a picture of Greek thought about philanthropy is that of an upper class regarding man-to-man relationships as defined by that class background.

Early Views about Helping the Stranger

Eighth century Greek society was built around the family or the clan as the basic unit. A king in the territory was the head of the strongest claim and had responsibility for the members of his unit, family and related clan members. Odysseus returning from his wanderings disguised as a beggar engages in a conversation about the responsibilities of the leader for his dependents or his workmen and says:

He (the leader) would have looked after me properly and pensioned me off as a kind master does for a servant who has worked hard for him and whose work heaven has prospered as it prospers the job I toil at here. Yes the King would have rewarded me well for this. (Homer, *Odyssey* xiv)

But even as early as the eighth century B.C.E., some obligation to the stranger was acknowledged. Some characters in *The Odyssey* argued:

My conscience will not let me turn away a stranger in a worse state even than yourself for strangers and beggars all come in Zeus' name. Take this food and give it to the newcomer and tell him to go the rounds himself and beg from each of the company in turn. Modesty still sits ill upon a needy man. (Homer, *Odyssey* xiv)

You did wrong to strike the vagabond. You are a doomed man if he turns out to be some God from heaven. And Gods do disguise themselves as strangers from abroad and wander round our town in every kind of shape to see whether people are behaving themselves or getting out of hand. (Homer, *Odyssey* xvii)

Man's life is short enough. A churlish fellow with no idea of hospitality earns the whole world's ill will while he is alive and its contempt when he is dead; whereas when a man does kind things because his heart is in the right place his reputation is spread far and wide by the guests he befriends and he has no lack of people to sing his praises. (Homer, *Odyssey* xix)

Such generous views were contested at the same time.

May I ask why you brought this fellow to town? Haven't we tramps aplenty to pester us with their wants and pollute our dinners? (Homer, *Odyssey* xvii)

Who would take it on himself to press hospitality on a wandering stranger unless he were some worker for the public good, a prophet, a physician, a shipwright, or even a minstrel whose songs might give pleasure? For all the world over such guests as those are welcome whereas nobody would call a beggar in to eat him out of house and home. (Homer, *Odyssey* xvii)

Reciprocity and Friendship as a Basis for Philanthropy

According to Hands (1968) and the sources he cites, most documents surviving from ancient Greece deal with exchange between peers. The giving of gifts was self-serving—the giver anticipated the receipt of something in return (a gift or help) at a later time. While this may seem only a prelude to an economic transaction, such gift exchange was more likely to be a basis for all kinds of intercourse and social interaction among peers. It was a way to confirm interrelationships and to knit social cohesion. Giving something to another had the purpose of establishing friendship as much as being "done for another."

Because of this background, the earliest usage of the term *philanthropy* meant the exchange of gifts between equals, between friends. The giver may not only have expected a return gift but even to have asked for it. One of Thucydides' fifth century aphorisms is:

> He who has done a favor is in a stronger position while he who is in the position of owing one finds that friendship has lost its edge since he is aware that by making a return he will not retain a response of gratitude but will merely be paying back the generosity. (Hands, 1968, p. 31)

But as early as 400 B.C.E. the culture had shifted enough so that it was no longer considered suitable for the giver to openly expect a return. Democritus (460–362) would declare: "The generous man is not the man who looks for a return but he who is predisposed to confer a benefit" (Hands, 1968, p. 31). Demosthenes (384–322) would write: "For the benefactor to remind a man of what he has received almost amounts to rebuking him" (Hands, 1968, p. 32). Aristotle (384–322) would say: "If you receive a favor keep it in mind; if you confer a favor forget it" (Hands, 1968, p. 3). Aristotle urged that the value of a gift is not judged by its intrinsic worth but by the spirit of the giver. By the third century there was a competition among those who did good, that is, outdoing one good turn by another. But gifts were probably made to others of one's class who were *able* to make a return even though it was not asked for or even expected.

In time there emerged insights into the psychological relationships between giver and receiver of gifts. Interdependence among people of a given class, the maintenance of friendships, was important for general stability and security in the city-state. It also served as personal insurance in that one individual depended upon the moral obligations felt by those who were considered to be friends. This sense of dependence was often grating against the sense of independence and freedom from dependence upon others. Public speakers, performers, orators, or educators had to receive payment to meet their material needs but would treat any fee as a reciprocal kindness, interpreting their performances as having at least of equal or greater value than the monetary fee they received in return thus obscuring the dependency on the exchange. This fee would not be "demanded" but was expected in the near future (Jones, 1957).

Aristotle's definition of a generous man suggested that his wealth was important not for its own sake but as a source from which he could give to others. "Wealth consists in its use as a means of securing friendships rather than its being possessed." (Aristotle, EN 1120, B7; Rhet. 1361, A28; see Hands, 1968, pp. 29–35).

Today one may wonder how the term *philanthropy,* which in current usage, suggests a one-way direction of benefits, evolved out of this original two-way meaning. The meaning of the Greek noun for philanthropy suggested love of *a* man (not of all men) by someone other than a man—possibly a deity. By extension, it came to mean gift giving by powerful rulers to their subjects or by wealthy persons to their dependents. This was elaborated on in Rome into a significant clientele culture as will be discussed later. Oriental despots distributed gifts, food, honors widely and often extravagantly although they did not depend on others, especially for the poor, for approval.

There was an expressed as well as latent recognition that friendship, upon which a high value was placed, was also a way of knitting societies together. Aristotle would say: "In the tyranny where there is nothing in common for the ruler and the ruled neither is there any friendship. . . . It is friendship which in fact acts as a bond within cities" (Aristotle, *EN* 1160a). In the course of time, holding public office was treated as an exchange for substantial gifts by the wealthy. In the later stages of Greek society the burdens of public office became too onerous and were seen as part of an unfair exchange. Public service also became compulsory rather than being a free honor; various devices were used to extract contributions from the wealthy for the good of the city. Over time the value placed on peer friendship among free (non-poor) citizens of the city-state working together towards a common end was converted into a more complex set of inderdependencies fixed in a clientele system between a patron and his dependents. The reciprocity or exchange over time became less and less equal.

Community Philanthropy Plus Friendship Reciprocity: Benefit to the State

As early as 594 B.C.E., in Solon's time according to Plutarch (Loch, 1938), a variety of collective or social group arrangements emerged for the poor. Money was lent in order to permit a client to maintain an occupation. Emigration was arranged to assist the needy in caring for themselves or to relieve the state of caring for numerous agitators (Loch, 1938). The city purchased corn with contributed or public funds and distributed it at reduced rates from public granaries. The state used gifts from wealthy persons to import food and to distribute it at reduced rates to keep prices low. Free corn was distributed to those who were physically unable to earn; special funds were established for war orphans for whom the city-state was responsible (Hands, 1968, pp. 63–76).

Givers distinguished between the personal giving of food or shelter to beggars and other more generalized gifts to the poor. Voting citizens, full members of the *polis,* could be paid certain sums to serve on juries, to attend festivals and to participate in plays—an indirect way to assure income without it being naked charity.

When Athens turned from the marketplace to purchase grain for distribution it was to protect citizens from famine. Demosthenes was elected corn buyer before 339 B.C.E. The only condition for the receipt of grain purchased by the state was citizenship. (Slaves dependent in a personal sense on their master, were therefore not included.) The poor as such are not mentioned as a particular object of such philanthropies but are considered part of a larger body of citizens. While the definition of citizenship excluded many groups, a kind of universality applied in distributing life's necessities to those who made claim.

In addition to general "income support" through grain distributions, the state appointed guardians to oversee the upbringing of children, whose fathers were killed in battle. They were raised at public expense. No reference is made to public support for widows. At no time did the doing of good necessarily imply an obligation to rescue or aid the poor. Aristotle (*Rhet.* 1361, A28) defined the giving as doing good for one's fellowman and not for the poor; good for one's fellowman involved the payment for public services, ransoming prisoners of war (Hands, 1968, p. 35). In fact the earliest evidence of sympathy to those not related by kinship or friendship is found in the treatment of prisoners, i.e., ransom for prisoners of war. Social, civil altruism emerged later.

The Rationale for Gift Reciprocity: The Nature of the Return

Surviving inscriptions from Greek city-states make it clear that philanthropy was not originally altruistic. Gifts were provided by or solicited from the well-to-do with the understanding that the donors would be honored in proportion to generosity. Much solicitation served the normal functioning of the city, e.g., rebuilding of walls, building of commercial boats and the purchase of grain for public granaries. The recognition of generosity was not so different from that which prevails today in voluntary philanthropy: donors of small sums have minor honors conferred, being listed in a book or on a small plaque, whereas donors of large sums are honored by having a building named after them. One major difference was the link between gift giving to the gods, as part of religious practice, and gift giving among humans. The religious shrines were showered with gift objects of great and of minor value.

Gifts for the well-being of the community were not limited to material goods or money for civil purposes. Gifts to build temples could take the form of labor contributed directly by dependents of the well-to-do assigned to the task. Even gentlemen contributed labor. The Acropolis was built, in part, through such gifts.

Voluntary contributions were solicited for the purchase of corn and oil which could be sold at below market price for the poor or distributed free to those who were entitled to it. The difference between the price paid for supplies purchased by contribution and the price at which they were distributed was a gift from the donors and was so recognized.

A form of supergiving attempted to assure a kind of "immortality" after death. In Greece a common maxim was: "Man likens himself to God in doing good." This association between supergenerosity on the part of kings and noblemen was elaborated in Roman society which treated kings and emperors as if they became divine while alive. Similar seeking after immortality is found in early Christian as well as Roman thinking.

Who Were the Deserving Poor?

The poor in Greek life were all of those who had to work by their hands as well as those completely dependent upon others because of sex, age or illness. But views about who is entitled to an altruistic act (gifts from person to person) require explanation. The Greek concept of philanthropy included concepts about what the twentieth century calls the "deserving poor." Greek writers would argue: "Do good to the good." Aristotle would say: "The generous man would not give to just any one." And Cicero in Roman times would say: "Give to the most deserving," or "Give to those who are worthy." Seneca would say:

> Give to those who are capable of being made good. . . . to certain people I shall not give even though there is a need because there will still be a need even if I do give. (cited in Hands, 1968, p. 44)

In ancient Greece the categories of persons to whom ethical obligations were acknowledged included one's parents, old people, one's friends, the stranger who was seen as a guest, fellow citizens, and unfortunate persons or suppliants within the limits described above. In the fifth century B.C.E. these suppliants were usually persons who had been banished from other states, the shipwrecked or prisoners of war. Able-bodied residents who took to begging were seldom referred to favorably. Plato's Socrates says:

> If you wish to be loved by your friends you must benefit your friends. If you desire to be honored by some city you must be useful to that city. If you desire to be admired by all the worthy men of Greece you must try to benefit Greece. (cited in Bolkestein, 1939, II–168)

These early foundations for caring for others were rooted in the concepts an educated and upper class held about the suitable character of the person to be helped. But the even earlier record in the *Odyssey* revealed the same emotion:

> Welcome to your home only those who work for the public good—physi-
> cian, shipwright, minstrel. Nobody welcomes a beggar who would eat you
> out of house and home. (Homer, *Odyssey*)

Aristotle considers the good and the happy man will consider worthy of
his love and friendship above all the person who is the closest counterpart
of himself. Cicero suggests that one should take into account the recipient's sympathetic and cooperative attitude toward the donor's way of life
and the contribution which he has made in the past to the donor's well-
being (Hands, 1968, pp. 26–36).

Such views about the character and integrity of the recipient survived in the thinking of some (but not all) early Christian fathers who
linked sympathy to "worth" in those who sought alms. In Greece, concepts about the recipient did not imply any sense of empathy with or pity
for the person in difficulty. Philanthropy meant first, as we have seen,
acts to benefit the community, the city or the commonwealth. Philanthropy to outfit a ship, to pay for a public drama, to ransom prisoners
was more valued than gifts to help individuals in distress. Socrates offered as a basic doctrine that one should live the good life in his own
home, do good to friends and benefit the state (Bolkestein, 1939). This
logic had little sympathy for the poor and the able-bodied just because
they were poor.

The able-bodied beggars received little encouragement and their
plight is not unlike that of able-bodied unemployed workers of the West of
today. The beggars are those who "entreat." The other poor who might
have small landholdings and even have one or two slaves did not "entreat" since they worked with their hands. They were the recipients of
gifts through the patron system discussed below or through a civic exchange process discussed above. Pity was reserved, if at all, for great
people overwhelmed by unavoidable disaster, as in the Greek tragedies;
or for a merchant who had all of his ships, and therefore all of his wealth,
wiped out in a sudden storm; or for soldiers captured by the enemy who
had to be ransomed but who returned home destitute; or for widows of
previously hardworking yeomen.

Philanthropy was for one's fellows not for "the poor." Aristotle argued that it is in the interest of the wealthy to give their surplus revenue
to the poor, but not as pity. Pity implies that there is no moral claim held
by the recipient. Giving is a way to ensure cooperation and civil concord—
the basis for all relationships. Gifts were not given to a man but to
mankind collectively. This differs from both early Old Testament and
later Christian thinking which emphasize the obligation to individuals as
much as to community.

While this was the general pattern, philosophical inquiry into altruism asked whether there is a place for genuine personal regard for
others. Philosophically, was man capable of being wholly altruistic, of
engaging in a wholly altruistic act? Aristotle refused to accept a purely

cynical interpretation of giving which compared benefactor and beneficiary to creditor and debtor. On the contrary, Aristotle argued: The benefactor has a sincere kindness and affection for the man he has assisted.
He loves his work of giving because he loves existence, it is part of the
nature of things. This may seem to be a secular extension of the religious
belief that one gives because of a desire to perpetuate in man's relationship to man the natural love which God has for man. In later Rome,
Seneca would say that benevolent action is that which gives pleasure and
finds pleasure in so doing, the outcome of a natural and spontaneous
inclination (Hands, 1968, ch. III–IV; Aristotle, *EN* 1159 A26–27).

Such views, generous in modern eyes, were not uniformly held, especially after the Peloponnesian Wars, 432–404 B.C., when the Athenian
empire virtually collapsed and the population declined as did the economy. Aristotle (*Politics* 1320a) would argue against the further appropria-
tion of public money for the poor on the grounds that it does not change
their dependency. He recommended sums be given to help them start
farms or to enter some kind of artisan activity. And Plato would recom-
mend that steps be taken to assure prosperity for all (citizens) rather
than making poverty permanent. Temperance, courage and justice (the
valued virtues of the early Republic) became the moral qualities desired
of all persons. These were not encouraged by charity. The good and tem-
perate man would never really be in want, regardless of what disasters
befell him, because his friends would help. Those able-bodied who begged
on the streets were not considered "good" in this sense, thus, were not
appropriate objects of pity. So Greece added: A secular base for altruism;
a principle of reciprocity: a record of tension for and against the stranger
and the able-bodied poor; and the beginnings of secular public mechanisms to relieve poverty.

SUMMARY

The earliest secular thought about helping others emerged out of small
face-to-face communities with a wide base of slavery and unenfranchised
persons and a relatively small percentage of the urban population considered "citizens." For the upper 12 percent, bonds of friendship, civic cohesion and a common citizenship origin bound people together. This network
of friendship was considered central to human relationships. Giving
evolved into more complex collective public means to satisfy a limited
range of human needs. Reciprocity in some form governed charity. Parallel
to this culture was a call to genuine generosity, good for its own sake. These
more generous views receded in times of great economic or political
decline.

CHARITY IN ROME

Ideas about charity and philanthropy in Rome, during the Republic and the Empire, continued many aspects of the Greek tradition but were modified. Rome, as a worldwide empire, had to accommodate many races, peoples and civilizations to sustain its (then) worldwide hegemony. Concepts of obligation in the clan or small city-state were enlarged to include diverse parties and members. Citizenship originally limited to clan descendants, extended to nonslave members in Rome and in the provinces. The idea of belongingness was enlarged. A borderline between the stranger and the family member was, for state purposes, blurred. Rights were conferred on groups, races and conquered peoples. The practices in helping others varied in the provinces, but a clear general picture can be described for Rome (the center of the empire) which adopted some ideas brought to the capital by slaves, artisans and merchants from the conquered territories.

Altruistic or helping practices continued to be of two kinds: those carried on for citizens by the state and those expressed in personal nonpublic relationships between wealthy patrons and dependents. The concepts which governed both types derived from common philosophical and political origins, but they changed over the centuries. What follows cannot capture either the richness of detail nor the long evolution of these ideas, but a few central elements of caring can be summarized. Understanding them requires a recognition that helping needy individuals was not more important than helping the collectivity. Gifts, contributions and deeds were governed by pride of the city and social pressure to benefit the city in its public and outward forms. Helping individual dependents was influenced as much by ideas of obligation to city as to individuals; it is possible that both had their origin in long past ties which bound members of an extended family or a clan to each other.

Patron-Clientele Symbiosis

A central feature of Roman society was the intricate pattern of rights and obligations which evolved around rich patricians and several classes of dependents. Most influential, at first, were patricians who claimed descent from the original Roman clans, which was the first basis for citizenship and nobility. People were divided between the patricians and the plebeians (Romans without claimed descent who made up a lower and proletarian working class). There is some speculation that the plebeians were descendants of a different race, the Ligurians (*Encyclopedia Britannica*, 11th ed., S.V. "patricians"). As the Republic prospered and an empire grew, the population was increased by slaves from all parts of the world. Those from the eastern territories were often more highly cultured, educated and skilled than their Roman conquerors. They provided much of the skilled labor and managed, as well as worked, the estates of the wealthy.

Close bonds of interdependency, and sometimes affection, developed between owner and slave along with publicized cruelty and exploitation. Owners often freed their slaves, or set them up in business enterprises. In addition, slave functionaries in a great household had many ways to earn enough money to buy their freedom under early Roman law. As a result a class of freedmen grew up alongside the patricians, plebeians, and slaves. There were also immigrants from other towns of the Latin league who had varying citizenship rights.

The freedmen over time became an important, upwardly mobile class, much like a new bourgeoisie, arising out of a then immigrant slave population, and acting not unlike the new immigrants who moved by more voluntary means in later centuries. The freedmen had manners and mores different from that of the earlier patricians and plebes. Many became enormously wealthy from trade since the nobility was by law and custom barred from increasing its wealth by commerce. Many flaunted their new wealth and bought political and social privileges. They also made the economy and the society vital and alive (Dill, 1905, chap. III).

A network of obligation developed between the better-off and the worse-off, between the great and the weak, which is captured in the patron's responsibility to those dependent on him for whatever reason. A slave was certainly cared for to some extent by his master. But when the slave was freed he could come to his patron's (former master's) home each morning to be given some work to do for the day, for which he was paid, or to receive some gift of money or a meal, food. The poorer relatives who made up the extended family of a wealthy personage would also come daily. Free or plebeian workmen would show up for their wages.

Obligation flowing from a superior to an inferior extended within the nobility itself. By the time of the Empire (first century B.C.E.), the nobility could be dependent on the largess of the Emperor for favors, while they in turn could be called on for some service to the head of state.

This network of patronage underpinned the functioning of a society in which an estimated 90 percent of the population was dependent on a wealthy 10 percent.

Public Provision for Dependents

As Rome grew in size and population, it became more and more dependent on imported food and other necessities. In good times, the normal processes of commerce, trade and craftsmanship, plus the clientele system, were sufficient to meet the basic needs of most residents. But in times of depression, trade disruption or civil strife, these methods were inadequate. Formal instruments to meet needs evolved. The most extensive and interesting device was the regular public distribution of grain and oil—the basic necessities of life. Publicly maintained storehouses were financed through gifts from the royal or public revenues or were supplemented by large gifts from the wealthy either out of a sense of obligation or as a way to buy favor and honors from the Senate or the Emperor. Charity was given to beggars but patronage and public distribution were the major mechanisms to sustain a vast dependency.

As early as 267 B.C.E. in the Republic, public granaries had been established and corn was sold at reduced prices to those common citizens who were considered Roman citizens, but by 58 B.C.E., corn was distributed free to most of the plebeian population of the city. By 5 C.E. the Emperor Augustus appointed officials to oversee a public apparatus in the city of Rome to distribute corn and oil free to 320,000 urban citizens. There was a systematic method for certifying who was entitled, as a legal resident of Rome, to foods distributed (Loch, 1938).

As the population of Rome expanded it became more and more difficult to maintain a reasonable control over the cost of general food distribution or the number of persons demanding access to low cost or free supply. Distribution was not according to a means test as the term is now used. Instead the distribution was open for all, other than for the wealthy classes, as a right of their citizenship, not because they were individually needy. Periodic efforts were made to abolish or restrict the free distribution of corn, especially when it was in short supply. Such efforts were generally ineffective. In a society with much violence and periodic large-scale disorder, especially in the late Empire, even an Emperor had to win public favor. To avoid violence, free distribution was usually restored.

Foundations and Other Public Provisions

A variety of subsidiary or secondary institutions and legalized practices evolved in both Republican and Imperial Rome. They are early ancestors of contemporary social institutions.

As the society became more elaborate, foundations and endowed charities (*Annona Civica*) were established. Wealthy individuals frequently endowed a foundation for a specific purpose with the expectation that it would continue after the donor's death. They celebrated the donor's birthday or death of a loved one. They often were created to underwrite a public event—the future costs of a national feast, of gladiators and public entertainments—but they also provided for the maintenance of poor freedmen or for the care of orphans.

There were also primitive efforts, as in Greece, to control the growth of population or to get rid of deformed or unwanted infants. Practices developed to expose some children at birth to die prematurely. This has been condemned as cruelty but was then justified on the grounds that parents had a loving concern—too many children condemned all to starvation; the reduction in the size of the family made it possible for the surviving children to live in something other than the direst poverty. The analogy between planned limitation of families in the contemporary period and this more primitive way of limiting the size of family population indicates the antiquity of the concept. "Exposing of children" may have referred mainly to weaklings and deformed children but abortion was also a known practice to limit the size of families in the time of Greece and Rome. By the time of Constantine (fourth century C.E.), when Christian influence had become significant, the practice of infant exposure was forbidden but parents were granted the right to sell newborn children.

The social concern for children expanded in two directions. Legal provision was made for adoption of orphans. The laws usually protected the property rights of families and were limited to the well-to-do. However, the Roman State undertook by law to care for some children, orphaned by war and other disasters.

There was legislation (*pueri alimentari*) by which wealthy landowners and others were given loans (sometimes forced on them) at low interest rates. The interest was paid into a fund to feed orphans and poor children. Much of this fund was used for the children of broken and poor families, presumably where the head of the family had died either in war or from illness.

A less formal adoption system also evolved. Abandoned children were often rescued to be brought up by charitable foundations. Children were placed in sites where they could be found. Families wanting children, or feeling pity, did take in such abandoned children for adoption.

Another way of dealing with the pressures of the poor in the urban centers was to resettle soldiers drawn from the Roman corps on land taken by conquest—an early form of economic relocation. As part of a much older tradition, going back to fourth century B.C.E., the proletariat or the poor of the city also sold their services to foreign generals or kings, sometimes in the hope of acquiring land by conquest, as a way of living.

Radical land reform was also attempted. As social and economic change became more and more threatening to old republican values and to stability in large urban concentrations, efforts were made to return the society to older practices either by force against the poor or by radical redistribution of land. In 133 B.C.E. Tiberius Gracchus, who was later assassinated, sought to redistribute land by enforcing laws which would limit the amount of land held by any one family. The aim was to return to an era when small farmers constituted the bulk of the population, each making his own living by his own labors on his own land holdings. This was a continuation of Plato's idealized conviction that under such an arrangement it would be inconceivable that any man possessed of a modicum of worth could be allowed to fall into beggary.

The use of private generosity for public purposes warrants attention for civic pride played an important role in classical Rome. Many of the monuments and public buildings and the amenities of urban life were provided by generous gifts of wealthy citizens, whose wealth was, for its time, as vast as that of kings of the past and of large corporations and bankers of the modern world. Temples, theatres, markets, bridges, aqueducts, roads, colonnades and public baths were built in all cities by these means. These donations commemorated the memory of a donor or publicized the "civic virtue" or general good which such contributions claimed to represent. The quality of urban life was determined by such means. One spectacular benefactor who lived in the second century C.E. and was tutor of Marcus Aurelius gave the equivalent of $200,000 to supplement an imperial grant for a town water supply. He built aqueducts, race courses and public baths in many cities; helped restore countless old towns; invited all the citizens and strangers among the tribes in his area to public feasts; built a public theatre for 6,000 in memory of his wife, etc. Before formal government and taxation evolved, city life was shaped by a class tradition, self-serving as its motivation now seems.

The Motives and Rationales of Giving to Others: Writing and Thinking about Doing Good

Within this cultural and organized framework attending to the needs of the poor, a number of ideas developed to justify doing something or nothing, or to provide some rationale for acts of caring for others. Except as embodied in actual laws, most writings are by literary and political figures who were part of an elite group. We can only speculate about how representative their views were of the daily practices, or how much they influenced the behaviors of others. But the writing opened doors to the thinking of the times. No attempt can be made here to deal with major writing or with the development of concepts in classical civilization over time. A few views are singled out because they seem to be intellectually linked with subsequent developments.

The Greek idea of reciprocity survived and was expanded in the political realm of the imperial period as high office and even kingship came to be purchased by the giving of magnificent gifts to "the people" for the good of Rome, of the Senate, of the State. For a long time, as the empire grew, the gift and the return or "purchase" of honor were reciprocals going hand in hand. Giving for public good was not necessarily associated with concern for the disadvantaged. This kind of political reciprocity differed from practice in Asian countries from which the basic practice was probably acquired. In the Orient it is more likely that gift giving by leaders, an emperor, or high officials was not linked to any expected return. Gift practices of a Pharaoh or an Emperor in ancient Egypt and Asian countries were beneficial to the poor, even though the poor played no part in election of the king (Hands, 1968).

More personal forms of reciprocity continued on a wide scale through the patron/client relationship which has been described. Underlying this was sometimes a real sense of patron obligation, owed to one who had been part of one's household, who had taught the master or served the patron well, and who could be well-beloved. For others only social pressure of noblesse oblige moved the wealthy to distribute money or food to secure the good regard of peers. For still others a real if minor economic exchange took place as when the client performed services for the patron.

The many Roman inscriptions which have survived to describe gifts suggest that donors acted out of love, out of honor or glory. Gifts were not neatly justified for selfish reasons only, but neither were they based upon selfless pity for the disadvantaged. Between such extremes lay a philosophical, ethical conception of man's relationship to others, the standards from which reputations and the good name of any person could be derived. Drawing from Greek and Asian sources as described earlier, the Roman philanthropists could well be conscious of Seneca's definition of "being beneficial" as "benevolent action which gives pleasure, and finds pleasure in so doing, the outcome of a natural and spontaneous inclination." There was one strain of socializing moral thought that treated the helping of another as being a virtue in itself, separate from self-regard. The honorable man was one capable of living for another as he wished to live for himself and to be not solely self-regarding. Gifts for the poor and others were not shorn of self-regard and self-gain but the motivations were also based on decent behavior—that it is natural to help another (Hands, 1968, chap. V–VI).

Cicero would say: "If we are truly liberal and beneficent we do not make a profitable business of doing good." And Seneca would say that certain benefits should be given anonymously. "On occasion the very person who is being helped is to be kept in the dark" (Hands, 1968, p. 30).

According to such writers to be honorable was to appreciate the truth; guard the social life—that is to give each person his due; strengthen the spirit; and be moderate in one's life. They define beneficence as a service given for the sake of the person given to. Giving is encouraged because it is a part of nature: "I possess all things but they belong to all men" (Seneca). Of course common sense entered into action based on such precepts. Thus Seneca concluded that if the recipient of help was not grateful "I must not be less liberal only more careful." He used the analogy of farming to suggest that farmers had to replenish the soil and in the same sense the giver of help to another person did so in order to restore the receiver to a state of independence rather than continual dependence (Hands, 1968, p. 45).

The Deserving Poor

In this reconstruction it is useful to keep in mind how the givers of charity viewed the poor they were helping. The image of the self-reliant independent person remained foremost in thinking. The widow, the orphan and the victim of war could be treated sympathetically. The able-bodied poor were not well-regarded—even when they were the object of a substantial widespread public help. Writers valued character and struggle for independence above pity. Cicero would write:

> Do you suppose that body of men to be the Roman people which consist of those whose services are hired out for pay? . . . a mass of men, a herd of slaves, of hired men, of rogues and destitutes?

He argued that the giver should be motivated by the recipient's sympathetic and cooperative attitude towards the benefactor's way of life and the contribution which the recipient has made to the giver's well-being. As remained true in later Christian doctrine and in much contemporary thinking, there was a demand for worthwhileness in those who ask for alms; begging by itself was not respected (Hands, 1968, p. 64).

Very few signs can be found of Roman writers who were really concerned about the condition of the very poor who were able-bodied and working in the most depressed circumstances. Only occasionally a writer would treat with sympathy the lot of miners in far stretches of the Empire and not be worried about the profits of those who exploited them. One, Diodorus (first century B.C.E.) wrote sympathetically of the slaves who rose against their masters on the large estates of Sicily (Hands, 1968).

Given the low regard in which the very poor able-bodied of the lower classes without land were regarded, it was easy for the concept of worthwhileness of a recipient to emerge early and persist. Character, dignity and the struggle for independence were always highly valued.

Despite generally harsh views about the able poor, there also existed more humane sentiments. The Stoics preached the brotherhood and equality of men as fellow citizens in one commonwealth. Seneca urged equality of the bound and the free and the entitlement of slaves to kindess and consideration. Horace would ask "Why should the worthy be in want when you have wealth?" Many of these ideas of the first century B.C.E. and the first century C.E. had been gestating for generations before (Hands, 1968, chap. V–VI).

In this evolution, the idea of pity was also examined. Pity could be threatening to the moral underpinnings of the society if too much stressed; generosity or the giving of help becomes a one-way street in which the recipient plays no role and is in effect totally dependent upon the largess of others. In place of pity reciprocity, with its real or implied quid pro quo, implied some form of contractual obligations between giver and receiver, maintaining the dignity and respect of each even though their material condition differs. The idea of reciprocity was originally bound up with friendship and cooperation in a closely knit community in which members have a contractual moral obligation to help each other, a contract in which each party has both responsibilities as well as rights, even though the rights were social expectations rather than legally enforceable.

According to this line of reasoning, mutual obligation and responsibility depends on the character of both the giver and the receiver. Human nature being what it is, it is not inconceivable that some members of a close knit community may, because of defects of character, take advantage of their friends and peers and in time would become in effect outcasts. The difficulties of transferring these concepts of reciprocity in a close knit society to a large and impersonal urban society are evident when confronted in Rome. The issue will recur as we discuss the evolution of thinking about the poor in later chapters.

SUMMARY

Roman society added the following to earlier experience:

1. It reinforced a triple-edge meaning of the word *philanthropy;* some feeling of caring and of decency between human beings; based in reciprocity and exchange; and a relationship between socially and economically superior classes and their inferiors.

2. In Latin a concept of *humanitas* was added to language late to express the idea of human sympathy for the weak and the helpless in a sense which philanthropy did not. It was a more secular and philosophical concept than Old Testament ideas of justice and of obligation sanctioned by religion.

3. Dependency relationships became more systematized, if informally, and reached through all social and class statuses. The idea of obligation of a more powerful person to help those dependent upon him was matched with obligation of duty on the less powerful to serve in some way.

4. An organized urban and public structure was installed to relieve the gross material and the basic social needs of predominantly dependent urban citizens. The generalized nature of food provision from public granaries and the extensive provision of public places for use by all, including the public baths and the public spectacles may have minimized the demeaning stigma of dependency upon others. The rich may have despised the masses of inferiors (although there is evidence of strong positive attitudes to slaves and servants in many great households) but it is not at all clear that the masses thought of themselves as mean and despicable because they received food and entertainment through the generosity of others.

6

EARLY CHRISTIAN VIEWS
Compassion, Brotherhood and Voluntarism

It is the season of kindness not of strict inquiry, of mercy not calculation.

ST. JOHN CHRYSOSTOM

Method must be observed in liberality.

ST. AMBROSE

The early record of philanthropic principles intermingles three major strands of thought: the Hebrew, the succeeding Christian philosophy and the Greek and Roman thought. Between about 500 B.C.E. and 100 C.E. the Old Testament, Asian, Middle Eastern, Greek and Roman civilizations slowly penetrated each other. After 100 C.E. ideas developed in the growing Christian church added a new strand of thinking—which was undoubtedly influenced by the nature of the church membership and its position in the Roman controlled world.

Adherents to the new religion were probably drawn from all levels of society, but were overwhelmingly poor, for most of the population was poor. The early centuries of the common era were also times of social disruption, decay in the Roman society and constant warfare against intruding Germanic tribes who settled in and were partly absorbed by the declining Roman culture. One consequence was that many privileged and well-to-do Romans sought refuge in new religious beliefs; in a slowly collapsing world the new religion promised dignity and identity. Although the new church consisted mainly of the poor, it also was fairly representative of the class structure of the times (Latourette, 1953). At

Many of the sources quoted in Chapter 6–9 were originally identified in the papers of Karl DeSchweinitz, at the Social Welfare Archives, University of Minnesota.

first it was simply one of many eastern sects which flourished in troubled times, but by the fourth century the Emperor Constantine (288–337 C.E.) not only tolerated but favored Christianity, either for political reasons or out of religious conviction. The church moved from its humble beginnings to become a major institution which shared power with secular leaders concerned with the affairs of this world as well as of the next. Simple beliefs about charity and the poor were elaborated during this evolution from institutional poverty to power.

At the beginning the church preached love of the poor, that men love others (or should do so) much as men love God and God loves man. The emphasis was often upon the regard and pity which men should have for each other as brothers, distinguishing it from the Greek concept of rational reciprocity and the Hebrew tradition of justice. The obligation to look after the poor and the disadvantaged was stressed, but it was either a personal obligation of one person for another or the group obligation of a collegium of the poor gathered together in small church associations. The motivation was love, one for another, not hope for reward or fear of punishment. Jesus is reported as saying:

> I was a stranger and ye took me in; naked and ye came to me. In as much as ye have done it unto the least of these my brethren ye have done it unto me; what is written in the law, thou shalt love the Lord thy God with all thy heart, with all thy soul, with all thy strength, with all thy mind and thy neighbor as thyself. (Matt. 25:35–36)

These precepts echoed in the moral views which had appeared earlier in Deuteronomy, Leviticus and Hillel, but the earlier concepts of mercy and justice were amplified by a new stress upon compassion, pity and identification with the poor.

The views about caring for each other, including the poorest, must have had a powerful appeal in an epoch of widespread insecurity when the stability and security of the Roman civil order was beginning to come apart under both internal and external pressures. Both security and meaning could be found in new forms of personal relationships within a collegium of like-thinking believers. This view about concern for each other whether consciously intended or not, must have helped bring people together in a social and religious solidarity because of identification with religious principles and leaders—not because of clan, family or formal citizenship ties in a civil society. Charity bound diverse individuals together. Their community was no longer limited to members of a family, of a clan tracing a common descent, or to those holding citizenship status in a political jurisdiction. It included all persons even the poorest and the most despised with any background and from any nation, bound together in communal relationships which required concepts and mechanisms as powerful as those of citizenship and clan descent.

Illustration of this sense of community building appears in Acts 5:34–35—written around 65 C.E.

> And all that believed were together and had all things common; and sold their possessions and goods and parted to all men as every man had need. And they continued daily with one accord in the Temple and breaking bread (at home) from house to house. Neither was there any among them that lacked: for as many as were possessors of land or houses sold them and brought the prices of the things that were sold and laid them at the apostles' feet and distribution was made unto every man according as he had need.

The encouragement of compassionate identification of all with the poorest is found in I Cor. 13:3: "And though I bestow all my goods to feed the poor now I give my body to be burned and have not charity it profiteth me nothing."

It is doubtful, in the earliest times, that any legally enforceable obligation was intended to look after the poor. Instead St. Paul said:

> Let each man do according as he has proposed in his heart: not grudgingly or of necessity: for God loveth a cheerful giver. (2 Cor. 9:7)

Here was a personal call—not a law—to serve one's neighbors in love (Ulhorn, 1883). Assuming that the words "brother" or "sister" refer to members, not blood relatives then James' plea is moving:

> What doth it profit my brethren if a man say that he hath faith but hath not works? If a brother or sister be naked and at lack of daily food and one of you say unto him go in peace be ye warmed and filled and yet ye give him not the things needful to the body what doth it profit? (James 1:27)

At the same time, narrower conceptions persisted. Some especially needy groups were singled out as being especially deserving of care, as was true in Hebrew and Greek thought. The belief that all shared equally in the goods of all was soon followed by more limiting identification, as in 1 Timothy, chapter 4:

> Honor widows that are widowed indeed. But if any widow hath children and grandchildren let them learn first to show piety first towards their own family . . . . let none be enrolled as a widow under three score years of having been the wife of one man if she hath brought up children . . . if any woman that believeth had widowed let her relieve them and let not the church be burdened that it may relieve them that are widows indeed.

The genius of the new formulation lay in its combining ancient beliefs about caring for one's family with a wider concept of "family" in which all are brothers and sisters to each other. Personal obligation to others was probably reinforced by the fact that the churches were, at first, small enough to meet in a single household in which all members were known to each other much as members of a family. All knew each other and formal institutions did not yet exist. There was not yet need for orphanages, hospitals, houses of hospitality or houses for foreigners so long as every Christian house was an asylum where traveling brothers and every Christian man and woman was ready to receive the indigent (Ulhorn, 1883, p. 123).

By the time of Constantine (288–337 C.E.), the first *xenodochium* (house for strangers, or hostel) had been founded as an institution outside of the home. Julian the Apostate (331–363 C.E.), a polytheist, ordered the establishment of a xenodochium so that "strangers may experience in our humanity and not our own people only but whoever is in need. . . . For it is disgraceful when there is not a beggar to be found among the Jews that our people should be without our help." (Cited in Ulhorn, 1883, p. 326)

By about 350 C.E., early church doctrine about responsibility for the poor had already evolved in two mainstreams—each with substantial rationale and justification. St. John Chrysostom (347–407) wrote and preached in the East most eloquently in favor of the uninhibited, unrestricted attention to the poor. In quoting the injunction from Ps., "Blessed is he that considereth the poor and needy" he asks what is meant by "he that considereth" and answers:

> He that understandeth what it is to be a poor man, that hath become thoroughly acquainted with the affliction of the poor man. For he that hath become acquainted with his affliction will certainly and immediately have compassion on him. When thou seest a poor man do not hasten to pass but immediately reflect what thou wouldst have been hadst thou been he. What would thou not have wished that all should do for thee? (Cited in Pusey, 1854)

St. John Chrysostom then goes on to deal with all of the arguments conventionally advanced, then and today, against generosity to the poor:

> Accusations are brought against him who applies (for help). For why does he not work you say? And why is he to be maintained in idleness? But (tell me) is it by working that thou hast what thou hast, did'st thou not receive it as an inheritance from thy father? And even if thou doest work is this a reason why thou shouldst reproach another? But what say they? He is an imposter. What sayest thou, oh man? Callest thou him an imposter for the sake of a single loaf or a garment? But you say, he will sell it immediately. And doest thou manage all thy affairs to perfection? But what are all poor through idleness? Is no one so from shipwreck? None from lawsuits? None from being robbed? None from illness? But you say he has means and yet makes himself this figure. But this is a charge against thyself not against him. He knows that he hast to deal with people, with wild beasts rather than with men and even if he utter a pitiable story he attracts no one's attention: or on this account he is

forced to assume also a more miserable guise that he may melt thy soul . . . if we see a person coming to beg in a respectable dress this is an imposter you say and he comes in this way that he is supposed to be of good birth. If we see one in a contrary guise him too we think dishonest. What then are we to do? . . . Stretch out the hand. Let it not be closed up. We have not been constituted examiners into men's lives. Since so we should have compassion on no one. Why is it that when thou callest upon God thou sayest, remember not my sins? So then if that person even if he be an exceeding great sinner make this allowance in his case also and do not remember his sins. It is the season of kindness not of strict inquiry, of mercy, not of calculation. (cited in Pusey, 1854)

A different view was expressed by St. Ambrose (340–397) and also by St. Augustine of Hippo (354–430), who argued that the church could not and *should not* provide for every person who was able to work; they considered that strong, able-bodied men who were certain of securing food without working would neglect acting in proper or just ways. St. Ambrose while insisting upon the obligation of individual Christians to give generously in charity had a concern about the wise use of resources which made prudent calculation necessary. St. Ambrose, at first a non-Christian government official, later became the chief executive of the Provinces of Liguria and Emilia-Romagna in Northern Italy. This was a period of civil upheaval at the same time that the capital was in a violent debate over the choice of a new bishop. Ambrose acted so well in his government capacity that he was elected as bishop even though not yet a professing Christian. He was subsequently baptized and consecrated as bishop.

Some years later St. Ambrose set down his reflections on ecclesiastical administration, addressing all the clergy as if they were his sons:

Let there be method in our giving for if the poor may not go away empty nor the substance of the needy be done away and become the spoil of the dishonest. Let there be then such due measure as kindness may never be put aside and true need never be neglected. Many pretend they have debts. Let the truth be looked into. They bemoan the fact that they have been stripped of everything by robbers. In such a case give credit only if the misfortune is apparent or the person is well known. Then readily give help. To those rejected by the church supplies must be granted if they are in want of food. (Nicene, 1900, vol. 10, ch. 15–16)

He argues strongly for generosity but with care.

We ought not only to lend our ears to hear the voices of those who plea but also eyes to look into their needs . . . method must be observed in liberality . . . so that the kindness one shows may be able to be shown day by day and that we may not have to withdraw from a needful case what we have freely spent on waste. (Nicene, op. cit.)

He goes on to define some of the special areas of concern as:

> In giving we must also take into consideration age and weakness; sometimes also that natural feeling of shame which indicates good birth. One ought to give more to the old who can no longer supply themselves with food by labor. So too weakness of the body must be assisted and that readily. Again if anyone after being rich has fallen into want we must assist, especially if he has lost what he had from no sins of his own but only to robbery or banishment or false accusation. (Nicene, op. cit.)

St. Ambrose seems to anticipate a modern concern for guidance and psychological help in his urge to be liberal in the giving of advice as:

> Money is easily spent: council can never be exhausted. It only grows the stronger by constant use. . . Money that grows less and quickly comes to an end has failed even kindness itself; so that the more there are to whom one wants to give fewer one can help; and often one hast not got what one thinks ought to be given to others. But as regards the offer of advice and active help the more that thou spend it on the more there seems to be and the more it returns to its source. (Nicene, op. cit.)

St. Ambrose also urges attention to the needs of the stranger, the noncitizen in much the same way as did the early Hebrews and Greeks:

> They too who would forbid our city to strangers cannot have our approach . . . they would refuse them a share in the produce meant for all and avert intercourse that has already begun; and they are unwilling in a time of necessity to give those with whom they have enjoyed their rights in common a share of what they themselves have. (Nicene, op. cit.)

Out of the twin approaches of open generosity and caution the church's ethics began to acquire an institutional base—especially under Gregory who entered the church, gave all or most of his fortune to founding and endowing monasteries and in 590 became Pope. Before he entered the church monastic life (while still in his early thirties), he had been Prefect and the chief governing officer of Rome. This was a time when want, poverty and distress were widespread and penetrated all classes of the population. There had been a long economic depression and a succession of invasions. Buildings were in ruins, business declined and the population of Rome had fallen from a million to scarcely more than 50,000. The wealthy families had moved to Constantinople—the site of the Eastern wing of the church. In this situation Gregory acted as an able administrator, building upon the pre-existing system. Dividing the city in districts, he placed a deacon of the church in charge of a base from which food was distributed to the poor. A ninth century biographer, John the Deacon, describes this method as follows:

> On the first day of every month he distributed to all the poor the store which had accumulated from the tithes. The father of the Lord's household would give away as each had need the fruits of the season . . . to the

higher in rank he respectfully offered pigments and other costly mer-
chandise so that the church, a common mother of all men, began to be
regarded as a common storehouse of all people. Every day he sent cooked
dishes through the hands of trusted courtiers into the different quarters
and streets of the city for those who were sick or maimed. And for those
who shyly hid their troubles before he himself dined he took care to direct
a dish with the Pope's blessing to their doors. (DeSchweinitz, part I)

There are intriguing echoes of early practices in twentieth century
philanthropy. Cooked dishes to the sick at home sounds very much like a
sixth century meals-on-wheels; and the giving of help in accordance to
need, which included recognition of the differing statuses of the poor,
echoes the principles derived from the early Hebrew testament and found
in twentieth century views about individualization of need. The class
difference was apparent as the upper classes were treated more generously if they fell into want.

The Book of Pastoral Rule was issued under Gregory for the use of
all bishops and became a philosophical and ethical essay on many subjects about helping the poor. It instructed:

It is needful for them to take anxious thought lest they distribute what
has been committed to them unworthily; lest they bestow something on
those on whom they ought to have spent nothing or nothing on those on
whom they ought to have spent something or much on those on whom
they ought to have spent less; lest by precipitancy they scattered unprof-
itable what they give; lest by tardiness they mischievously torment peti-
tioners . . . he however who gives his bread to one who is indigent
though he be a sinner, not because he is a sinner but because he is a man,
does not in truth nourish a sinner but a poor righteous man because
what he loved in him is not his sin but his nature. (Nicene, 1900, vol, 12,
p. 45)

In comparing the teaching of Chrysostom with that of Ambrose and
Gregory, St. John emerges on the radical fringe of thought and the others
on the conservative side. The Book of Rules prepared by Gregory sounds
very much like an early description of the professional principles of the
twentieth century; "professional" standards are to be used in assessing
need and giving of help, striving to achieve good ends without doing too
much, too little, too soon or too late. By contrast, for Chrysostom every
denuciation of inordinate luxury is coupled with an exhortation to the
relief of distress. He not only perceives the moral wrong of profuse luxury
and extreme destitution side by side, the only method which he could
suggest for rectifying the evil was to impress on the wealthy the duty of
alms giving on a large scale (Stephens, 1872).

St. John argued that wealth is not a possession, it is not property, it
is a loan for use.

For when thou diest willingly or unwillingly all that thou hast goes to others . . . . property is in fact but a word; we are all owners in fact but of other men's possessions. Those things only are our own which we have sent before us to the other world. Our goods we have are not our own; we have only a life interest in them, or rather they fail us during our lives. Only the riches of the soul are properly our own as alms giving and charity, for we cannot take our wealth with us when we depart hence but we can take our charities. (Nicene, 1900, vol. 13)

With a wealth of moving concept and language, early Christian thought added new dimensions to Western concepts about helping others; it did so by building on the antecedent experience of the Middle Eastern and Hebrew and Greco-Roman world. To the earlier concepts was added an embracing concept of men's relationship to each other, a universalism albeit one which probably was first intended to embrace those who entered the new church, but from wherever they might come. Psychological insights into relationships between giver and receiver of help began to be elaborated. And an institutionalized form of helping slowly evolved, based not upon government nor the mechanisms of a monarchy, but upon a voluntary, religious institution—the church. Within that new institutional structure two views about helping emerged: one focusing on need with few questions asked; the other, more administrative, focusing on need combined with inquiry into personal causes for distress. The latter predominated in time. As with the past, the widows and the clearly helpless received preferred attention. Able-bodied persons were treated with some skepticism, a skepticism perhaps suitable for an era of sharply limited resources and very great want. Work was urged and private property was not discouraged.

The early Christian church enriched and elaborated ideas about care for others by wedding several contradictions, e.g.: all men are brothers or family and kin responsibility, open sharing of wealth with prudent caution and formal institutions alongside personal acts of kindness.

The main features of early Christian thinking about philanthropy and care were: all adherents, rich and poor, are obligated to give what they can for others; the motivation is love for another, not hope or fear; objects of beneficence emphasize the widows, orphans, the sick and those put out of work or imprisoned for their faith; the nameless stranger fallen on misfortune is to be helped; and giving is a personal and voluntary matter (Latourette, 1953, p. 247). The second and fifth of these represent clear variation from earlier experience; the rest are elaborations of concept first introduced in the Hebrew Scriptures.

DEPENDENCY IN THE FEUDAL WORLD

Insecurity and Personal Charity

> *The poor, widows, orphans, and pilgrims shall have consolation and defense so that we . . . deserve the reward of eternal life.*
>
> *CHARLEMAGNE*

The major intertwined themes of personal responsibility, justice, compassion and reciprocity were all shaped in Mediterranean society. After the fourth century Rome divided between East and West. The Western half began to fragment and change as alien tribes settled, or invaded, the old empire. Rome fell, not at once but through a long-drawn-out decentralized transformation. Not much is known about caring except that charity was provided by the church (one major institution of the era) and by monarchs. Catholicism slowly penetrated to England, France and Germany, the onetime outposts of the centralized Empire. The Catholic Church assumed authority with some secular powers in what remained of the Roman Empire. The belief in sharing what we own with the poor and that all is held in trust for God, coexisted with more dominant realities of life in the period called the Dark Ages when life was uncertain, harsh and cruel. Society fractured into innumerable small political units built around the power and strength of a warrior-cum-noble class, each nobleman controlling a small or large territory and imposing authority primarily by power over a complicated social structure made up of kinsmen, associates, peasants, artisans and traders.

Power was only slightly moderated by civilizing or softening influences of the Catholic Church. Changes in climate, crops and disease led to constant moving, marauding, invading and fighting across Europe for some groups. Most people remained tied to land on which they survived in spite of constant warfare. Although wealth was present, poverty prevailed for most of the population. The society was strictly graded between the rich and the agricultural poor with many levels in between. The homes of rulers were the center of official activities, the administration of justice, reward or punishment, and such charity as existed. The population was largely agricultural, serfs, or freemen, plus craftsmen and court functionaries. They depended for their security on the strength of their lords. Society was bound together by ties of kinship and lordship, the obligation between a superior to an inferior. Loyalty between lord and subject and among kin were the primary safeguards and personal allegiance was a powerful instrument of community.

This feudal society provided the environment in which concepts of caring for others were transformed. Church philosophies transmitted through a church structure, which shared authority with secular authorities, sought to combine ethical teachings with power and rule.

Two social institutions, or social conventions, expressed the impulse to care for or help others. Bishops of the Catholic Church dispensed alms throughout the period, supplemented by the monastaries which also gave alms and sheltered travelers. At the same time, giving to the poor was a living social ideal moving both rich and poor. The ideal was rooted in part in religion, but was also in the economy of the times. Some historians consider the early Middle Ages to have been basically a "gift economy" held together by bonds between all levels of society (Labarge, 1965; Little, 1978; Duby, 1974). The lords were responsible for their peasants and, as a part of economic necessity, tried to feed them in times of famine. This practice survived in later centuries as a social convention when lords maintained household almoners who dispensed alms from the amounts regularly set aside for that purpose. While most of this charity was voluntary, although compelled by both economic and religious influences, there were occasional rights commonly respected. The poor were entitled by custom to glean the village fields after the harvest and before animals (livestock) were let in to graze (Homans, 1942).

In this violent period safety of person was an overwhelming concern in England. A social legal structure grew up to recompense individuals for personal injury done by others. Aside from one's personal strengths there existed in the early Middle Ages a legal principle known as Wergild in which the property value of each person was determined by his station in life. Injuring the person required compensation from the offending individual as a way of protecting human beings viewed as property. Killing another or destroying their sight or a limb, or raping a woman all had a cash value—much as insurance does today—but the value was graded according to the position the injured person held in the social structure. Responsibility for payment was placed upon the aggressor or his family and all types of crime had penalties attached to them. Much of this legislation evolved less out of concern for the injured individual than as a means of developing a stable social structure in which members were relatively secure in the pursuit of their social and economic activities. This may be likened to the Egyptian concept of negative confession in which virtue was found in not injuring others. But in this era the virtue was legally enforceable in this life.

If we use England as an example, this situation prevailed from the Roman withdrawal in the fourth century until the late sixth century when Catholic priests were sent from Rome on missionary tasks. St. Augustine of Canterbury was sent by Pope Gregory in 597 c.e. to convert the Anglo-Saxon population of England, and begin the transmission of Roman and Judeo-Christian concepts to the feudal society of England. Gregory specified that a third of the payments made by converted members to the church (these conversions began with the king and powerful noblemen) were to be used for the poor, with the church as the ministering instrument. Concepts of help for the poor remained a tradition of personal charity from those who had a great deal of surplus.

Illustrative of the conception that powerful individuals with great surplus should be generous to the poor is a record by the historian the Venerable Bede (673–735):

> On an Easter day King Oswald had placed before him a silver dish filled with royal delicacies and they were already about to put forth their hands to bless the bread when there entered suddenly his thane to whom was committed the charge of receiving the poor and he informed the king that a great multitude of poor people come from all quarters were sitting in the streets begging some alms of the king. He at once ordered that the food placed in front of him should be carried out to the poor and also that the dish should be broken up and divided in portions among them. (Bede, 1954)

By the end of the seventh century in England the country was divided into several separate kingdoms in which the secular and religious life was joined through cooperation between king and bishop. The lord of one kingdom made contributions to the church a legal obligation, imposing fines on those who did not make the appropriate payments (Bede, 1954). Such edicts ordered that widows and children be cared for by tithes to the church although the responsibility for support was placed first upon relatives:

> If a husband and a wife have a child together and the husband dies the mother is to have her child and rear it and she is to be given six shillings for its maintenance, a cow in summer, an ox in winter; the kinsmen are to take charge of the paternal home until the child is grown. In the case of foundlings or full orphans the King in his person assumes the responsibility for contributing to the support of the child for a fixed number of years. (Hadden, 1871, p. 371)

By 747 a church council not only prescribed but regulated alms giving:

> Alms must be necessarily given daily by the faithful in order that for sinners and those who in turn who do penance by fasting be more quickly and more fully remitted by God. But these gifts ought not to be given when it may be lawful for anyone the more freely to commit any sin he pleases . . . Let not alms besides be given to a hungry person so that he may gorge himself unduly on food and elicit drinking. (Hadden, 1871, p. 372)

The basic foundations for responsibility for the poor were early laid on individuals and for limited categories of persons, orphans and widows and, later, for pilgrims.

These developments were more systematically evolved by Charlemagne who was the Emperor of what became the Holy Roman Empire. For example, one royal decree ordered:

> Bishops, abbots and counts shall be mutually in accord in order to render a just judgment with all charity. . . . the poor, widows, orphans and pilgrims shall have consolation and defense from them so that we through their good will may deserve the reward of eternal life rather than punishment. No one in our whole kingdom shall dare to deny hospitality to rich or poor or pilgrims. . . . Concerning beggars who wander through the countryside it is our will that each one of our subjects shall support his own poor whether on his estate or within his own household and shall not allow them to go elsewhere to beg. And where such vagrants are found when they work with their hands let no one think of giving them anything. (Munro, 1923, vol. 6, pp. 16–17)

In order to assure that such wishes were carried out Charlemagne established a position known as *Missi* consisting of two persons, an ecclesiastic and a layman, who:

> Make a diligent investigation wherever any man claims that an injustice has been done him . . . they shall administer the law fully and justly in case of the holy churches of God and of the poor of wars and widows and of the whole people. (Munro, 1923, vol. 6, p. 19)

Such conceptions were received with interest in England and church advisers sought to promote these ideas. It is unlikely that the efforts to mandate care of the poor penetrated widely or deeply throughout any nation. Countries were largely rural, populations lived in small villages frequently inaccessible and the officers either of the church or of the king are unlikely to have travelled persistently and widely to any area to see that the rules were enforced. In 734 the Venerable Bede would write:

> We have heard that many villages and hamlets are situated in inaccessible mountains and dense woodlands where there is never seen for many years at a time a bishop to exhibit any ministry . . . nor is it only a bishop

who is lacking in such places to confirm the baptized by the laying on of hands. There is not even a teacher to teach the truth of the faith and the difference between good and evil conduct. (Bede, 1954)

In the late eighth century increasing raids by the Vikings from the North and other physical disasters led church leaders in England to attribute these disasters to a failure of the king, the church and of the people to observe the rules of right living. Such events stimulated new efforts, Alfred, in the ninth century, divided all of his revenues into two parts. The part devoted to secular uses was used to compensate the persons who fought or worked for him or for his kingdom. The spiritual part was "to be purposely dispensed to the poor of every race who came to him."

Do not give little to whom you should give much or much to whom you should give little nor nothing to whom you should give something nor anything to whom you should give nothing. (cited in Asser, 1904)

The difficulties persisted. One biographer of Alfred reported that:

For except for him alone (Alfred) the poor have no helpers throughout the kingdom or indeed very few; since almost all the magnets and nobles of that land had turned their minds more to the things of this world than to the things of God; indeed in the things of this world each regarded more his own private advantage than the common good. (Asser, 1904)

By 959–975 under Edgar the secular law sought to enforce the giving of tithes by severe penalties for failure. Those who failed to give one-tenth of their income for church purposes would have all of their possessions taken from them except one-tenth (Attenborough, 1922, p. 395). And between 970–1016 Ethelred decreed that "with regard to tithes the king and his Council have agreed in accordance with the principles of justice . . . the third portion to go to God's poor, to poverty stricken slaves" (Robertson, 1925).

The Anglo-Saxon and early English Christian experience was limited in its attempts to introduce a system into charity. Society remained structured in a hierarchy of classes ranging from king to slave with reciprocal rights and obligations based on personal loyalty and dependency. The relief of poverty remained a matter of voluntary personal charity usually mediated through the nobility and through the Church via its tithes and limited to devout persons traveling as pilgrims, widows and orphans and the clearly helpless. The able-bodied poor were protected mainly by the strength and generosity of their overlords to whom they were bound. However, the primary responsibility for the impoverished remained vested with relatives.

The sense of responsibility which a nobleman felt to his dependent subordinates was partly induced by the bonds of lordship, by the nature of the economy and encouraged by the extent of his religious conviction. But the relationship of giver and receiver was based upon dependence and subservience. The generous giver was motivated beyond this partly for fear of his position in an afterlife as seen in Charlemagne's edict: "So that we through their (the poor) good will may deserve the reward of eternal life rather than punishment." Dominant motivations were concern about sin and heavenly retribution plus social and economic reality. An early popular poem read: "When you may help through wisdom and skill and will not help but holdest you still; when you speak sharply to the poor that some good asks at you door; . . . be it without be it within yet it is a venial sin" (Morris, 1863, p. 94).

Personal conscience encouraged by fear often found expression in special events to celebrate an important date in the life of the giver. When much of the charity was royal largess, it could be generous for a day and not beyond. For example, King John on Christmas Day in 1206 would buy 1,500 hens, 5,000 eggs, 20 oxen, and 100 pigs and 100 sheep for the Feast of Christmas which was accompanied by a mass feeding for the poor. In 1216–17 Henry III on a January holiday might feed 6,000 people. But the king's retinue also included one acknowledged official, the "Almoner," who was:

> to gather up the fragments left from the royal meals every day and distribute them to the needy; he is to visit for charity's sake the sick, the lepers, the captives, the poor, the widows and others in want and wanderers in the countryside and to receive . . . other gifts bestowed in alms and to distribute them faithfully. He ought also by frequent exhortations to spur the king to liberal alms giving, especially on saints day. (Johnstone, 1929, p. 155)

In this society most people were bound to the land by their serfdom but travelers, especially pilgrims who traveled for religious reasons were entitled to special charity and were invited into the household for feeding. After the twelfth century with the emergence of universities, students were often armed with letters from university authorities testifying to their worthiness. They would wander the country begging not in the name of charity but to support their learning and their search for wisdom. There were also mendicant friars who came at the beginning of the thirteenth century in the footsteps of St. Francis of Assisi. They withdrew from the material world and dedicated themselves to a life of poverty as an example of human personal relationships unencumbered by the search for wealth and power. They were sustained in this vocation by their begging. During the eleventh to thirteenth centuries the conventions of giving remained so strong that Europe supported a subculture of beggars. This subculture included several types of dependents: freelance monks, poor preachers, students, probably displaced persons of all kinds, discharged soldiers, and failures of many kinds.

Writing much later, in 1513, Machiavelli summarized what may be one of the motivations for secular giving in this period:

> It is necessary for a prince to present the friendship of the people; otherwise he has no resource in times of adversity . . . a wise prince will seek means by which his subjects will always and in every possible condition of things have need of his government then they will always be faithful to him. . . The prince may either spend his own wealth or that of his subjects or the wealth of others. In the first case he must be sparing but for the rest he must not neglect to be very liberal. . . You may be very generous with what is not the property of yourself or your subjects. (Machiavelli, 1952, p. 44)

Medieval Evolution of Formal Institutions: Civil and Religious

In addition to personal charity carried out through the household of the king, of bishops or of individuals, more formal institutions began to develop later including almshouses and a parish structure. By 1123 combinations of almshouses and hospitals were well established on both an inpatient and an outpatient basis to perform many of the functions of caring for the disabled, the sick and the mentally ill. The motivation for initiating one such great institution, St. Bartholomew's Church and Hospital in London, was a deep sense of guilt felt by its founder, Rahere. Rahere undertook a pilgrimage to Rome because of a feeling of personal guilt. He had become ill and vowed that if he could recover he would erect and maintain a hospital for services to the poor in all things. He is reported as saying:

> Oh man, what and how much allegiance would you pay to Him who would help you in such a moral crisis? (Webb, 1923, p. 7)

The people who were intended to be helped were described as follows:

> They that can do no labour, old people, sick and impotent; poor women in childbed, weak men wounded by great violence and eaten with pox and pestilence, wayfaring men and maimed soldiers. (Webb, 1923, pp. 7–8)

Reference is often made to other able-bodied poor but with the limitations that they be "honest folk fallen in great poverty" (Rotha, 1909).

As civil organization took on more formal shape in Medieval society so did the Church elaborate its structure for benevolence. The motivation was captured by William Langland (1330–1400) in *A Vision of Piers the Ploughman:*

> So I counsel all Christians to cry for God's mercy, praying Mary his mother to mediate also that God give us grace now before we go hence; such works for to work, even while we are here, that after our death day then do—well may witness such a great day of doom that we did as he bade. (in Langland, 1913, p. 126)

The structure of the Church continued to evolve and was always used to carry out charitable tasks. A body of canon writing was incorporated in papal pronouncements and in enactments of church councils. The giving of alms was not only the personal expression of faith and of virtue, but it was supported by a growing body of ecclesiastical law which imposed legally enforceable taxes. A kind of Medieval Church Poor Law emerged.

> In general the bishops shall provide necessities for the poor and those who cannot work with their hands . . . bishops ought to assist widows and orphans seeking the help of the church. . . Hospitality is so necessary in bishops that if they are found lacking in it they ought not to be ordained. (Tierney, 1959, ch. 1)

Such obligations and the specification of officials to carry them out were repeated by Pope Innocent IV (1243–1254). Execution of these duties was entrusted as before to the bishops and to the local parishes.

Parishes were also considered as benefices, that is a source of income due to individuals appointed to the head of each parish. In time these appointments became items of patronage. The appointees in charge were not necessarily parish priests charged with helping the poor and performing other churchly duties. They might be a civil servant, a wealthy individual, a nobleman or even a monastery. These "proprietors" were able to divert church tax funds ostensibly levied for the poor to their own personal needs and there was no effective mechanism to control the diversion. Even where monasteries controlled the income of certain parishes it was frequently reported that the monks of the monasteries saw to their own needs before using these funds for the discharge of obligations to the poor.[1]

Over several centuries criticism flourished about the way in which the church discharged its almsgiving duties. Between 1284 and 1327 the Bishop of Durham reported that hospitality was not shown and alms were not given to the poor. In 1342 Archbishop John of Stratford reported that:

---

[1] Is this an early forecast of two tendencies in modern welfare states: (1) for employees of large welfare programs to improve their own income position as a first charge upon resources; (2) the persistence of unsatisfactory institutions?

> The monks and nuns of our province procuring appropriation of churches strives so greedily to apply to their own uses the fruits and revenues of the same that they neglect to exercise any works of charity whatsoever among the parishoners. (cited in Coulton, 1930)

In 1455 Archbishop Thomas Bourchier pointed to the failure of clergy to fulfill their obligations to the needy (Leonard, 1900; Coulton, 1930; Gee, 1921).

At the same time continuous efforts were made by some bishops and through royal decrees to revitalize the parish system of almsgiving. While most of these efforts at efficiency were directed at the obligations of royal or church officials, there is an intimation in 1432 that some church lawyers believed that the individual poor might have certain rights of redress:

> Ask whether this assessment having been made by the bishop arises from any right or suit by the poor? It would not seem so since the persons of the poor are unspecified it is impossible to establish to which of them the obligation is applicable. . . . Nevertheless I think if in a parish there were a corporate body of the poor that then an action would belong to them as to be a sufficiently strong determinant person. . . . If there was not a corporate body then just for the sake of piety a bequest to the poor is valid although made to unspecified persons. So it might be said that as a specially privileged group a right of action belongs to them since the poor in our case are specified, namely the poor of one certain parish. (Lyndwood, 1432)

Despite this intimation about rights, the following is a more likely description of daily practice. While there was a firm mandate in ecclesiastical law to provide aid to the poor, the execution of the mandate depended on the personal character and disposition of individual persons. Assistance was intimate—almsgiving was voluntary charity, not an established grant of aid. It is doubtful that the poor man had much *right* to relief. He probably felt himself to be the beneficiary of the kindness of the rector. The justifications for personal giving or through taxation to support almshouses were probably mixed. Some of those who helped the poor did so not so much to relieve the hungry as a matter of inward religious conviction but as a penance imposed for the breach of religious duty. In fact, the occasion for almsgiving other than that through tithing was often carried out in the celebration in some rite of transition: weddings, births and funerals of the great or the rich.

At the same time, there was the social institution of lordship which formalized and carried out the functions of caring whether inwardly felt or not. And equally, individuals were moved to acts of compassion because of deep religious conviction.

By the late fourteenth century a wealthy middle class had become sufficiently affluent to establish foundations for charity. The wills of businessmen began to record bequests to provide food or care for the sick or the disabled. A not uncommon type of will is that recorded in 1395 by a William Barnaby who left £ 100 to be distributed among the beggars, poor householders, and prisoners and for the dowries of poor girls or to send poor boys to school or the mending of highways. In 1422 another will funded an annual dinner for 2,400 poor men, householders of the donor's city, as a memorial. Whatever the motivation—guilt or charity—the giving was determined by the mood of the benefactor and not the need of the poor alone (Commissary Court).

Alongside these civil, royal and church developments there also grew up in the Middle Ages a body of writing arguing a more secular, social rationale to govern the relationships between the rich and the poor. John of Salisbury wrote:

> Then and then only will the health of the commonwealth be sound and flourishing when the higher members shield the lower and the lower respond faithfully and fully in like measure to the just demands of their superiors, so that each and all are as it were members of one another by a sort of reciprocity and each regards his own interest as best served by that which he knows to be most advantageous for the others. (Salisbury, 1927, p. 244)

This is a twelfth century formulation of the Greek and Roman concept of reciprocity, but no longer reciprocity among peers and members of a common tribe or with common descent but translated to a feudal, hierarchical society of superiors and subordinates in which the bonds of reciprocity are still powerful.

The feudal system, being a complex of many different parts, each with its own function, was still intended to work towards the general welfare as well as that of each individual. Inferiors owed it to their superiors to provide them with the things necessary for their protection. The feudal society involved an intricate network of obligations which each class owed to its superiors and to its inferiors. Within this rigid, defined structure of duties and obligations evolved concepts of charity due to those above and those below. While this was a society with many social gradations, of extremes of powerful landowners and servile cultivators, it was the latter who were expected to be assured of food, at least, since those to whom they owed their loyalty had it in their personal interest to have them well enough to be able to give service in return. However degraded the condition of the mass of the people might be they were presumably assured of the bare necessities of life (Eden, 1797).

The failures of this system, in its reality as against its theory, is captured by a long succession of protests. An extreme example of that is

John Wycliff (circa 1384) who wrote after the Black Death—which over-turned lord and peasant relationships. When the economic position of English nobility was thus undermined it reacted with exceptional greed-iness. Shortly after a revolt of peasants in 1381:

> And thus lords devour poor men's goods in gluttony in waste and pride and they perish their mischief and hunger and thirst and cold and their children also and if their rent be not readily paid their beasts are dis-tressed and they are pursued without mercy though they be never so poor and needy and overcharged with age, feebleness and with many children. And yet lords will not meekly hear a poor man's cause and help him in his right but suffer seizure of goods to destroy them but rather withhold poor men for hire for which they have spent their flesh and blood. And so in a manner they eat and drink poor men's flesh and blood. (Mathews, 1880, p. 234)

The means by which that society could impose some restraint upon this exploitation was limited. It had not changed much since the thir-teenth century when Albert Magnus would write:

> The duties which lords lay upon their serfs cannot be called robbery however grievous since a serf possesses nothing save in his lord's name. (Coulton, 1925, p. 118)

The appeal to more decent human relationship was often only an unenforceable appeal to avoid religious sin. Not many worried that the lord can sin by excessive demands for forced service or by oppression of his serf, even though the community was interested in the way in which a man used his own property (Coulton, 1925, 1930).

The reciprocity of which John of Salisbury wrote and which echoed in new form the older ideas remained an aspiration rather than the law in the Middle Ages.

SUMMARY

Between the decline of the Roman Empire and the enactment of the Elizabethan Poor Law, society was characterized by a hierarchy of feudal relationships, of obligation between different classes of society in which rights and obligations from and to each class were carefully defined in theory but were quite different in practice. The concepts about caring for the stranger were limited. Help for others was first of all a matter of royal beneficence or of personal charity of the wealthy for the poor—who had no claim to that beneficence. The charity was generally erratic. Institu-tions developed in the form of religious parish relief and almshouses. The motivations were a combination of religious conviction, economic necessi-ty, fear of punishment in an afterlife, and appeals to the simple pity that human beings should have for each other's condition. There was also a continuing conviction that a stable society requires some attention to the needs of the poor on a reciprocal basis if the well-to-do were to be assured of their position. Much of this appeal to stability was argued philosophically within the framework of a hierarchical society of subservience and dominance.

What persisted and was reinforced was the limit of help to certain groups of helpless persons and some form of reciprocity. What was new was the continuous evolution of a religious institution as the main instrument for charitable actions, even if it sometimes acted through a secular monarch influenced by religion. New also was the modification of the concept of reciprocity from exchange between peers, or persons with some mutual interdependence, to reciprocity based on a hierarchy of subservience and domination. Concern for the life after death continued and became as powerful a motive for charity as memorializing of one's life through ancestor remembrance. With the mixing of civil and religious structure for taking care of the poor, there was a continuous criticism of deficiencies and a search for reform.

8

THE SIXTEENTH AND SEVENTEENTH CENTURIES
Nation-States, Commercial Capitalism, and Government Responsibility for Poverty

> *By this means the wealth of the nation will be increased and everybody put into a capacity of eating his own bread.*
>
> *SIR MATHEW HALE*

The next stages in the conscious development of governmental responsibilities for the disadvantaged took place in Northern and Western Europe and in England. Nation-states were formed out of groupings of smaller, regional fiefdoms, with more sophisticated national controls. Government responsibility for poverty became embodied in law, but intended to serve the nation more than to help individuals. The poor were an accepted part of local community life and, except for able-bodied strangers, not yet rejected.

In pre-commercial-capitalist Europe, charity was dominated by the Church or the tradition of generosity of powerful individuals. In the fifteenth century people who were singled out for care as poor or as paupers, in the language of the time, were dependent beyond the dependency of lordship, tied to land owned by another. They were mainly the physically disabled, the mentally deficient, orphans, or widows, the aged and occasionally the religious bound by vows of poverty in the Catholic Church. Most others were also poor but able-bodied. Poverty was a normal way of life and almsgiving, the basic structure of charity, directed and restricted to categories among the poor.

Context and Social Change

Change in the sixteenth century did not come quickly, nor everywhere at the same pace. Early forms of human organization persisted and were modified incrementally. Change was forced by cycles of crop failure leading to starvation; by plague which decimated populations; and by waxing and waning economic activity or commerce which led to increase or decrease in the degree of poverty and the acuteness of misery. Centers of wealth and power shifted, although most people, the peasants and urban craftsmen, lived in a poverty considered normal.

For the purposes of this volume, government responsibility for the poor replaced the personal obligations of feudalism only after perhaps 200 years of demographic, economic and political change and upheaval. Cumulatively these crises made the older forms of caretaking unworkable—a new form had to develop to meet new conditions.

By the fifteenth century the old feudal society was already breaking down and being replaced by the new form of economic activity, by primitive industrialism, commercial capitalism or mercantilism. The ties and obligations in a strict hierarchy, the tying of individuals to the land were relaxed. Economic development in the form of exploration and new crafts created new social disparities. Many persons were released from or forced off the land by economic disaster or by new powerful classes. Not everyone could any longer count on the social protection of the village or town community. Many ended up as wanderers or anonymous strangers in cities. Continental wars displaced farm workers to the army and then returned them to no home or secure community.

The use of coinage began to displace in-kind exchange of services between subordinate and superordinate classes. Money substitution for personal services accompanied the development of manufacture and trade. Between the end of the twelfth and the beginning of the fourteenth century mills substituted water power for human power, towns began to develop near the sites of power and people began to cluster their work and craftsmanship and trade around these centers (Carus-Wilson, 1934). Towns began to secure more freedom from local feudal lords through negotiation with the king. The wars on the continent led to a transfer of manpower, which at the end of the wars returned home displaced from their land.

The conditions of life continued to change slowly, but widespread poverty persisted. Peasants, even when freed from serfdom, remained tied to the most precarious existence of agriculture; plague, famine, and continuing wars not only killed many noblemen but destroyed the continuity of ownership and class relationship. Land on which freed peasants depended was either untilled when population declined, or it became more economical to enclose small land holdings in larger ones when profitable commerce demanded it. Pasture for sheep could change land use in order to supply the new textile industry. A new wealthy class appeared here and there based on trade and manufacture with sufficient surplus to reinvest and acquire further land and further wealth. But the craftsmen and farm laborers were often displaced, dispossessed and frequently unemployed. In 1514 Henry VIII was advised "an infinite number of the king's subjects for lack of occupation hath fallen and daily do fall into idleness and consequently into thefts and robberies" (DeSchweinitz, chap. XV, p. 182). A stronger central government began to arise to replace the great variety of feudal aristocracies. The multiplicity of private armies maintained by the feudal barons was no longer as necessary and in their uselessness the soldiers became surplus.

The increasing rootlessness and economic uncertainty separated people from others who could be responsible for their care. Those without the means to care for themselves turned to more assertive and demanding mendicancy. This was not a sudden state of affairs. In the fourteenth century farmers, artisans and noblemen were also harassed by the unscrupulous behavior of pilgrims, students, friars and "vagabonds." Some of the resulting concern and distress was a popular reaction to a change from old and accustomed ways of living, with mutual, if hierarchical responsibility for each other. Strangers, sometimes threatening, appeared in communities where residents once knew each other. To the English poet, William Langland, the mendicants:

> hope to sit at hot coals to spread abroad their legs or lie at their ease to drink deep and dry and then betake themselves to bed and arise when it pleaseth them. When they are arisen they roam about and spie right well where they may soonest have a meal and a round of bacon and sometimes both and carry it home to their cottage and cast about how to live in idleness and ease while others travail . . . For the beggars live in no love nor keep no law . . . They go falsely begging with children forever after. (Langland, 1913, pp. 127–151)

He distinguishes between people who suffer poverty in their own homes and vagrants who beg falsely.

> The most needy are our neighbors . . . such as prisoners in dungeons or poor folk in cottages burdened with children and the landlord's rent . . . that turn the fair sight outward and are abashed to beg and would not tell their neighbors what they need at noon and eve. . . And yet there are other beggars in health but they want their wit: and wanderers mad more or less . . . such manner of men Matthew teaches us we should take to house and help them when them come. (Langland, 1913, pp. 148–150)

The economic conditions were also affected by the succession of plagues which periodically devastated the population and created a shortage of manpower which in turn led to demands for higher pay or better conditions. This upset customary class relationships and obligations. All in all there were successive, cyclical social and economic shifts which threatened the security of landowners and merchants and the poor. Misery, poverty, and precarious life balanced on the edge of subsistence was still considered the natural fate of most people. The more comfortable life of a few noblemen, merchants, skilled artisans or large landowners was rationalized by religious views about hierarchy and by political power.

Change in the form and value of work was also antecedent to the Poor Laws in England and on the continent. From the fifteenth century onward the importance of work was constantly emphasized; the distinction between being able-bodied and out of work or impotent and unable to work, became more and more clear.

A major religious change also divided Europe as Protestantism, in its several forms, challenged both the power and the theology of the universal Catholic Church.

The Protestant Reformation introduced significant changes in both religious and theoretical views about the poor and their relief. When Luther attacked the efficacy of "works" for salvation he in effect also demoted almsgiving from a transcendental act capable of earning one's salvation in a future life to a duty to the community in this life. But reformers often held much harsher attitudes about the poor, especially the Calvinists and Puritans, in whose eyes the poor were probably damned anyway. Putting the poor to work, when they were not at work in the normal course of events, became the popular solution, first among Protestants and soon after among Catholics (Davis, 1975; Chill, 1962; Pullan, 1976). Love and concern for the poor, as a central element in human relationships, sanctioned by religious belief was replaced, in theory, by a more material and perhaps more self-serving interpretation of human relationships. Old and new beliefs about obligation and charity contended and led to new forms of charitable or caring effort.

Attempts to Improve Welfare: Foundations, Mutual Aid, and Failed Attempts at Legislation

Despite widespread misery, some groups prospered. In prosperous periods, trade and commerce increased the numbers and types of better-off citizens: traders and merchants, an increasing number of governmental functionaries in city and capital. A small but prospering bourgeoisie arose in cities. They were interested in their security and were also moved by the stimulation of new religious doctrines. It became not only necessary but morally urgent to create new charitable institutions to relieve the new social distresses. Secular as well as church-controlled charities increased. The concern of the newly well-to-do for charitable acts outside the Church of Rome followed the Reformation with its evangelism and reinterpretation of the Old and New Testaments. Schisms divided the established Church; concern for the afterlife was matched by concern for conditions in the earthly life and for current safety. As early as 1423 the executors of the will of the Lord Mayor of London would record:

> The best intention of a prudent, wise and devout man shall be to . . . make secure the state and the end of the short life, with deeds of mercy and pity: and namely to provide for such poor persons which grievous penury and cruel fortune have oppressed and be not of power to get their living either by craft or any other bodily labor: whereby at the end of the last judgment he may take his part with them that shall be saved. (Brewer, 1856)

The objects of charity were members of urban groups, sometimes the distressed members of guilds and artisans or of merchant corporations residing in a named parish or a town. Economic aid to members was characteristic of many fraternal orders, some of which were based on parish neighborhoods. Some of the guilds maintained a primitive form of insurance in which regular payments were made by the members to cover infirmity, blindness, deafness and illness whether it be lasting or temporary. Others were more truly charitable making gifts for "thirteen poor goldsmiths in the greatest indigence" or "thirty-two poor householders, free men and women of the Fishmongers Company" or "for the sustenation of one hundred poor men."

These voluntary, guild or charitable efforts did not address underlying trouble in society. Neither private foundations nor church parish charity were adequate to cope with the increase in so-called "vagabond labor" and with economic dislocation, although government tried to control and punish the "vagabonds and knaves" who were thought to be preying upon the public. Henry VIII was reported to have executed over 70,000 petty thieves and rogues. An earlier statute of 1388 complained:

> Servants and labourers will not nor by a long season will serve and labour without outrageous hire and much more than hath been given to such servants and labourers in any time past so that for the scarcity of such servants and labourers the land tenants may not pay their rents nor live upon their lands should great damage and loss as well of the lords as well as all the commons. (DeSchweinitz, chap. 14)

As the conditions persisted, voices against punitive efforts were also raised. Sir Thomas More noted:

Neither is there any punishment so horrible that it can keep them from stealing which have no other craft whereby to get their living. (De-Schweinitz, chap. 15)

In 1380 John Ball, a priest would say:

By what right are they who we call Lords greater folk than we? . . . Why do they hold us in serfage? If we all came of the same father and mother how can they say or prove that they are better than we? If it be not that they make us gain for them by our toil that they spend in their tithe? They are clothed in velvet and warm in their furs and ermines while we are covered in rags. They have wine and spices and spare bread and we eat oatcake and straw. They have leisure and fine houses, we have pain and labour and rain and wind in the fields and yet it is of us and of our toil that these men hold their state. (cited in DeSchweinitz, p. 173)

In 1548 the Bishop of Worcester charged that "London was never so ill as it is now. In times past men were full of pity and compassion but now there is no pity for in London thy brother shall die in the streets for cold, he shall lie sick at the door and perish there for hunger." And a chaplain to Lord Somerset would say, "All good men have ever pitied the poor and sought all means possible to do them good. But the contrary is found among us nowadays for men are lovers of themselves and not of the poor, they are covetous to themselves and not liberal to the poor, they heap to themselves, they provide nothing for the poor" (DeSchweinitz, p. 240).

Agricultural and tenant farming organizations sprang up, but protest was met by repression and imprisonment. The attempt to control vagabondage and laborers by a combination of punishment plus private charity and church almsgiving continued for a long time. The newly wealthy and rapidly growing merchant class in England substantially increased its benefactions between the late fifteenth and the early seventeenth century. Between 1480–1660 in ten representative English counties there were almost 35,000 donors whose giving rose from £50,000 between 1481–1490 to £430,000 from 1621–1630. Over an 80-year span the benevolence increased tenfold and 40 percent of the gifts went to the poor (W. K. Jordan, 1959).

Attempts to meet social and economic change with punishment and private charity continued to be insufficient. In 1536 Thomas Cromwell, an ancestor of Oliver Cromwell, became the key adviser to Henry VIII. He prepared a memorandum of remarkable scope to deal with the problems of poverty by royal edict. This document identified the classes of persons entitled to help—including even those who might be poor because of laziness. The remedies were a massive program of nationally administered, tax-financed public works for highways, canals and harbor building. The poor who did not enroll for work and remained vagabonds could be arrested. The ill were to be provided with medical care and cared for in hospitals. For the first time, there was included aid to "all those in misfortune—honest men who cannot live on their earnings by reason of multitude of children or other honest cause or who have come to extreme poverty through sickness, fire, water, robbery and otherwise" (Elton, 1953).

For various reasons this ambitious program was not adopted at first; instead older means were maintained for another generation. Efforts of the Crown to deal with the problems of poverty remained minimal for many years while concerned individuals searched for and argued over better ways to adjust to new conditions.

New Approaches by Government: European and English Poor Laws

Some of the most significant and interesting attempts to deal with the changing times and with the theology and morality of Protestantism appeared in the Continental Lowlands. At Ypres and Bruges, experiments and practices were introduced as early as 1530; they were read about and known in the English Court by the middle 1530s.

One of the most forward looking plans for relieving the poor was prepared for the Mayor of Bruges by Juan Luis Vives in January 1536 when he wrote:

> It is much more important for the magistrates to devote their energy to the producing of good citizens than to the punishment and restraint of evil doers. For how much less need would there be to punish if these matters were rightly looked after beforehand. (Salter, 1926; DeSchweinitz, chap. 17)

He proposed attention to three categories of poor: (1) those who live in hospitals including abandoned infants, the insane and blind; (2) the poor who suffer privately in their own homes; and (3) beggars without fixed dwellings. He proposed that officers of the municipality systematically ascertain the requirements of each category. The fundamental approach to dealing with poverty was the provision of work. "This principle must be accepted which the Lord imposed upon the human race as a punishment for its sin: that each man should eat bread that is the fruit of his own labor." The poor who did not have a trade would be taught one and if some trades are too difficult for those of slow wit they should be assigned to easier tasks. It was suggested that even those who dissipated their fortunes in riotous living must be relieved for no one must die of hunger, but to them more irksome tasks would be assigned and smaller rations that "they may be an example to others and be led to repent of their former life and not relapse easily into the same vices being restrained by lack of food and by the severity of their tasks. They must not die of hunger but they must feel its pangs" (DeSchweinitz, chap. 17). Government-sponsored employment was proposed for the able-bodied who were out of work for no reason of their own. Apprenticeship was modified for the physically handicapped for "nor would I allow the blind either to sit idle . . . There are a great many things at which they may employ themselves." The elderly and infirm "should have light tasks furnished to them suited to their age and strength. No one is so feeble that he completely lacks strength for doing anything." For the mentally ill it was proposed:

> Since there is nothing in the world more excellent than man nor in man than his mind, particular attention should be given to the welfare of his mind; and it should be reckoned the highest of services if we either restore the minds of others to sanity or keep them sane and rational. Therefore when a man of unsettled mind is brought to a hospital first of all it must be determined whether his insanity is congenital or has resulted from some misfortune whether there is hope for recovery or not. . . . It is of the utmost importance that treatment be such that the insanity is not nourished and increased . . . what could be more inhumane than to drive a man insane just for the sake of laughing at him . . . Remedies suited to the individual patient should be used.

> As the soul animates and quickens not one part but the whole body so the government may neglect nothing that in the entire compass of the state. For those who care only for the rich and despise the poor act just like a physician who should not think of it much important to heal the hands or the feet because they are at a distance from the heart but even as this would cause serious harm and suffering to the whole man so also in the commonwealth the weaker may not be neglected without period to the more powerful. (Vives, 1917).

Proposals directed towards relieving and rehabilitating the poor rather than punishing them, were also advanced by Thomas More, Martin Luther and others. By 1513 Machiavelli writing in *The Prince* described practices and principles which probably were drawn from experience in a number of cities. Referring to unemployment which might be experienced in a city besieged by an invading army:

> These cities have all the necessary bastions, sufficient artillery and always keep food, drink, and fuel for one year in public storehouses. Beyond which to keep the lower classes satisfied and without loss to the commonwealth, they have always enough means to give them enough work for one year in these towns in these employments which form the nerve and life of the town and in the industries by which the lower classes live. (Vincent, 1935, p. 48)

He concluded that "It is necessary for a prince to possess the friendship of all the people and then they will always be faithful to him."

Luther in 1520 proposed more traditional methods to reduce begging. His solution was to keep foreign or alien beggars out of each city and that every city should support its own poor. He called for a central depository for voluntary contributions to which would be added certain fines and church-ordered penances. "And there shall also be a box or two wherein money may be put for the upkeep of the common chest." Employees who have parish rights would be forced to contribute a certain sum collected by their employers. The chest was administered by overseers elected at a general parish meeting; orphans were supported by guardians elected for them; and young women were endowed for marriage with reasonable help. There was also provision for the purchase of corn in times of shortage so that lower priced grain was made available for the poor (DeSchweinitz, chap. 17).

In all of the proposals to relieve poverty under public or communal authority, stress was placed upon the good character of the recipient. Zwingli in an ordinance for the town of Leisnig said that alms were "not to be given to any person of whom it is known that they have spent and wasted all their days in luxury and idleness and will not work but frequent public houses, drinking places and haunts of ill repute" (Salter, 1926).

The Poor Law in England: Progress but Not Generous

Throughout the sixteenth century England searched for ways to cope with the economic distress which continued as mercantile capitalism replaced earlier feudal forms of society. Ways were sought to coordinate policies toward the poor, employment or its lack, and taxation to finance policies. While much royal government action was based on punishment and private or church controlled charity, other forces advocated more positive approaches which included, perhaps incidentally, more humane concern for the poor.

The Poor Law Act 43 Elizabeth I, 1601 was the culmination of a century of searching. Voluntary action had been first relied upon. Henry VIII in 1536 referred to "their free will and charities." Edward VI proposed in 1551 personal solicitation supported by persuasion from parsons and churchwardens. Elizabeth I in 1563 proposed that bishops refer cases of obstinate contributors to local justices of the peace. In 1572 Elizabeth I edged to a public responsibility by ordering local officials to tax inhabitants in their local jurisdictions to relieve the poor.

Over the same time some local communities organized work projects. Raw materials were purchased by town officials, given to unemployed adults to work over and to return, when they were paid off. The officials sold the finished product to finance the work. By 1601 such separate initiatives were brought together in one comprehensive law which became the framework for public attention to poverty for 300 years. A national policy was enunciated which combined relief for the poor, work, and a taxation method. Translating policy into program was assigned to local justices of the peace and they in turn appointed churchwardens and local citizens to oversee the program.

The main provisions were:

1. local administration and taxation authority
2. work for the able-bodied
3. relief of the old, blind, impotent and others unable to work
4. apprenticing of children of the poor
5. building of houses (or a house) for the impotent poor
6. filial and parental responsibility for each other
7. taxation by justices of wealthier parishes to help parishes too poor to sustain their responsibilities.

The manual, "An Ease for Overseers of the Poor," was issued in 1601 to guide public officials charged with administering the new Elizabethan version of a Poor Law. It called for speedy inspection of the poor indicating "what poor must be sent to work. The overseers must tender the poor and lay no more upon them than they are able to bear." But they must also "hold the poor to work for most are so by nature given to ease that it is hard to bring their bodies to labor as the ox that has not been used to the yoke to draw" (DeSchweinitz, chap. 21, A262).

The first intent of those trying to improve administration of the Poor Law was generally benign. The instructions, for example, point out that people can and should be relieved with money because the term *relief* itself means an ease or lightening of a burden and "who knows not that the poor endure many burdens and that a little thing will ease where there is want or oppression." The guidelines point out that ill-trained workers will spoil their materials at first and that this wastage is to be tolerated for "everyone must have a beginning and while there are many learners there will be much loss, as the scholar wasteth much paper before he can well use his pen." The author urges "tender the poor but do not tyrannize over them; for it is no more glory to triumph over the poor then to treat of a worm; it is better to deserve commendation by discreet government than exclamation by rigorous dealing." At another place the author counsels "Let your taxation be made as well with discretion as affection, and endeavor to proportion the rates by the necessities of the poor, and not the poor by the discretion of your rates." In time it became apparent that such guides to individual discretion did not work out as benignly as hoped for, but they capture the intent of this milestone legislation by a national government (DeSchweinitz, chap. 21, p. 262ff).

Mercantilist Concepts: The Ends and Limits of Government Generosity

While it is difficult to generalize about mercantilism which comprised so many conflicting and differing developments in the sixteenth and seventeenth centuries, certain elements are clear. Mercantilism was a secular concept suitable for the growth of national states in which the interests of the state were paramount. The state was defined as royal government with the hierarchy of privileged estates which held powerful influence in that state. It built on the millennium-old concepts of hierarchy, class and status. Laborers were viewed as serving the national political interests. But they also served the interests of the new economic activity: increased trade, trade in world markets of the time, and manufacture. There could be relatively generous social programs but their purposes were always to further the interest of the state—not evoke compassion for the poor. The writing and political activity of a few citizens may have helped to soften otherwise selfish class economic policies. The moderating voices had religious, as well as political or secular humanist roots.

Mercantilist doctrine considered a large, healthy population to be essential for the economic wealth and strength of the nation. It therefore encouraged keeping people healthy, growing in numbers, free movements of workers, frugality in the poor, and labor. At the same time it was committed to a belief that wages must be kept low in order to maintain competitive advantages in trade. A nation was wealthy and powerful because it had a large number of industrious and disciplined workers who were kept fully employed. Mandevil wrote that in a free nation where slaves are not allowed the surest wealth consists in a multitude of working poor.

On the continent, this concern for a large and industrious laboring class was encouraged in France by the development of family allowances in 1666 to directly increase the number and size of large families (Cole, 1939, p. 464).

But through this period there was also a belief that the working classes had to be kept in control. Cardinal Richelieu observed:

> All political opinions are in agreement that if the poor were to live too much at ease it would be impossible to keep them within the rules of their duty. (Hauser, 1944, p. 145).

And Arthur Young as late as 1771 would say: "Everyone but an idiot knows that the lower classes must be kept poor or they will never be industrious" (Furniss, 1920, p. 118).

Whatever one may think about these moralizing views, however, mercantilism was significant in the evolution of the welfare state because, whether unemployment was due to individual or social causes, it still was considered the duty of the state to intervene. "If working people are idle it is for want of being rightly governed" (Johnson, 1979). And the persistence of idleness was often taken as proof that the state had been remiss in its duty to its subjects.

A number of enlightened businessmen saw that in the poor lay an important and untapped source of national wealth. Thus, Sir Joshua

Child, Chairman of the East India Company, proposed the creation of a municipal corporation to set the poor to work on whatever manufacture they saw fit. He argued:

> Whether it turns to present profit or not it is not much material. The great business of the nation being first to keep the poor from begging and starving and inuring such as are able to labour in discipline that they may be hereafter useful members of the kingdom. (DeSchweinitz, chap. 25, p. 297)

Another anonymous writer proposed to Parliament ways to keep laborers in their place and wages low, in the pamphlet "The Grand Concern of England":

> If men, women and children were set at work . . . had to manufacture the staple commodities of the kingdom at cheap rates and thereby bring down the wages of handicraftsmen which now are grown so high that we lost a trade of foreign consumption . . . we shall quickly come to sell as cheaply as foreigners do and consequently engross the trade to ourselves. (DeSchweinitz, chap. 25)

Another businessman argued:

> Is it not a pity and shame that the young children and maids here in England should be idle within doors, begging abroad, tearing hedges or robbing orchards and worse. On these and these alone are the people that may and must if ever set up this trade of making fine linen here. After a young maid hath been three years in the spinning school she will get eight pence a day and in these parts I speak of a man that has most children lives best . . there the children enrich the father but there beggar him. (DeSchweinitz, chap. 25)

Thomas Firman in 1678 proposed a combination school where children would be taught to read as well as to spin. And in 1696 the municipality of Bristol organized two workhouses in the first of which "we received 100 girls and set them to work at spinning of worsted yarn, all of which we first caused to be stripped by the mistress and new clothed from head to foot which together with wholesome diet and set hours and good beds to lie on so encouraged the children that they willingly betook themselves to their work." A second workhouse was "devoted to the remainder of the poor, ancient people, boys and young children where they learn their ABC's and grow up to go into the working rooms." The city program went beyond work for it authorized a physician to visit the poor at home and were relieved at home till they were able to work. Those who had been ill but needed a stock of goods or money for rent would be helped until they resumed employment (DeSchweinitz, chap. 25).

SUMMARY

Why did the specific device of the Poor Law of 1601 emerge as the method for dealing with poverty when it did? The answer must be speculative at best. The Poor Law was not at first a radical change from the past, but over time it led to far-reaching changes in social caring. It was a device which confronted the change overtaking the more static community life of the past with its formula of personal obligation. The local community was still a basis for national life, but it was faced with more and more strangers. The amount of poverty did not materially change, but the expectations of life did change as mobility increased, as a wealthier middle class emerged and as cycles of good and bad times were governed by trade as much as by crop success and failure. The social changes required some response at a time when the concept of national government was being strengthened. National government acted to introduce a coherence which innumerable local conditions could not assure, but it relied on the tools of local administration to carry out a wider national purpose. At the same time the religious beliefs of Protestantism combined the values of work with those of a charity which could be secular and collective as well as personal. The Poor Laws were a reasonable synthesis to emerge from the social and economic and political context of the times.

By the seventeenth century poor relief was no longer discontinuous and undifferentiated assistance as a charity—it had become a continuous and selective system usually administered by an official body which had power to raise the necessary funds and was not dependent upon voluntary contributions. A publicly sanctioned method replaced voluntary charity. At times primitive elements of a welfare state were tried out. Work, training, and prevention of poverty were ideas in common usage and even attempted from time to time, but without much success. The motivations were as much a concern and a desire to avoid civil unrest as charity. The avoidance of civil unrest was also accompanied by religious beliefs about man's destiny and by secular conviction that an able-bodied population was a source of wealth for the state. Charity or caring and labor duty coincided with the national interests of the time. This approach persisted until the reform of the Poor Law in England in 1834. The poor were an accepted part of local society, to be relieved in cases of need, not necessarily rejected. Able-bodied "beggars" and strangers were frequent exceptions to such acceptance.

The Mercantilist Era, the poor laws and the age which succeeded feudalism created new boundaries for caring for the stranger, while rediscovering forgotten concepts from the ancient world. For the first time not only was concern articulated for the needy, the helpless and the stranger, but this concern was matched with a permanent government mechanism and structure to carry out those concepts—no matter how limited they seem in retrospect. The government mechanism, while local in character, was activated by and carried out in accordance with principles laid down by a national government which could claim to speak for all the forces within a nation or state.

The motives and the rationales for helping were a compound of selfish interest and benevolence. Obligation toward the weak or poor was part of a hierarchical society. Concern for one's soul was still a powerful motivation. But the Reformation revitalized belief in a society based on morality and a Godly design for mankind. Concern for the collective well-being was defined in national state terms. Reciprocity became more abstract, less personal, flowing between subject workers and distant or impersonal owners and government. For the most part, the able-bodied were not well treated, but some provision was made for them through emphasis upon work opportunity.

The system remained fundamentally a paternalistic one; individuals could seldom claim rights, except by threatening violence. And with the passage of time the system became overbureaucratized and rigid, inappropriate for later industrial and social developments. When the time came again for a major change it was guided by ideas about liberal economics. Utilitarian philosophy and personal freedoms became dominant motifs within which social caring programs were reshaped.

Despite shifts in outlook and policy, the threads of personal obligation, about what men owed to each other in their basic human relationships, were kept alive by a few generous men although their views were only occasionally incorporated in the official action of governments.

9

ESCAPE FROM PUBLIC RESPONSIBILITY

Eighteenth and Nineteenth Century Economic and Political Liberalism

> *For the idle man there is no place in this England of ours. He that will not work and save according to his means let him go elsewhither; let him know that for him the law has made no soft provision.*
>
> *THOMAS CARLYLE, 1840*

In the eighteenth century the Poor Law framework came under attack from the advocates of a new science of economic and political liberalism who found the paternalism of the mercantilist state unacceptable and unsatisfactory. In addition, the failures in the administration and functioning of the Poor Law itself became overly burdensome and restrictive.

As early as 1608 the English Lord Chancellor already complained that there were more vagabonds and wanderers than before passage of the Poor Law and that the parishes and Justices of the Peace did not perform their duties satisfactorily. In 1609 the King's Council wrote to the Justices of Devon that "there was a want of good correspondence between execution and direction" (DeSchweinitz, p. 270).

The eighteenth century brought many changes in the economic and political shape of Europe, but the condition of most citizens remained one of poverty and insecurity. It is not wise to generalize with confidence since conditions varied from place to place, but, in general about 85 percent of the population continued to be rural and agricultural; the remaining 15 percent rested in large part on the tax paying propensity of this rural base. At the same time, wealth also increased and made possible the purchase of more goods and increased investment in other wealth producing economic activities. Economic depression and prosperity, at least for the wealthy, alternated. When times were bad, farm prices fell and it even became profitable for landowners to change to less labor intensive uses of land—at the price of displacing peasants and tenant farmers. Land tenancy was shortened so that agricultural workers and peasants had less security in their access to traditional land and work.

At the same time the overall population began to increase steadily as loss due to plague and war declined. Unfortunately population seemed to increase faster than food produced, so that the pessimistic views of a Malthus about the inevitability of poverty and starvation seemed justified by the then available evidence (Hufton, 1980). As population pressed against food supply, prices rose, thus forcing more rural workers from farms to cities in a search for work or some relief.

A survey in Sheffield in 1615 found that out of a total of 2,007 people 725—the begging poor—were not able to live without the charity of their neighbors. There were 100 households which helped the others, but 160 householders were not able to help others with their tax payments and were unable to survive "the storm of one fortnight's sickness and would thereby be driven to beggary. And 1,222 servants of these householders were ill-provided for" (Leonard, 1900). Conditions did not much improve with time. The number of poor seeking relief in England continued to rise and by 1790 it was estimated that as much as 25–35 percent of residents in local communities received relief out of the local taxes and about one-half of local taxes were devoted to poor relief (Bahmueller, 1981).

In England, 30 percent of the population were reckoned as paupers. In Sweden, the proportion rose to 50 percent in 1815, rising from 25 percent in 1751. In France it was estimated that, overall, paupers and "exposed" elements in the city stood as high as 60 percent (Hufton, 1980).

Against this background poor relief administration was blamed more often than government policy. During the seventeenth century the King and Council sought to improve administration, and at first blamed the growth in relief not upon economic conditions but upon maladministration of poor relief. The national government tried to maintain its minimum national responsibility by issuing more orders to be executed by local jurisdictions. This was a survival of the late Middle Ages when royalty was idealized to be paternalistic and the King was philosophically believed to be responsible for the welfare of all his people, above the interests and self-interests of local lords and noblemen. These orders did not affect the course of events.

Widespread unrest, only partly due to economic difficulties, led to civil war, and the overthrow of Charles I. And it was not until 1660 that the monarchy was restored. Charles II had a quite different view of national responsibility. After the Restoration, legislation punitively limiting movement as a way of controlling poverty was introduced. The Law of

Settlement of 1662 affected almost everyone in England over the age of 40. As Adam Smith noted in the next century, no poor man would venture to leave his home to take advantage of opportunities elsewhere when he ran the risk of being returned enforceably to the community from which he had come, no matter how sound the reasons for the move, no matter what the economic circumstances in his place of residence and no matter his willingness and ability to work.

This controlling view was replaced by the evolution of quite different concepts about economics, the economy, and the political relationship of the Crown to local jurisdictions. The new ideas were reinforced by a wave of religious evangelism which sanctioned rewards for economic achievement. Morality became tied to material success. The promise of *this life* as well as of the life to come, became important. The belief in duty to work and the rewards which came with it were applied not only to those who succeeded in trade or in farming but those who were poor as well.

Slowly the Poor Law of 1601, which originally intended not only to control vagabondage but to relieve the poverty of the distressed, was transformed into an instrument for enforced work and enforcement of a specific morality in which poverty was considered one of the wages of presumed sinfulness (Mandevil, 1924). The poor were less seen as deserving of help from their neighbors and more as sinners. During the eighteenth century critics of a generous Poor Law joined forces with new advocates of economic and political freedom—the liberalism of the eighteenth and nineteenth centuries. In the new liberal view too much monarchical control and bureaucratic government was responsible for the ills of society, including poverty. The Poor Laws were considered by economists as simply one example of a way of enslaving workers, keeping them in their parish or in workhouses, preventing them from moving where there were opportunities for work and controlling their wages. The conviction emerged that the solution was to free the poor and rich alike from bureaucratic constraints on economic and political activity. Without a Poor Law all would be as free to make their own way in the open and freer economic and political society. A new world of opportunity would be opened up. Even if the poor did not yet have the vote, they should be given the same economic freedom as others possessed. Each should be free to contract and to arrange for his affairs as he was able and the sum of these individual efforts would prove more beneficial for the nation than any attempt at planned control of the poor. The mercantilist goal of the well-being of the nation, not of individuals, would remain shorn of governmental interference.

In the late eighteenth century several agricultural parishes adopted the *Speenhamland* policy whereby local taxes were used to subsidize wages to help the poor meet the rising cost of living. It may be seen as an early effort to help poor workers combat poverty by further liberalizing the administration of Poor Laws which had over the years fallen into abuse, neglect and which stigmatized the poor. In an unsophisticated way, the market economy for labor was subsidized by taxes during serious depression and inflation. A table was developed of the necessities of each family from which was derived a judgment about the weekly income necessary for the industrious poor. This income was determined by the price of bread and as the price of bread increased so would the scale of income. Individuals and families who were at work but earned less than this scale would be eligible for relief but instead of being treated on a charitable basis the worker was entitled to supplement his wage. In 1782 this concept was incorporated in an act which proposed to assure relief payments at this scale to anyone out of work and to continue to subsidize the difference between wages earned and the minimum. The bill was defeated on several grounds: a man with a small family might have too much income and a man with a large family would make too little; such a scheme might encourage idleness; and the labor market was too complex to permit a guarantee of work for all. The initiative lost against the more persuasive arguments of those opposed to government regulation and of those who blamed the poor for their poverty (Mencher, 1967).

The debate which began with Adam Smith, Hume, and others in the eighteenth century radically altered the way in which a population and its government viewed the problems of poverty. The debate continued into the 1800s. The problems were redefined. Poverty became associated either with incorrect habits which in turn were associated with particular classes of people hampered by public rules; or they were the so-called "dangerous" classes of moralists. The problem became not so much ignorance, which could be remedied by education and training, but corrupt knowledge; schools began to be seen as places to inculcate good moral habits rather than training in skills.

While this debate was under way, humanitarian compassion and pity persisted mainly in concern over children. A few reformers were appalled at the rate of infant mortality, especially in the poorhouses. One survey found that, between 1750 and 1755, of 1,265 children born in the workhouses of London's 14 largest parishes only 168 were living by 1755, and death rates were as high as 82 percent for children under one year of age. Scores of pamphlets appeared attacking the maladministration of the poorhouse and proposing various reforms and appealing both to the necessary protection of the young as the workers and citizens of the future (DeSchweinitz, p. 309).

The humanitarian concern as distinct from the economic argument did not address the fundamental reordering of the Poor Law—but accepted its premises and sought remedies in better organization and administration. One remedy tried by Poor Law reformers during the eighteenth century was the consolidation of small parish relief units into larger districts with a stronger administration for the Poor Law. An interim Act of Parliament in 1782 permitted consolidation of the parishes for Poor Law purposes. It also ordered guardians of the poor to combine their administrations better to secure employment of poor persons who were able and willing to work but who were otherwise unable to find employment. It was obligatory to maintain and provide for such persons until employment could be procured. The belief in a humanistic and civil approach to poverty was expressed by Samuel Johnson who was quoted as saying: "Where a great proportion of the people are suffered to languish in helpless misery that country must be ill-policied and wretchedly governed: a decent provision for the poor is a true test of civilization" (Boswell, 1957).

De Tocqueville in a related vein would write:

> And if you think it profitable to turn man's intellectual and moral activity toward the necessities of physical life and use them to produce well-being, if you think that reason is more use to men than genius, if your object is not to create heroic virtues but rather tranquil habits, if you would rather contemplate vices than crimes and prefer fewer transgressions at the cost of fewer splendid deeds, if in place of a brilliant society you are content to live in one that is prosperous and finally if in your view the main object of government is not to achieve the greatest strength or glory for the nation as a whole but to provide for every individual therein the utmost well-being protecting him as far as possible from all afflictions then it is good to make conditions equal and to establish a democratic government. (De Tocqueville, 1980)

But the interpretation of these humane aspirations required attention to unpleasant and practical details: how to deal with poverty, with economic unevenness in the society; how to assure a cohesive society in which all elements feel bound together and yet work together rather than taking from each other. The self-centered class-focused attitudes and beliefs proved more powerful than more generous ones.

The western world in the late eighteenth and early nineteenth centuries, welcomed and was dominated by the coming of industrial capitalism to replace commercial captialism. Displacement and distress increased among the poor; there was more wealth and also more poverty. In 1834, reform of the Poor Law summed up the change. It was based upon moral concepts of a middle class which defined poverty to be the result of personal defect and sinfulness. The political and economic liberalism of that class and of the day argued that the constraints of monarchy and or bureaucratic government also had to be dissolved and that, once dissolved, all persons would have an equal opportunity to find the happiness to which their labors entitled them. If they did not find that happiness it would then be due to their failure rather than to failure in the economic or political structure which was no longer considered responsible. A 1786 pamphlet on the Poor Laws captures the flavor of argument which led to the change. It urged:

> To promote industry and economy it is necessary that the relief which is given to the poor should be limited and precarious. Unless the degree of pressure be increased the laboring poor will never acquire habits of diligent application and severe frugality. (Townsend, 1886)

Thomas Robert Malthus in 1803, writing on the principle of population wrote:

> If the Poor Laws had never existed in this country there might have been a few more instances of very severe distress but the aggregate mass of happiness among the common people would have been much greater than at present. . . The Poor Laws powerfully contributed to generate that carelessness and want of frugality observable among the poor who seem always to live from hand to mouth. (Townsend, 1886; Malthus, 1926)

In this time the wealth of England increased enormously but the tax structure leveled taxes inequitably and weighed especially heavily on farmers, squires, village shopkeepers and the like. New manufacturing districts escaped heavy taxation. A combination of inequitable tax distribution and rising poverty in a period of great economic growth was accompanied by agitation by workers, especially agricultural workers, and other poor who sometimes resorted to violence in attacking the new machinery.

1834 Reform

As newly articulate voices were raised, a regressive and punitive reform of the Poor Law was achieved in 1834. The terms of this reform conformed to the economic and political liberalism of the time, namely concentrating on: the dismantling as much as possible of a once relatively generous Poor Law system and its replacement through forced means to drive the poor to work by making poor relief as unattractive and punitive as possible. A three man commission was appointed, no member eligible to sit in Parliament, to shield its work from political pressures. The commission which developed and administered the Poor Law Reform concentrated primarily on the unemployed or the partially employed and gave limited attention to extreme youth, old age, infirmity or disease (Report on the Poor Law Commissioners, 1835).

The commission concluded that only stern treatment would demonstrate to the poor the desirability of self-support which would keep people in the active labor force. The legislation authorized parishes to voluntarily combine into larger unions for administration. While the law itself did not ban relief in the home, the report of 1834 on which it was based had stated "All relief whatsoever to able-bodied persons or their families, otherwise than in well regulated workhouses . . . shall be declared unlawful." The report provided the detail which the bill did not elaborate on; the commissioners appointed to administer the new law were its strong advocates; they and their assistants were for the most part men of superior education, and of a higher social class than the old Poor Law officials. They were committed to the new economics.

Within five years the Poor Law consolidations were completed; 13,641 out of 15,635 parishes were formed into 587 unions. Two-hundred and fifty-two new workhouses were built, 175 remodeled, and 113 planned for. The flavor of the reform is captured in these extracts from the first report.

The Commissioners in 1835, in their first annual report, describe the operation of this system. After being examined for "disease of body and mind" which would require reception in the "sick ward, or the ward for lunatics and idiots not dangerous," the incoming pauper is to "be clothed in the workhouse dress." The members of the family are then to be classified according to sex, age, and physical condition. Each class shall be confined in a separate part of the building or buildings, husbands in one place, wives in another, the aged and infirm, children under seven, the able-bodied from thirteen years upward, each sleeping at night in its own, large, open ward.

"During the time of meals, silence, order and decorum shall be maintained." The diet shall not "exceed, in quantity and quality of food, the ordinary diet of the able-bodied laborers living within the same district." "No person shall be allowed to visit any pauper in the workhouse, except by permission of the master . . . provided that the interview shall always take place in the presence of the master or matron." The paupers were not permitted to leave the institution on Sunday to attend church but "divine service shall be performed every Sunday in the workhouse." The disorderly or uncooperative pauper "shall be placed in an apartment provided for such offenders, or shall otherwise be distinguished in dress and placed in apartments provided for such offenders, and placed upon such a diet as the board of guardians shall prescribe." The pauper could give up his residence in the workhouse on three hours notice but, if able-bodied, he could not do so without taking his family with him, a condition difficult for him to meet if, being jobless, his purpose in leaving was to find work (DeSchweinitz, p. 352; Report, 1835).

Later reports emphasized the Commission's view that it was vital to make the condition of the poor worse than that of independent workers:

> An inmate of a well-appointed Union workhouse lives in rooms more spacious, better ventilated, and better warmed; his meals are better and more regularly served; he is more warmly clad; and he is better attended

in sickness than if he were in his own cottage; moreover, all these benefits are supplied to him with perfect regularity, and without any forethought or anxiety on his part. Thus far, relief in a public establishment violates the principle above adverted to, and places the pauper in a more eligible condition than the independent laborer. And yet humanity demands that all the bodily wants of the inmates of a public establishment should be amply provided for. The only expedient, therefore, for accomplishing the end in view, which humanity permits, is to subject the pauper inmate of a public establishment to such a system of labor, discipline, and restraint, as shall be sufficient to outweigh, in his estimation, the advantages which he derives from the bodily comforts which he enjoys. (Report, 1840)

One result of the reform was a marked drop by one-third in public expenditure on welfare, between 1834 and 1837. The local tax rate for welfare, with some fluctuations up and down, dropped from 8 shillings 9½ pence per head in 1834 to 5 shillings 5½ pence in 1852 (Nichols, 1898).

The official Report summarized what the tax-paying and voting public (which at that time did not include many workers) wanted to hear; it expressed the moral beliefs and prejudices of the time with authority and assurance in a manner which fixed for a generation the environment for dealing with poverty:

Each opinion entertained by men at a given era is governed by that whole body of beliefs, convictions, sentiments or assumptions which for want of a better name we call the spirit of an age. Deeper than opinions lies the sentiment which predetermines opinion. (Dicey, 1948)

A second, delayed result of the reform was political. The new Poor Law was not without its critics. William Cobbett vigorously attacked the legislation and argued:

The right of the English poor to relief . . . was the right by law founded in nature and on the principles of civil society; and if this were not a right what right had they (the wealthy) to call on the poor to become militiamen to defend their estates? (Hansard)

But these defenses of generosity and sharing did not succeed and the reformed Poor Law introduced the concept of lesser eligibility as the basic principle for public relief of want—that the poor should under no circumstances live in conditions equal to or better than that of any independent laborer. While some shred of elementary humanity was retained in the concept of lesser eligibility it was combined with a relief system which limited help to "incarceration" in a poorhouse as a necessary condition for receiving any assistance and admission was made as demeaning as possible. Disraeli, later prime minister, in opposing this approach argued: "It announces to the world that in England poverty is a crime" (1881). He argued that the Poor Law was based on a basic moral error—that relief to the poor is a charity. Disraeli maintained that it was a right.

Those who argued for a right to humane maintenance encountered counterarguments from those like Herbert Spencer who asked:

> What is maintenance? Is it potatoes and salt, with rags and a mud cabin? Or is it bread and bacon in a two-roomed cottage? . . . does the demand include meat and malt liquor daily? (Spencer, 1886)

They succeeded in persuading legislatures that agreement about what constituted a decent humane standard of living required acceptance of the concept of lesser eligibility—the standard must be lower than that of the lowest paid full-time worker. This conformed sufficiently to common belief to prevail.

CONTRADICTIONS IN POOR LAW REFORM

The new relief structure with its centralized and more punitive character contained internal contradictions. In the first place, while the old Poor Law concepts with its relative liberality was dismantled in favor of a more punitive one, the new system required national and central administration and control just at a time when economic and political theory argued in the opposite direction. Between 1834 and 1846 the bureaucratic structure grew exponentially as it did elsewhere under later welfare states. Unpaid overseers in 1834 were replaced by almost 14,000 persons in the controlled workhouses who functioned as investigators (Nichols, 1898).

Although the most powerful forces behind the reform lay in the imperatives of the new industrialization which replaced the old commercial capitalism, removing laws which inhibited labor mobility and workers' commitment to an urban industrial life did not take care of the realities of life in the new industrial world. Adam Smith objected to the poor relief system as a hindrance to the free circulation of labor, however, he also recognized the need for some provision for those who were "impotent." The reform failed to meet this test.

One intellectual current of the times favored an indissoluble community to build a nation and a sense of unity based upon sympathy and mutual interest. Unfortunately, the new economic liberalism, as then defined, tended to split society. Malthus objected that the Poor Laws tended to increase the population of the poor without increasing food for its support and that even the provisions consumed as the most valuable part (i.e., not working) diminishes the shares which would otherwise belong to the more industrious and worthy members which in turn forces those worthy members to become dependent. He argued for the moral principle that rejection of dependence and rejection of protection given by society to the individual were both based upon natural law. "There is one right which man has generally been thought to possess . . . . a right to subsistence. . . . Our laws indeed say that he has this right and binds a society to furnish employment and food for those who cannot get them in the regular market but in doing so they reverse the laws of nature" (Rimlinger, 1971, p. 40). In arguing for an abolition of government responsibility Malthus argued instead for strong action by government and by voluntary means to improve the moral character of the poor.

Nassau Senior, a leading member of the commission to reform the Poor Laws saw the reform not in the stark terms enunciated by Malthus but rather as a way of emancipating the working class. The old Poor Law limited the freedom of the worker and thus conflicted with the utilitarian belief that the greatest social happiness and progress was achieved by leaving each individual free to pursue his self-interest. He pointed out that the old Poor Laws were basically an attempt to maintain the older elements of a system in which workers were tied to the land. The right of support given by the Poor Laws was only "part of a scheme in defiance of reason, justice and humanity to reduce the laboring classes to serfs, to imprison them in their parishes and to dictate to them their employement and their wages" (Rimlinger, 1971, p. 43). Senior, as a leader of the commission, wanted to free the poor from this kind of servitude and believed that the poor were either too ignorant or degraded to perceive or resent their enslavement. He wanted to free the industrious from having to support the indolent. To a significant extent Senior and his colleagues retained the belief in supporting the impotent, sick and elderly although now only in the workhouses with the punitive nature of the reform directed at the able-bodied person presumed capable of finding employment.

Similar action occurred in France where the paternalism of the old regime was replaced by the new liberalism. There the liberals believed that with free competition for individuals would come the diffusion of prudence and forethought, capital per head would accumulate, wage levels would rise and the lot of the masses would steadily improve (Rimlinger, 1971, p. 44). In 1840 the Minister of the Interior wrote to all prefects in the kingdom that they must not ignore the objections which enlightened economists had advanced against legal (or public) charity. He thought it dangerous to let the poor classes get the impression that they had some legitimate claim against the wealthy of the country. He did however favor private charity on the grounds that the poor man would not ever get the idea that he can claim that as a right (Schaller, 1850, p. 41).

The essential flaws in the new reform were found not so much in intellectual arguments as in the realities of the growth of poverty which they ignored: structural unemployment, technological unemployment, cyclical fluctuation, and the groveling mode of living with its squalid living quarters, unsanitary working conditions which were hardly propitious for the development of virtues of forethought, industriousness and sobriety (Allen, 1947, p. 52).

The consequences of this punitive and rigorous adherence to libertarian plus moral concepts about poverty led within a short time to strong reactions. In the United Kingdom such reactions took the form of political protest, union organization, and private and voluntary philanthropy based upon a concern for human beings. The latter differed from the former in the belief that the remediation of poverty had to be accompanied by a moral reconstruction of persons whose moral fiber was destroyed by their poverty. This led to concepts of social protection which in time were joined to the eighteenth and nineteenth century concepts of political and economic freedom. This evolution was hastened by the shocking revelation of widespread destitution in the midst of unprecedented national wealth. These led to a succession of demands and wide public debate about fundamental economic and social reforms which separated advocates from each other. Voluntary efforts, such as those of Charity Organization Societies, remained the most influential determinant of middle-class opinion about the poor. These agencies attempted to maintain the thrust of a free market society while solving the problem of poverty without government. It was soon clear that the size of the problem vastly exceeded the capacity of voluntary effort. Massive studies by Charles Booth, Seebohm Rowntree and others provided abundant evidence and testimony (Booth, 1970; Bruce, 1961, pp. 143–146). At the same time union and political organization sought to mobilize government in a restructuring of class and economic relationships.

SUMMARY

It is out of this environment that we can move to the development of welfare thinking in the United States. England and industrializing Europe added to the backlog of welfare thought a clear national role, a permanent national responsibility for the poor carried out by a local, publicly administered apparatus and a paid bureaucracy. But the execution added a legal differentiation between the working poor and the "relieved" or non-working poor, stigmatizing the latter, relying on punishment, not loving kindness, training or concern.

10

SHAPING A RELUCTANT WELFARE STATE: U.S.A.

The preceding chapters summarize a pool of ideas about welfare and about caring for others which evolved at different times in Mediterranean and European history. There is no suggestion of a linear evolution in thinking, however, the different ways of relieving distress add up to a cultural heritage which could be drawn upon by later generations as each confronts poverty and suffering in its own social and economic circumstances. Some of this heritage is made available through writings, some through a less systematic absorption of values fostered by social organization, by religion, or by economic and political doctrines, and by oral transmission.

Settlers in the new America brought some of these ideas with them in the seventeenth century, and other ideas were introduced in the eighteenth and nineteenth centuries. However, the special circumstances of the American settlement introduced their own shaping influences in the charitable actions taken by settlers and citizens. This context for welfare in America was a compound of several often conflicting beliefs which evolved and changed during four periods: the early colonial settlement; late eighteenth and early nineteenth century growth; the progressive era of 1890-1920; and the pre- and post-World War II flowering of federal welfare energy. Before considering the change in welfare thinking which the late twentieth century requires, it is worth reviewing the stages in welfare effort in the U.S. This American welfare past, when added to the

145

pool of belief derived from the European past, may explain, in part, the emotional beliefs and values on which an American citizenry will draw as it confronts the next decades. A national welfare program evolved out of the past, but slowly and with much reluctance. Will America continue to be a reluctant welfare state?

Poverty as distinguished from dependency is not a recent American phenomenon. It was a widespread condition in the earliest settlement, and has persisted as a theme in American life, contrary to popular views about frontier society. Most citizens were poor in early colonial America, but not many were paupers, or dependent on public help. The town of Watertown, Massachusetts, population 1,000 in 1708, recorded 32 individuals receiving relief between 1700 and 1709. Salem, population 2,500 in 1700, recorded 29 cases in the 1690s (Lee, 1982, p. 564). Evidence is not consistent, nor easily come by, but several reconstructions of the colonial years indicate that well under 1 percent of the population received help from non-family sources. In Massachusetts in 1784 the figure has been calculated at 0.88 percent; in New York City before 1740 at 0.9 percent; in Philadelphia in 1709 at 0.52 percent (Byers, unpub. mss; Nash, 1976, pp. 556–560). In one Virginia parish only 97 cases of help were recorded between 1709 and 1749.

Conditions changed in the late eighteenth and first half of the nineteenth centuries. The population grew and economic conditions were periodically disrupted—bankrupting many and throwing others into dependency. Later in the nineteenth and early twentieth centuries, immigration increased the working class populations and industrialization transformed the economy—creating great wealth while it left more citizens without secure or stable work or income. Dependency increased steadily, but fluctuated widely as a proportion of the population at any given time.

Illustrative is the data for Massachusetts (Byers, unpub. mss.):

TABLE 10.1   Massachusetts Average
Annual Growth Rates for Absolute
Numbers of Poor Relief Recipients as
a % of Population, 1784–1970

1784–1850	1.68%
1850–1860	0.08
1860–1885	3.50
1885–1925	negative
1925–1970	1.28

In any one time period, economic depression increased the growth rate of poor relief recipients or rapid population growth reduced it. But cumulatively these rates led to the following proportion of the Massachusetts population being dependent in a given year (*Statistical Abstract,* 1974):

1784	.88%
1819	1.36
1925	5.78
1970	10.

Colonial America

Colonial America, in contrast with much late twentieth century thinking, did not resist government as the chosen instrument for collective action on human problems. True the government was local and small scale, but the right to use it to override personal interests was well accepted. Later events inhibited the extension of this beyond its early Poor Law foundations.

The very earliest settlements in 1620, the Massachusetts Bay and the Plymouth Colonies started out with communal views which would be radical today. John Winthrop counseled that the supplies, joys and labor of any one member must be shared by all in "our common Commission and community." Poor relief symbolized a well-ordered community and commonwealth. Regard for the poor was a civic virtue brought by a dissident religious sect from a less egalitarian Europe. While such radical views of community were soon replaced by the practicalities of social and human interaction, the seed of sharing did not wholly disappear although its form and rationale did (Lee, 1982, p. 564).

The English Poor Law provided the framework for treating the poor and helpless. Poor Law concepts were formally adopted as the legal foundation in 1642 when the Massachusetts Bay Company voted that every township "shall make provision for the maintenance of their poor" (Lee, 1982, p. 564fn). In 1683 the General Assembly of New York "enacted that the commissioners of every town, city, parish and precinct shall make provision for the maintenance, support of their poor respectively" (Schneider, 1983, p. 36). Two years after the Declaration of Independence the General Assembly of Pennsylvania voted "to revive and put into force" a provincial statute of 1771 "levying local taxes for the relief of the poor" as did other of the new colonies (Statutes at Large of Pennsylvania, vol. 8, pp. 75–96). Until the end of the eighteenth century these legal provisions were applied for the needy poor who were not viewed as different from their neighbors. People helped the poor because they were helping their own kind.

People lived in small frontier communities, closely knit associations of individuals thrown together by location and a need to survive. Conditions and arrangements varied among the Colonies so that generalization is risky. But all people found ties not only in family but in being thrown together in frontier conditions. They often shared a common religious faith or a common European area of origin. Face-to-face community life was a combination of individuality, independence and mutual interdependence. Hazards of survival could be overcome only by reliance on each other to supplement what each did for him- or herself.

Formal organization remained uncomplicated for a time. Records from New England are full of evidence about the way uncomplicated local government acted on its poor members' needs. One Rhode Island town meeting voted to provide for the maintenance of "Old John Mott in 1644." "Old John Mott" lived with a Mr. Baulston who in turn received a cow and some grain from Mott's son and in addition received in-kind grain contributed by the town fathers to the caretaker. A year later the town agreed to build "a small house" for the comfortable being of "Old John Mott" in the winter, for effecting of which the townsmen "do here promise and upon the call of the overseers to come in and help forward the work." Over a period of 13 years at least five different householders undertook Mr. Mott's care and the townsmen ordered paid from the treasury such sums as were necessary for his keeping beyond that contributed by voluntary means (Creech, 1936, pp. 284–286). The kinds of difficulty handled by such neighborly arrangements were the obvious needs of persons who could not help themselves— the sick or injured, very aged, infirm, widows, and orphaned children. The numbers too were not large and in some towns no resident poor were noted in the town record during the first hundred years of the town's existence. Or, if there were any, less than a dozen might have been identified over a hundred years of time in a community which consisted of between 50 and 110 families and up to 600 inhabitants. Similar approaches were recorded in Virginia and elsewhere among the Colonies.

In the early years, laws of settlement were not rigorously enforced. Strangers who could bring some strength to the community (in labor or other assets) were welcome—especially if their behavior endangered no one. Most were soon absorbed and became accepted members of the community family (Rothman, 1971). Casual deviant newcomers were not welcome. The Poor Law and custom made such judgments possible. Helping acts were those one would expect to find in a close-knit tribe or clan; those who became accepted members of intimate communities were assured of help because their neighbors would rally to relieve them. For the most part, poor people were accepted members of these communities, neither strangers nor ostracized. Weakness in character, as long as not threatening to others, was tolerated much as physical or material disaster was a part of normal existence.

Vagabonds and others who were perceived as "rogues" were not acceptable in these communities. People who were lazy, or who lived a corrupt life by the standards of the community, were punished or expelled. Popular beliefs and local law discriminated between honest hard working folk who fell on hard times and those who, while able to work, chose not to. Strangers from other communities were welcome, laws of settlement to the contrary, if the newcomer added to the economic and social life, but not if he exploited it.

Religious beliefs played an important role in shaping colonial settler behavior, along with the earthly reality of staying alive. Especially in New England, clergy preached the Old and New Testament injunctions about obligation to the poor, while at the same time acknowledging the material calculations involved in fixing the tax rate which had to pay for some of the obligations. One premise behind the preaching was a belief that the existing social order, in which all classes, including the rich and poor had to be accepted, because their presence was part of a divine plan, just as the more secure had an obligation to relieve them as part of the same plan. The opportunity to do good and the condition of poverty furthered the design (Leiby, 1978).

Philanthropy, carried out personally or through taxes, served many purposes in this theological view. Men rose above self-interest and pride by helping others; charity brought neighbors together and social love or care increased the cohesion which bound a society together. Men were less likely to fear their poor neighbors if helping them had divine blessings. Benevolence also justified the pursuit of wealth, since wealth was essential to the rest.

Religious sanction was sometimes divided over the extent of obligation. Some theologians were harsh about those who would not work though able; other ministers urged care for any in distress, no matter whether due to accident, illness, idleness or even vice. By and large local behavior did not punish the poor because of their poverty; they were accepted and often cared for positively.

Local judgments were relied upon to decide whom to help and whom to punish in a context which accepted poverty and crime as natural to man born in sin or living out a divine plan. Neither implied a flaw in the community structure.

This approach was made easier by the relatively small size of most communities. As late as 1765, the population in most towns in Massachusetts was less than 1,000 and these residents would attend the same church, intermarry and work together.

One practice often overlooked in later experience was the firm acceptance of the right of government, especially locally controlled government, to override privilege and to act for the general welfare. Local government was given wide power over both the economy and of education, so much so that children not properly educated by their parents at home could be removed by public action to families which would give them a "decent Christian education." Responsibility extended to widows, orphans, the aged, sick, insane and those needy by force of circumstances.

Local taxes provided funds. Decisions about spending were left to local judgments (without too much formal rule or regulation) but expense was always controlled. Officers relieved need in the most practical ways.

Home relief and boarding out in the homes of neighbors were common. Some modest payment was made to caregivers—who were not themselves necessarily the poorest trying to earn money but sturdy neighbors willing to help neighbors. Contracts for indentured labor were also common.

Urban areas did build almshouses, as in Salem, Boston, New York and Philadelphia, but they served a special purpose. They received people too disabled to be really cared for in private family homes or they were insane and considered dangerous. The almshouse was also used for strangers who fell ill or were injured; their number was growing as the cities became centers of trade and shipping. In some ways the almshouse population was not unlike that of a modern nursing home if combined with a convalescent home for short stays. Orphan children were sometimes placed in the almshouse, but usually for a short time until relocated with a family or as an apprentice or indentured worker, unless they were quite handicapped.

Popular views about the poor were influenced by both secular and theological opinion. Benjamin Franklin, neither atheist or deist, wrote influentially about the virtues of work, saving and sturdy self-independence.

The Late Eighteenth and Early Nineteenth Centuries

After the War of Independence, several developments slowly changed the public perceptions about poverty, and the views of how to handle it. There were depressed economic conditions as a consequence of the Napoleonic Wars in Europe and the War of 1812 with England. Normal population growth was accelerated by increased immigration, especially of those escaping the devastating famine in Ireland. Cities were growing, there was more mobility and urban life was less static and self-contained. In spite of economic difficulty the cities offered more opportunity than did many rural farms, thus, families came to the cities seeking work or relief. Crime increased and there were more extreme cultural differences to absorb.

Religious and intellectual ideas also began to change. People began to think that earthly woes were not part of a divine and immutable plan; many ills were due to environment, to defects in the social order, and to individual weakness. Reforming ideas were imported from Europe. A growing middle class became simultaneously less content with the results of a benign relief at home or in an almshouse and more concerned about the costs of dependency, which had grown noticeably.

Comfortable citizens began to think that they and the poor were significantly different, less brothers under God and more separated by different behaviors judged against a standard which called for educating the poor in ways of good moral character. However, the country did not reach the situation which Disraeli later described for England:

> Two nations between whom there is no intercourse and no sympathy; who are ignorant of each other's habits, thought and feelings as if they were dwellers in different zones or inhabitants of different planets . . . the rich and the poor. (Disraeli, 1881, p. 76)

But a gap did grow up between the poor who had to be relieved and the rest, who paid for it.

The pattern of helping changed in this period. More reliance was placed on the workhouse as a way to relieve poverty. The size of institutions increased and in some places such as Salem, Massachusetts (by 1750) and New York City (1824), public outdoor relief (relief outside of institutions) was nearly abolished. Relief required entry into a workhouse. By 1845, Boston relieved its poor approximately half in institutions and half at home (Byers unpub. mss.). The extent of this shift may be exaggerated, however, since it is based on public payments which may list separately the grants to private charities. In New York, for example, almost half of town appropriations for charity went to private agencies that may have helped some additional poor people at home.

Partly because of dissatisfaction with the Poor Law provisions a number of concerned citizens established the first voluntary association—A Society for the Prevention of Pauperism—in December 1817. Its objectives were: "first amply to relieve the unavoidable necessities of the poor; and secondly to lay the powerful hand of moral and legal restriction upon everything that contributes to introduce an artificial extent of suffering" (Griscom, 1859, pp. 157–158; Society for the Prevention of Pauperism, 1818, pp. 12–24). This association enunciated in the clearest form the basic premises for ameliorating efforts which evolved in the nineteenth century, whether under public or voluntary auspices. The Society emphasized: ignorance among the foreign poor; idleness, "a tendency maybe more or less inherent," "intemperence and drinking, want of economy, imprudent and hasty marriages." Attitudes of "we" and "they" became widespread, along with a concern about costs. The Society believed that "one of the most powerful incitements to an honest and honorable course of conduct is a regard to reputation or a desire of securing the approbation of our friends and associates. To encourage this sentiment among the poor, to inspire them with feelings of self-respect and a regard of character will be to introduce the very elements of reform." While the Society only lasted until 1825, the basic ideas were carried forward in a variety of voluntary efforts in succeeding decades including that of the New York Society for the Prevention of Pauperism, the Community Organization Society, and the Association for Improving the Condition of the Poor. Citizens became concerned about ways of preventing an increase in pauperism and believed that education, religious instruction and moral supervision of individuals and neighborhoods were the main safeguards to be used.

In the same period the Poor Laws themselves came under vigorous attack for reasons which echo the liberal economic justification for the English Poor Law reforms of the early nineteenth century. Josiah Quincy, who became the sixteenth President of Harvard University and was a former legislator, completed a report in 1821 which asserted:

> The pernicious consequences of the existing system (the Poor Laws) are palpable . . . the poor begin to consider it as a right . . . the stimulus to industry and economy is annihilated. (Committee on Pauper Laws, Commonwealth of Mass., 1821)

However, Quincy and his committee concluded that the then existing system of making some compulsory or public provision for the poor was too deeply ingrained in the affection and in the moral sentiment of the people to be loosened by such strong theories, no matter how plausible they would be. The committee therefore recommended, consistent with ideas embodied in the English Reform Law of 1834, that major provision be made for pauperism, to the extent that it was going to be inevitable, in the almshouse. They were to be converted into houses of industry rather than "abodes of idleness" (Commonwealth, 1835). Home relief was less and less trusted.

Similar official enquiries led to like recommendations in New York and elsewhere. In New York State in 1824 the Secretary of State recommended that houses of employment be established where paupers would be maintained and employed and where their children could be instructed at the expense of each county. The Poor Laws were maintained and persons were entitled to claim relief but only in the county where they became sick or infirm. The report took note of what had become a common practice in the early nineteenth century of farming out, contracting out or in effect "selling" the poor to those who would bid for their labor (Senate of the State of New York, Journal of the 47th Session, 1824, pp. 1–154).

Within a decade these restrictive approaches were followed by a widespread reaction against the conditions which developed in the almshouses or the public infirmaries. By 1833 a Commission appointed by the Massachusetts Legislature found that:

> It has become at once a general infirmary and an asylum for the insane and a refuge for the deserted and most destitute children of the city. So great is a proportion of the aged, infirm, of the sick, insane, hideous and helpless children in it that all of the effective labor of the females is required for the care of those who cannot take care of themselves. (Report of the Commissioners on the Pauper System of the Commonwealth of Massachusetts, 1835, pp. 39–45)

The attempt to convert the almshouse into a house of industry and work was frustrated by the fact that the people who were dependent and poor were those who were by reason of their physical and mental state incapable of working. Nevertheless, relief continued to be made as unpleasant as possible. Concern over the moral basis for poverty and the costs of relieving dependency competed with more generous reforming efforts.

Up to the middle of the nineteenth century there was no national responsibility for the poor. Local government responsibility was tempered by the beliefs that poverty and distress were examples of moral weakness and deficiency of character which demanded re-education; and the poor were to be taken care of in the most economical way possible.

The nineteenth century was full of other currents of thought which may have affected middle class life but did not much alter the welfare system. For example, Ralph Waldo Emerson urged that each individual should realize himself, to realize his potentials. This meant, in his view, a moral realization, a reaching for a dignity of high moral standards rather than the pursuit of pleasure or ease but it certainly encompassed the concepts of self-realization with the necessary economic means assured.

More generous attitudes were not absent. Many comfortable people involved themselves voluntarily with the poor and the nature of human relationships. The more liberally minded concerned themselves with the condition of the mentally ill and of the children. Others entered the fight between the almshouse and outdoor relief (local general relief in the twentieth century). Some argued that outdoor relief cost only half as much as care in an institution. Others argued for the economy of scale in an institution with its deterrent effect on willingness of the poor to turn to public aid. The arguments have some of the color of contemporary arguments about home care versus nursing home and mental hospital.

Illustrations are numerous. The American Society in 1824 reported:

> While the temporal necessities of the poor and the afflicted are affectionately enquired into and relieved the Christian enlightened from above to view the state of man as an immortal being is most concerned for his eternal blessedness. This is a grand object he is called to pursue with sevenfold ardour. (American Tract Society, 1824)

A number of voluntary visiting societies grew up in which lay visitors as part of their church obligations visited the poor bringing charity and Christian instruction. Reverend Joseph Tuckerman, who became the minister of the American Unitarian Association in 1826, treated the young, the people in almshouses, prisons, and hospitals as a kind of parish of which he was the minister. He approached the needs of children and of families as well.

From the beginning of my ministry, therefore, I have always had my poor's purse. I could not have carried out my ministry without it . . . . I could not have obtained the access which I have obtained to their hearts.

Its design is to awaken and give excitement to a sense of human relations . . . . it proposes to make the great classes of the rich and the poor, the strong and the feeble, of the wise and the unwise, of the virtuous and vicious known to each other. (Tuckerman, 1838, pp. 85–88; DeGrando, 1833, p. 4)

Some of the intellectual motivation was stimulated by the importation of thinking of devout Catholics in France after its revolution. Antoine Frederic Ozanam became the president of the Society of St. Vincent de Paul, and wrote in 1834:

Go help the poor each in your special line yet let your studies be of use to others as well as to yourself . . . help humiliates when there is no reciprocity, when you give the poor man nothing but bread or clothing when in fact there is no likelihood of his ever giving you in return . . . but it honors when it appeals to him from above, when it occupies his self with his soul, his religious, moral and political education, and with all that emancipates him from his passions . . . when it treats a poor man with respect . . . . since he is a messenger of God to us for him to prove our justice and our charity and to save us by our works. (O'Meara, 1876, p. 103)

In retrospect, it is interesting to wonder about this blending of an ancient appeal to reciprocity between giver and receiver with a belief in the inevitableness of the poor who exist in order to give the more privileged an opportunity to show their piety by being charitable. The concept of reciprocity might be seen as a decayed version of that appeal to reciprocity which characterized Roman and Greek thinking about philanthropy. Reciprocity becomes abstract; the giver is repaid by the beneficiary's acceptance of the moral standards and beliefs of the giver.

The Mentally Ill and Other Special Categories of Dependents

Treatment of the mentally ill and of the criminal received special attention as these behaviors were more and more perceived due to causes other than God's providence or an immoral life. New scientific theories challenged older opinions and methods of treatment. European theories about human ways to treat the mentally ill and the criminal initiated by Pinel in France, Tuke in England, and Beccaria in Italy, were picked up in the U.S. The mentally ill and the criminal were both threatening to others, and also unfit for customary adult working responsibilities. How should they be treated. The punishments of the past were barbaric in the new enlightenment which science promised, but the costs of trying out new methods were high.

Concerned citizens such as Samuel Gridley Howe (a distinguished educator) and Dorothea Dix (a philanthropist) became aroused as early as 1840 by the insufferable conditions of mentally ill persons in the almshouses. They led citizen movements directed at state governments—not voluntary helping. They began a nationwide campaign based primarily upon new science and human compassion for the helpless. Dorothea Dix wrote:

> I come as the advocate of helpless, forgotten, insane and idiotic men and women; of beings sunk to a condition in which the most unconcerned would start with real horror; of beings wretched in our prisons and more wretched in our almshouses . . . . of insane persons confined within this Commonwealth in cages, closets, cellars, stalls, pens, chained naked, beaten with rods and lashed into obedience. (Dix, 1843)

While character building plus relief for the poor occupied the attention of many voluntary associations, efforts of those who concentrated on special problems such as mental illness were more often directed at government. In time this led to the spurt in state level responsibility for special categories of distress, e.g., for the insane, the retarded. A foundation of support was built for modern scientifically staffed institutions which were built later and operated by state agencies, increasing the scale and scope of government.

Throughout much of the nineteenth century, the types of persons entitled to local public aid did not change much although their numbers increased steadily: dependent children, blind adults, the feeble-minded, deaf and blind children, deserted or abandoned children, orphans, insane persons, bastard children, other minors, cases of desertion and abandonment, etc. But these customary Poor Law activities were perturbed by crises such as great epidemics which killed many wage earners and left widows and orphans; by the depressions of 1837–43, 1854–55, 1857–58; and by the Civil War. Such crises were dealt with by local mechanisms which combined Poor Law administration and voluntary agencies. Appropriations by local governments had to be increased periodically, for a short period of time. The threat of violence was real as the unemployed poor gathered in large numbers demanding some relief. Local governments also responded, by increasing the volume of public works to provide employment in buildings, streets, sewers, reservoirs, etc. (Breckenridge, 1939; Schneider, 1938). Periodic economic crisis accounts for the periodic surge in dependency and public appropriations. After each ebb in the crisis the remaining poverty grew incrementally so that absolute numbers of dependents had increased at a steady rate of between 1 and 2 percent annually.

The Progressive Era: New Ideas Within Old Constraints

After the Civil War industrialization and urbanization accelerated the pressures for more satisfactory and efficient arrangements. States expanded the scope of their welfare with programs for the mentally ill and retarded. It was not until the early twentieth century that a few states enacted Workmen's Compensation Laws to cope with the severe industrial injury. A few states adopted statewide mothers' aid programs, and later still a few states adopted old age pension programs. Most of these late developments resulted from the stimulation which the Progressive Party injected into political life during the Progressive Era (just before World War I) and from the growth in trade union organization and industrial unrest.

These late efforts were limited to a few industrialized states. They included a major shift in the rationale for public programs at a state level. Certain classes of need were acknowledged which did not arise from moral defect, lack of effort, to to divine providence. The neighborly acceptance of the poor in colonial times was slowly replaced by impersonal legislation more suited to an urban and industrial and mobile society.

The growing scope of state, and later, national government responsibility for welfare took place within the limited boundaries for action which the nation's previous history approved. However, the legislative agenda of the Progressive Movement, which penetrated both the Republican and Democratic parties, called for legal mechanisms which promised greater dignity to the poor. Their benefits would be sanctioned by laws which specified the details of entitlement rather than by the judgment of neighbors as under the old Poor Laws. Also the financial bases were deepened by access first to state government tax power and, much later that of national government.

These improvements did not change other limiting conditions to development of a welfare state. The old categories to be relieved remained the same: widows, orphans (and other neglected children), the disabled and the aged. The distressed had to find their way into the specialized welfare programs, where rules and regulations made it increasingly difficult for administrators to be flexible. Also, most benefits were work conditioned in some way. The able-bodied without work, and the disabled without a work history were treated no better now than before, except in times of economic crisis.

The machinery for welfare was much improved but the theoretical framework was not much changed. The tangible results of agitation and pressure in the twentieth century were due to compromises which conflicting interests made inevitable. A few of these interests are worth recalling. Caution and skepticism about distant national government power, reluctance to pay taxes for activities which did not benefit taxpayers directly, and concern over government expenditures were all at work.

At the same time a loose grouping of different interests was arrayed on the side of increased government responsibility. There were muckraking exposers of the terrible conditions in which the new immigrants and the poor lived in the big cities, trade unionists, political activists, academics of the then new social sciences (sociology and economics and psychology), liberal church members, women's, men's rights and temperance groups, social gospel believers, and many more. Some, like the legislatively appointed Tenement House Committee of New York in 1894, were convinced that government had to intervene powerfully. Only government regulation could improve housing for the poor and this, by itself, would reduce and ultimately eliminate high mortality rates, immorality and concentration of deviant and slothful behavior (Lubov, 1962).

Religion also continued as a force shaping public opinion. The social gospel wing of Protestantism urged the view that Jesus taught a social and not an individual ethic. It became part of what McLoughlin called the third great awakening (McLoughlin, 1978). In his view of American history there have been three periods which he calls "awakenings." They are characterized by:

1. the emergence of a deep and not well-focused popular anxiety and concern about changing conditions
2. a great awakening to these developments
3. an initial reversion to older accustomed ways of thinking, which in the American context were primarily religious
4. finding the old ways unsuitable to the new conditions, the creation of a wave of reform more suited to the new circumstances.

Such awakenings are identified in the period 1730 to 1760, 1800–1830, and the third from 1890–1920.

In the third awakening one wing of Protestantism joined forces with a variety of disparate groups, including Socialists, to bring religion and science together to improve the conditions of masses of individuals. Moral behavior remained its guide, but collective responsibility to create healthy conditions for men to grow in replaced belief in a fixed pattern to God's will, in the market, in voluntary or personal charity. Revivalist preachers drew large crowds and moved them by their passionate preaching to be saved either by deeds or by faith in a Protestant belief. At first the deeds which people were exhorted to respect were moral ones, e.g., abstinence from drinking and sex—but they also included obligations to help the needy. The sects were in the forefront of opposition to slavery.

After the Civil War, the social gospel movement altered its scope and direction. As the gap between the rich and the poor grew and as urbanization spread, these groups actively opposed the consequences of the new industrialism. By the 1880s and 1890s revivalism and municipal reform frequently went together, although both were accompanied by a strong desire to impose certain kinds of socially and church approved norms upon everyone. In 1880, B. Saye Mills argued that socialism and Christianity were not incompatible, that socialism was only an expression of human brotherhood and cooperation, and that quite possibly this cooperation could be secured through laws and government. In 1898, Samuel O. T. Jones ran for mayor of Toledo and publicly favored public ownership of the utilities, withholding of city franchises from private interests, and a minimum wage on the basis of Christianity not socialism.

People motivated by religious conviction divided over means and ends in the twentieth century. The Social Gospel movement moved out of the churches and became more and more secular while the churches reverted more and more to their original concentration upon moral behavior, defined as sexual and familial probity, hard work and abstinence from drink. The Social Gospel adherents hived off their activities into mission work in the slums. One of their leaders, Josiah Strong, provided leadership in creating both the Federal Council of Churches and the American Institute of Sociology. His aim was to recreate the social ideals of Christ on earth as in heaven and emphasized the laws of service or the laws of sacrifice. His aim was to save men—not souls—and he was opposed by those in the country who sought to keep the Negro in his place and the poor in their tenements.

The traditionalist wing of church organization continued to believe that the English-speaking people were the chosen carriers of Christianity and all its virtues, slightly moderated by a vague belief in social service as an ethical responsibility. The differentiation could not be made more sharply between views of the Social Gospel and those of Warren Kandler, who saw his church competing with all the rest in an attempt to secure universal dominion, in which all other church forms would be eliminated and "the earth becomes more uniform in religion and in moral government" (McLoughlin, 1959). He saw America as having an Anglo-Saxon destiny in which the church served to assure the survival of the fittest. In contrast, Strong viewed a church which introduced a moral check on social Darwinism through its efforts to preserve and elevate the poor, a church having an obligation to "save men" and not their souls.

One of the intellectuals of this movement, Lester Ward, a professor of sociology at Brown University, argued against the view that evolution worked best by laissez-faire. He pointed out that man controls his environment as well as simply adapting to it, that even Darwin found the existence of a social instinct in biological determinism which was more important than individualism and that some kind of cooperative effort or "fraternalism" is the basis of the political order and progress, not competition.

The joined religious and intellectual forces concluded that man was able to influence his own evolution and in the course of doing so evolve social institutions which rely on common activity. Planning and cooperation for the future became thinkable for individuals and organizing groups: socially controlled activity became more respectable again.

This evolution was reinforced by reports of the contradictions embedded in the new industrialism with its growth of wealth and the accompanying growth in the numbers of the poor. A laborers' organization emerged to challenge the inequitable distribution in the new industrial state. However, there was no strong political foundation for such organization nor any tradition of a strong active national authority. Attention to human needs had to be legitimized within the framework of a more individually oriented society. Forces such as those just mentioned began to coalesce in the Presidential campaign of 1912 when not only tiny socialist groupings but a major political party, the Progressive Party of Theodore Roosevelt, called for state and national intervention in such areas as workmen's compensation, protection of life against the hazards of sickness, irregular employment and old age through a system of social insurance (Porter and Johnson, 1956). Theodore Roosevelt in 1901 argued that "it is impossible to have a high standard of political life in a community sunk in sadden misery and ignorance" (Croly, 1965). And the platform of the Progressive Movement for 1912 called for "the conservation of human resources through an enlightened measure of social and industrial justice" (Porter and Johnson, 1956, pp. 189–190).

The numerous critical voices of moral and human outrage against the insufferable conditions under which large numbers of the poor and helpless lived, did not yet represent a sufficient consensus to achieve a real change in national responsibility (Bremner, 1956).

Such views were not yet acceptable to the electorate and Woodrow Wilson won the Presidency on a platform which attacked social programs of the national government or of any government which claimed to look after the interests of individuals. He argued for justice and opportunity over benevolence. What *was* acceptable was any program which could be justified as maintaining the conditions compatible with individual self-help. Any attempt to adapt to the requirements of an industrial society which depended upon cooperation or national government effort could still rally support only in the most limited areas and in times of crisis.

1935–1970

The period 1935–1970 was such an era-of crisis, depression and World War, followed by the national euphoria of victory, economic boom and world power. It is in this period that the national welfare activity reached its peak, as summarized in Chapter 1. The support for an ever growing national welfare state began to recede during the 1970s. This ebbing of support may be temporary, or it may reflect a return to the conservatism and limits which the temper of American life has kept around its social welfare activities. If the latter is the explanation, then the next decades will need a reformulation of objectives for government intervention. Rather than attempting to sum up the national mood, the next chapter considers two specific dimensions of late twentieth century thinking in America. It will review public and political opinion which shaped the social programs between 1935 and 1975 as reflected in repeated opinion polls taken of samples of the American population and review the legislative history of selected social programs enacted since 1950.

PART

III

THE WELFARE STATE RECONSIDERED

CONTEMPORARY RATIONALES FOR CURRENT WELFARE PROGRAMS
Some Empirical Evidence

As we approach the contradictions about public welfare policy which characterize the late twentieth century debates, it is worth turning to various social sciences to see whether their work throws light on the questions raised thus far. A few examples are used to indicate how sociology, political science and psychology approach the subject, but it is necessary to caution that with the exception of survey research, the social sciences seldom deal directly with the questions we have been exploring. We begin with the reality that the array of publicly funded social programs established by the 1970s did not grow as a result of any conscious, systematized, well-thought-out philosophy about welfare state responsibility. Instead the growth consisted of an accumulation of ad hoc programs designed to deal with narrowly defined and specific problems in a pragmatic way. However, when looked at in the aggregate, and after the fact, certain attitudes begin to emerge which may explain or justify government action acceptable in American society. These are the effective dynamics which control the evolution of social programs. The source of information used in this chapter to identify these attitudes are: statistically based opinion polls about citizen attitudes toward welfare questions, the legislative history of some key social programs, and a few social science analyses other than opinion polling.

The Opinion Polls: Pro-Programs; Anti-Welfare[1]

Opinion polls have been conducted periodically on a national and regional basis since 1935. Public attitudes about welfare and who is entitled to it are remarkably consistent over time on a few items. Certain inferences can be drawn about the rationales which will be supported by an electorate.

Schiltz found a measurable rise in public support between 1935–1965 about extending Social Security coverage. The proportion of respondents who believed that more people should receive Social Security coverage rose from 66 percent to 76 percent between 1938–1945. Domestic and manual workers were most supportive and farmers and white collar workers least supportive. Those with more education were slightly more supportive of increased Social Security coverage, but as the respondents increased in age there was a slight decline in support. Understanding about Social Security was limited, but a very large majority of respondents continuously supported the principle of employee contributions (Schiltz, 1970).

Over the decades, a high level of support also persisted for Old Age Assistance. Beginning in the period between 1935 and 1941, 75–85 percent of all persons polled favored "pensions to the needy," not distinguishing between medical or income security. This weight of opinion persisted until the 1980s. It is possible that this strong support for programs for the elderly as "pensions for the needy" evolved into the later treatment of all elderly as a class needing help as in Medicare insurance regardless of the real distribution of need.

Between 1939 and 1946 the percentage of respondents who approved Social Security and Public Welfare, even if it meant a rise in public taxes, increased from 52 percent to 66 percent. While the older and the richer in the respondent sample were relatively less supportive, fewer of the wealthy respondents would withdraw their support if a tax increase were required (14 percent) compared with the percentage of poor who would withdraw their support if a tax increase were required (23 percent). Such support continued to be conditioned on narrow concepts of "the needy" which excluded the able-bodied worker. The belief prevailed that most persons on relief could get a job if they really tried. This was a time when memory was fresh about insecurity in depression and war. But between 1964 and 1965 when depression memory faded and the economy boomed,

---

[1] Information in this section is summarized from Schiltz, *Public Attitude to Social Security,* 1935–1965; Natalie Jaffe, *Attitudes Toward Public Welfare Programs and Recipients in the United States,* A Review of Public Opinion Surveys 1935–1976; The Institute of Public Sciences and Public Affairs, Duke University, Spring 1977; and Fay Lomax Cook, *Who Should Be Helped?,* Sage Library of Social Research, Beverly Hills, CA, 1979.

the percentage of respondents who thought that individual poverty was due to lack of personal effort increased from 33 percent to 40 percent.

Unemployment insurance has had less support than social protection for the elderly; in the post-World War II era many respondents preferred programs which promised work rather than assistance. Fewer people considered that being unemployed constituted "need," whereas during the 1930s the observable facts were seen to explain "need" for unemployment protection. The reduced support for unemployment insurance was possibly a continuation of an age-old doubt about the desirability of supporting the able-bodied.

Employment, whether by government or in the private market, remained a basic criterion underlying support of public programs. In 1961 and 1964 polls 84 percent of respondents agreed that all men on relief who were physically able to work must take any job offered which paid the going wage. Complementing this approach was the opinion of 85 percent of respondents who approved a Supplementary Income Program for those working poor who do not earn enough to meet their basic needs despite full-time work (Jaffe, 1977).

Another analysis of public opinion surveys found that American respondents generally identify "poor Americans" as fellow citizens who were disabled by age or physical infirmity, the hard working but low paid heads of families and the unemployed who are diligently looking for work and willing to take any job (Jaffe, 1977). Persons identified as "welfare recipients," were generally viewed as unworthy although this view was modified when polls described the specific characteristics of the welfare population. Illustrative of this divided view is a Harris Survey of January 1973 which found that two-thirds of respondents favored an increase in spending to help the poor, but an equal number was opposed to increasing spending for people "on welfare."

Most support favors public programs which help dependent populations become productive and economically independent; there is less support for those whose condition is not remediable or whose behavior is antisocial. A University of Southern California 8-state study in 1972–73 found that 93 percent of respondents favored tax supported but controlled programs even after a long period of economic affluence (Jaffe, 1977). Fifty-four percent supported help at "a decent level of living" provided there was a clear demonstration of need and compliance with stringent eligibility requirements. Respondents were almost equally divided between those who opted for higher benefits and those for reduction of benefits to a bare minimum. Of those who supported more generous approaches to public welfare almost 85 percent favored mandatory training for recipients. Sixty-seven percent of respondents in one state believed that there were plenty of jobs and over 50 percent of all respondents believed there were jobs for all who wanted to work. When specific proposals for welfare reform were presented four out of five respondents agreed that any cash relief program should require that a recipient take any job or enter training. This is not much of a shift in attitude from 1937 when a Gallup Poll found that nearly 80 percent of respondents disapproved of cash relief as a substitute for public works; and in 1938, 90 percent favored work relief over cash assistance.

Older, moral views about who is "entitled to assistance" are also found in a series of surveys which reported a widespread belief that single women without a husband at home who have children and those who have illegitimate children should *not* be helped; only 10 percent of respondents believed that they should receive help or if they are given help they should not be forced to work as a condition for receipt (Jaffe, 1977). Some punitive suggestions were offered by respondents, including compulsory sterilization and institutionalization. The punitive view is further reinforced by the four out of five respondents who would spend what is necessary to help welfare children become productive but disapproved of providing help for their unproductive parents.

Some of these views apparently persist regardless of race. A study of both black and white women in Baltimore in 1971 (Kallen & Miller, 1974) found that both black and white women generally agreed with each other, but three-fourths of black women thought that too many welfare recipients waste their money on liquor while less than half of white women believed this. There is a deep-seated belief that whatever assistance is advanced should be accompanied by some effort to change the character of the recipient. This was supported in the U.S.C. survey in which three-fourths of the respondents preferred that increased welfare programs be in the nature of direct client services rather than cash income transfer, even if such increase in services meant a reduction in cash income grants.

A 1976 Chicago study attempted to identify the bases for support of social programs by interviewing a random sample of black and white informants of all age groups and asking the respondents to allocate a hypothetical sum of money among various categories of possible recipients (Cook, 1979). Respondents revealed a clear hierarchy in their thinking about which classes of persons are entitled to more or less help. The disabled were considered more "worthy" of help than the generic "poor," and among the disabled and the poor the elderly were considered more "worthy." Adults under 65 are preferred over children if the adults are disabled, and children are preferred over adults if the adults are only poor but able-bodied. There was substantial sophistication in these respondents' willingness to discriminate not only among beneficiary groups but between the kinds of programs most suited to their needs. Respondents gave a higher priority to nutritional help for the elderly, to transportation for the disabled, and to education programs for able-bodied adults under 65. Being able-bodied and poor was the characteristic least likely to attract substantial sympathy and support.

Some longitudinal analyses of opinion polling come to more optimistic views about public attitudes. Auclair (1984, pp. 139–144) found that the percent of respondents to one series between 1972 and 1982 who thought that too much was spent on social welfare declined from 60 percent to 48 percent. The greatest decline in opposition (58 to 48 percent) occurred in the steep recession years 1980–1982. Opposition dropped most among the very young and the very old, among those with the least education, among minorities, and among those with lower incomes. Opposition remained stronger among workers age 46 to 64, among whites, among the better educated, and among those with incomes above $20,000.

In a more generous mood a 1979 national survey of American freshmen (Astin, 1980) found that entering freshmen listed their priorities for approaching life; first, stability of work for themselves; second, raising a family; and third the aim to "help others in difficulty"—64 percent of respondents. Is it possible that this taps a reservoir of youthful generosity, or is it an artifact of the student status? Anecdotes, and daily observation indicate a widespread generosity in personal relationships, although in recent years this has been expressed in support for many single issue causes: abortion, migrant workers, women's health, child abuse, etc. Although it has encouraged the turn to federal help for all causes, this has not coalesced into a more general approach to welfare policy.

A 1980 survey of 1,202 Americans (Harris, 1980) highlighted the contradictions which persist in all opinion polls over time. While 84 percent of the respondents generally favored cuts in federal spending, 74 percent were opposed to cuts in Social Security, 63 percent were opposed to federal cuts in education and 61 percent were opposed to cuts in health spending. At the same time, 69 percent wanted cuts in "welfare"—ill-defined as a general category.

These polls also indicate how much opinion polls are influenced by the climate for opinion which is created through the media, public debate and election campaigning. It is not clear how reliable these polls can be for long-range planning because the criteria used in them change with changing conditions, e.g., a deep depression, a war or period of affluence. Also a change in public sensibility may be introduced by a widespread media campaign publicizing either scandals or neglect in welfare. But underlying these secular changes in attitude to program there may also be a basic clash in attitude which divides respondents. Some seem to consider human existence to be harsh, unpredictable and unalterable—where individuals are innocent victims; others believe that conditions are not harsh but are changed by individual or collective effort. These views are supplemented by a further set of contrasts. Do individuals believe that human beings are fundamentally kind, caring, altruistic in their relations to others or do they believe that individuals are essentially individualistic, grasping, thoughtless of others unless forced by external circumstances to be kind.

Aside from these basic views about life, there are also politically formed lenses or filters through which the world is perceived. Marxist analysts generally use a lens in which class structure and the exploitation of classes and each other constitutes a major dynamic for analyzing what exists or what does not. A classic marketplace lens would emphasize permeability between classes—the opportunity to move from class to class and the individual character and capability which determine one's distribution in society. There are also differing social attitude filters: some can tolerate collective efforts of a nongovernmental character and believe these efforts are sufficient to meet most human needs; others can only accept collective efforts requiring the force of government.

Whatever the reasons, opinion polls are consistent over time in reporting Americans' readiness to help the clearly helpless (although not why they want to), and suspicion that the able-bodied are less worthy and need to be treated in some controlling fashion. Attitudes shift slightly in reaction to major economic changes. Consistently voters are in some doubt, supporting specific programs for clearly dependent people but antagonistic to general appeals to welfare.

Social Science: A Mixed Record about Generosity

A few social scientists have studied concepts of altruism and caring between humans. A few examples of these inquiries may indicate whether such science can help resolve some of the dilemmas inherent in popular attitudes as revealed by opinion polls.

Angell, a nonquantitative sociologist, examined values in American urban areas. He distinguishes between values which an individual holds for himself but which happen to be similar to those held by others and *common* values which are shared for and by the group—that is, by society as a collectivity. Moral values held in common are "acceptance of the rightness of human relations of a particular kind in pursuit of any goal." This seems close to the Greek Stoic view about behavior which is right and just, different from pity, compassion, or compulsion. Angell believed the common American values held in 1950 were: the dignity of persons before the law, civil and religious liberty, the control by people over their *common* life, opportunities for all without favoritism, and humanitarian friendliness. These values, he argues, were necessary if society as a collection of individuals and a collectivity is to function satisfactorily. Any society is subject to a variety of contradictory pressures and recurring crises through which a common core of values needs to prevail in order to keep that society coherent rather than disintegrating. Approaches which are limited solely to solving problems ad hoc will polarize society and divide its members from each other unless certain common values are held by all or most citizens (Angell, 1958).

Similar views are shared by anthropologists who, in their studies of primitive societies, have found that food gathered by hunters is shared by all members of the tribe as an unwritten "law." Even members of the group who are not otherwise productive (the elderly, the disabled and children) are entitled to their share. One interpretation is that these primitive societies intuitively recognize that the part of the population thus "helped" will return the favor through efforts in the future or are being repaid for past efforts. Another view suggests that this fundamental law of primitive society is a means of keeping the tribal group intact, avoiding its reduction and fragmentation.

Sociobiologists have recently speculated that there is a genetic base to human life which makes the survival of the species dependent upon altruistic and collaborative effort, especially in circumstances where the survival of individuals is threatened. This is inferred from a threat to the gene pool of any species which arises when many of its members are threatened. It is postulated that instinctual responses to such threats are triggered or activated to assure survival of an appropriate mix of personal survival, reproduction and group survival, thus suggesting an instinctive base for altruistic behavior (E. O. Wilson, 1975, chap. 5).

While this sociobiological view is highly controversial, many sociological views emphasize the recurrence and importance of cooperative behavior in primitive societies or in small closed groups insulated in the modern world. Pitrim Sorokin conducted a series of studies about altruism and the technical means by which belief in altruism was inculcated. Some of his studies dealt with groups far removed from the center of highly industrialized and urbanized society. The Mennonites were studied as one religious minority continuing to function within the modern society but with a fundamentalist adherence to New and Old Testament tradition. This group views itself as an historically oppressed minority which developed a strong sense of in-group belonging together with mutual aid necessary to preserve its existence. Doing good was initially undertaken for "those of the household of faith," although occasionally this altruism spread to others in times of great crisis. The Mennonites expanded their altruism to other oppressed groups when the needs of the others resulted from famine, war and flood. The study, based on anecdotes, identified numerous individual examples of selflessness as when one member gave his life willingly not only to save a member of the sect but to save an enemy. One such reported case occurred in 1569 in the Netherlands when a policeman, chasing an escaped convict, fell into the ice; the convict turns back to save the policeman but is then captured and later executed. The study concludes that the Mennonite Central Committee limited its help to others and primarily helps in whatever effort furthers Mennonite ideals and adds its work as a witness of Christian love (Krohn, 1954). Other reports about communal communities in South America found that tribal education was based upon responsibility of individuals to the whole group, emphasizing the rule of spirit and of altruism (Eberhard, 1954). This type of communal selflessness is similar to the tribal sharing which can take place in small intimate face-to-face groups even where there is no blood association.

Sorokin also studied various Oriental beliefs and practices, e.g., Zen and yoga, in which individuals seek to find a oneness with some universal by draining oneself into another worldly state of mind. He concluded that this process of introspection is an attempt to find an identification outside oneself, which ultimately leads to humanitarian human behavior toward others. This effort is comparable to treatment of the mentally ill which uses friendly relationships in a friendly atmosphere, to produce a friendly response.

In contrast to these selective views about more simple cultures, studies in advanced societies produce less clear-cut evidence. Some studies of cooperatives, not based upon blood or tribal relationships, indicate that members may be concerned with their personal membership benefits which does not in turn lead to a wider cooperative view of the public interest. One such study found that cooperative workers in the plywood industry in the American Northwest were highly committed to competitive, individualistic values, more so than workers in conventional employer-employee firms. The members of the cooperative joined for pecuniary reasons or job security and were involved in other community activities only when self-interest was involved. The conclusion of this line of inquiry suggests that collective decision making and participation does not necessarily lead to a wider appreciation of public interest (Greenberg, 1981).

Psychologists have studied the subject of social and psychological exchange and exchange theory, a modern-day expression of the early Greek and Roman views about reciprocity. One study of this subject examines concepts of equity and fairness (Gergen, 1980). It reports on Eskimo village life and its "myth of reciprocity" and concluded that, while reciprocity did occur and was an accepted convention of the society, it was also often violated. For any given act of generosity a long time may elapse before the opportunity for a reciprocal response occurs. In order that the belief in equitable relationships be sustained, some kind of record keeping of this time lag in reciprocity is necessary, but this is very difficult for it requires more abstract mechanical and organizational structure than the conventional beliefs about immediate spontaneous human interaction.

A journalistic review of psychological attempts to understand "why some people turn away from others in trouble" brings together a variety of interesting, contradictory psychological attributions. One group found that people experiencing joy for themselves because something nice has happened to them are more likely than others to help someone else. But as something wonderful happens to a friend there is no such self-joy effect. In fact the good fortune of a friend seems to lower the altruism level (Rosenhau, Solvay & Hargis, 1981, pp. 899–905). The authors of another survey of student volunteers conclude that if a population feels that it is being constantly ground down by the social pressures and economic pressures of its time, then it is unreasonable to expect that population to be kind to others. In periods of great stress this would suggest a decline in altruism. The complex regulations of the modern state lead to a sense of being hemmed in and exploited by impersonal outer forces and may add up to this kind of stress as much as economic want. This view is offset by numerous counterobservations of generous helping in the Great Depression, and in behavior of some people during physical disasters of flood and fire.

A self-regarding view is supported by investigators who have used tests of student volunteers. They suggest that self-gratification and altruism are interchangeable and conclude that there is no innate urge to help others without regard for our own welfare (Kenrick, Baumann and Cialdini, May 1979, pp. 747–755). Such a self-regarding view is in its turn offset by sociological and biological studies which conclude that altruism is useful to the survival of oneself, one's species, and one's inner-group. A study of 300 children found that they, as early as 12 months of age, exhibit some helping behavior, such as patting or giving some other sympathetic gesture to another who is in distress (Radke-Yarrow and Wexler, 1977). This study also concludes that short-term altruism may be motivated by guilt but that long-term altruism is primarily influenced by parental models in which parents have exhibited qualities of perseverance and courage. The decline of positive parental role models in society has led some psychologists to conclude that the disappearance of this quality in our society explains the Genovese case in which a 28-year-old woman was attacked and killed while 38 residents of surrounding apartments looked on and took no action (Rosenhau, Solvay & Hargis, 1981, pp. 899–905).

From these few examples it appears that social sciences, new as they are in modern life, throw some fresh light on altruistic behavior, but fail to resolve any of the policy questions. Some, as Angell, provide general concepts about people living in collective society, but their insights are very general and reflect a preformed abstract conception about human interactions. Others base most of their work on more primitive or organizationally less complex conditions than we find in a continental urban and industrial world. Nevertheless, such work does indicate that a coherent complex world in which humankind can live and survive probably requires the widest acceptance of a few governing principles about the obligation of members for each other. As supporters of welfare programs in the U.S. may note—the complex America of today has not shaped or widely enough accepted such principles as regards welfare.

The social sciences also clarify the extent to which altruistic behavior cannot be taken for granted, that selfish motivation coexists with the generous. Although we make pragmatic ad hoc adjustments as we go along, striking a balance between selfishness and generosity still escapes us in any comprehensive sense. And finally social scientists indicate that in less complex societies, cooperative and sharing behavior is consciously taught to youth as a foundation for adult behavior and has continuous reinforcement through social institutions, in the case of primitive societies, through religious or tribal ceremonies.

Changing Social Perceptions: As Much Selfishness as Generosity? Or More?

Opinion polls and most social science research tends to be backward looking. Can changes in public attitude and sentiment be captured by available tools of social science? By 1980 it became conventional wisdom that a change had occurred in the opinions of the American electorate about their government and about the responsibility of government for the disadvantaged. Aside from the 1980 elections, there are other clues that attitudes have changed as the burden of social programs has risen and become more visible to wider segments of the population. Some analysts have found that, in a period of economic decline, voters who have experienced a worsening in their conditions do not necessarily become more tolerant but rather become less tolerant. Rather than only the wealthy being unhappy with the burden of taxation those who are directly affected may also adopt a tougher and a more authoritarian view about a variety of social issues (Alt, 1979).

Some political analysts during the 1970s reexamined nineteenth century liberal economic doctrines as a way of reevaluating what was happening to the American society after the rapid and vast growth in federal responsibility. One approach considered whether the foundations of the nation were better served by a continuous system of interacting and contending rival interests rather than trying to impose uniform national solutions based on assumed good motives. Madison argued that a multiplicity of factions would make the American Republic unique and more humane (in Will, 1979). But a recent reanalysis argues that the U.S. is the only country whose founders did not require public spiritedness even of those in public office, and public spiritedness is not even presupposed (Will, 1979). In this view citizens are encouraged to do what they desire most on the assumption that loose institutional arrangements will manipulate the most powerful human impulses toward social good although none aims for the public good. People who are taught that they need not govern their own actions by any personal calculation about what was in the public good will in time come to blame all social and economic difficulties on the government as the agency of collective consideration and thus absolve themselves of personal responsibility (Will, 1979).

Supportive of this view is an opinion poll conducted by the University of Massachusetts in 1981. Seventy-five percent of respondents who thought there was room for more budget cuts believed that *essential* services had already been reduced; and 57 percent of those who agreed that essential services to the needy had already been reduced would still opt for a further reduction in welfare assistance if as a result, more state aid to local towns for uses of everyone (that is for roads, police and fire protection) were to be the result (O'Malley, 1981).

Another study tending to the same conclusion reanalyzed 1959 and 1970 multination survey data. In 1959, 28 percent of a British sample in a five-nation survey thought that most people were altruistic and would help others while only 15 percent of the Mexicans believed this. But in 1979, 20 years later, only 16 percent of the British thought that people would look out for others. The elderly tended to view the British as being most altruistic perhaps because they both give and receive more help, but the young adults, 25–44, tended to view their culture as grasping and individually oriented, perhaps because they are concerned with their own jobs and their own careers (Almond and Verba, 1979, p. 480).

Accompanying this pessimistic view about altruism is a view about government. In 1959, 89 percent of the British expected to have even-handed treatment from official agencies while only 32 percent of the Mexicans believed that. West Germany and Italian populations were somewhere between these two extremes. This confidence in even-handed treatment remains stable 20 years later. On the other hand, nearly one-third of the respondents believed that hostility between classes had increased in the 1970s and three out of five respondents thought that restrictions and government bureaucracy had grown. Seventy-five percent thought that the willingness to work hard had declined during the 1970s and that a desire to have leisure time to do what one wanted had grown during the same period. The proportion of persons who think there is more opportunity for individual freedom had also increased to 46 percent. However, the most educated class in the respondent group had the least satisfaction with their achievements (Almond and Verba, 1979).

Another changing condition is the shifting relationship between resources, population and environment. The exponential growth in the size of the Earth's population has in the view of environmental analysts led to such crowding and overuse of physical space that access to resources is more difficult. This argument is used to explain a believed reversion to more selfish behavior. But this view is contested by those who suggest that human ingenuity and technology have led to a great increase in the exploitation of resources, at least in the short term.

Another approach suggests that values may have been modified over time by changes in the size and nature of the American society, especially the identification of minorities with poverty and welfare (Miller, 1977). Within this framework of analysis, Miller suggests that giving and altruism found their roots in both religious sources and a secular democratic view about helping fellow creatures, who were "like ourselves." This level of giving was often personal: the generous giver helping the less fortunate. However, this generosity was frequently "perverted" in the sense that the act focused upon the goodness of the giver and the need of the recipient, but as the problems of poverty outran the generosity of individuals with the growth of an urban industrialized nation and an uneven economy there has been less gratification in helping others. Despite this development, most citizens accepted that difficulties the nation was confronting were primarily social and that the response should be social and increasingly national (Miller, 1977).

The bias of race has been a potent, if changing, element in American behavior. The early American foundations for generosity, whether through individual or voluntary giving or collective action, have probably been distorted by the minority status of the poor. The poor not only lack resources but they also lack the fundamental support of membership in a broader community of fellow feeling. Edwin Witte writing on the development of the 1935 Social Security Act wrote:

> At least some Southern Senators fear that this measure (the Social Security Act) might serve as an entering wedge for federal interference in the handling of the Negro question in the South. The Southern members did not want to give authority to anyone in Washington to deny aid to any state because it discriminated against Negroes in the administration of Old Age Assistance. (Witte, 1962)

This prejudice confronted any person concerned with the framing of the original Social Security Act and continues in less open form today.

The American culture has always discriminated, not always consciously, about how its public generosity will be allocated to certain classes. For example, one kind of reciprocity has been implicit in the special preference always given to those who served in wartime, since military services in wartime constituted an advanced premium payment by the veteran in return for which an emergency account was created upon which he had a right to draw forever in case of need (Steiner, 1971). By contrast the Aid to Families and Dependent Children (AFDC) population and other poor populations have never been perceived as having made a prior "payment of premiums." When the poor AFDC population became weighted by black clients, it generated even less sympathy than during its early 1935–40 days when its clientele was viewed as made up of poor white widows. There is no convincing myth in the American society which engenders sympathy for a minority population. Moral relations in the American society rest more securely on claims of right than of generosity or charity. In the long view of history one would think that the aged, the disabled and mothers of dependent children might fit into a model similar to that of the veterans, but reliance upon work programs continues in part due to the fear that somebody is "getting away with something" (Steiner, 1971, pp. 239–240).

In the 1960s an attempt was made by some groups to overcome the special disadvantage which the welfare population labored under by asserting welfare to be a matter of right rather than benevolence. However, the definition of reciprocal rights and duties necessary for a doctrine based on rights had not been developed. There was no clear recognition of or evidence advanced for any duty performed in return for the right. The assertion of rights became not a moral argument which enlarged the sensibilities but an act of power, in its most literal sense. Groups disagreed about the responsibility of government to assure equality or to reallocate wealth. The welfare state becomes implicated because, while it does not clearly articulate the objective of absolute equality for all citizens, it is directed towards reducing the levels of disparity between the disadvantaged and the more affluent classes in society.

Despite the foregoing evidence, social science has documented the facts of race as a major confounding welfare issue. Far-reaching race-related policy changes took place between 1940 and 1974 through judicial and legislative action. Social movements released in the aftermath of World War II used legal documentation and political action to forge a set of rights without recourse to reciprocal obligation by mandating minority rights in voting, open access to facilities and equal treatment by bureaucracies.

If we look beyond the achievements with regard to race, the social science evidence suggests change of a less promising nature: mixed evidence about normal human behavior as being generous or selfish; a possible decline overall in generous and helping attitudes which people expect of each other. The bitterness of such an interpretation is moderated by the arguments that individual freedom has been greatly enlarged in recent decades and that there are generational differences in weighing the balance, with the young being happier with the freedom but also being

less committed to collective public generosity. There are also clues that
the changes in public attitude may be a complex function of age in relation to economic conditions: older people who lived through economic
hard times when public action was highly valued still value former attitudes. Another generation which did not experience the same conditions
has less accepting views about public action.

The Rationales of Specific Legislative Enactments

Although problems are encountered, another approach to the wellsprings
of American action is to study the reasons used by supporters of welfare
as they appear in the written record of specific legislative history. There
is the uncertainty whether the recorded reasons given by spokesmen in
the legislative process represent their real convictions or whether they
represent self-justifications before an electorate. The same can be said
about the spokesmen from various advocacy constituencies arguing for or
against particular legislation since lobbyists for welfare programs can be
accused of self-interest which biases what they say publicly about their
organizations. Nonetheless, it may be instructive to examine the legislative history of several recent social programs to see what light, if any, can
be thrown on what Americans believe in for welfare.

Initial justification for federal action in the middle 1930s was the depth
and scope of the Great Depression. Unemployment, hunger and disease
were so widespread that emergency action was clearly called for and
would be supported on any of the traditional grounds of charity, of compassion, or protection of society. But rationales which justify the institutionalization of a set of social programs as a permanent part of society,
cannot depend on emergency conditions. Most analysts of the 1935 Social
Security Act agree it was shaped in the older American tradition of the
work ethic and it was heavily influenced by a concern with work opportunities. The Old Age Retirement program was defended in committees
on the grounds that this would facilitate the removal of older workers
from the workforce and make more opportunity available for younger,
more vigorous persons. This argument was also coupled with an appeal
for compassion for our elders and for recognition of the return due them
for their past labors which had advanced the earlier development of the
American society. Some modest assurance of minimal income could be
seen as a payment for past services rendered. Unemployment insurance
was a recognition of the unevenness of employment opportunity which
required that a stable workforce be maintained during temporary periods
of unemployment. Aid to Families and Dependent Children was early
supported as a means of maintaining family integrity, carrying forward

the old belief that widows and children were generally helpless and justified help from others who were working. It may be a commentary on the blind spot in the American social conscience that in the 1930s there was little recognition that dependent women might not be widows or that the bulk of them might consist of minority women whose needs had hitherto been given so little specific attention.

While these issues were being argued and debated on their merits in the 1930s, legislation was also enacted or supported by legislators not only on the grounds of economic or moral principle but for more selfish reasons. Legislators may have ethical commitments of their own and to their constituencies but also they are conscious of what behavior is likely to attract support at election time. It does not require cynicism to accept that congressmen try to help as many people as possible because that's what the elective political act depends on. Other congressmen take a very real personal satisfaction in "making life a little more pleasant for millions of beneficiaries" (Derthick, 1979). Political advisers to all presidents and all elected officials make a strong effort to show what good has been done or what people have been taken care of. This is similar to the ancient Roman practice of providing goods for the residents or citizens of a town in order to be perceived as generous and to justify election.

Despite these evident political truths anyone concerned with the deeper roots for social programs will want to ask: is there not something more to helping others than crisis or election to office? A random selection of federal legislation was reviewed, in its legislative history, to see if the arguments advanced on behalf of these enactments have a pattern of rationales which can explain American choices about caring for others. The following acts were reviewed: Federal Housing 1937, Community Mental Health Centers 1963, Child Health 1967, Supplementary Security Income, Juvenile Justice and Delinquency Prevention 1974, Assistance for the Developmentally Disabled 1975, Title XX Social Services, Child Welfare 1980. For the most part this sample was not affected by depression or war crisis.[2]

This review suggests that much of the generous social legislation has been justified by arguments that action will save public expenditure in the future, will reduce dependency, will return recipients to work status and the labor force. There is evident a willingness to try many approaches to helping those in some personal trouble—provided these other ends can be also promised. Arguments about the extent or severity of human distress, about the vulnerability of some groups, about the possibility of preventing trouble arising in the future, about improving the

---

[2] A summary of this legislation and further detail about rationales advanced in the debates over adoption are found in the appendix.

life conditions of the disadvantaged are equally mixed with arguments about abolishing dependency and reducing public costs. Pleas for social and individual rights are mixed with stigma and rejection.

The arguments which justify federal action, rather than state or voluntary effort, are seldom explored in detail—it being assumed that past failure of the states to act, or unevenness in state and local provision or imbalance in resources among the states constitute an adequate justification for national and federal intervention.

Other persistent rationales are:

1. To raise the level of living for all citizens as in housing. Although increased well-being is assumed for all who work, the poorest are entitled to some share in the improvement if they are helped through housing to return to work. Housing equals health equals work which means less taxes for dependency.

2. Prevention of social problems. Prevention is seen as a good primarily because it leads to more work and less expense for dependency.

3. All persons, especially children, are entitled to an opportunity to realize their full potential. But federal action is urged if it can help them to be economically self-supporting, although the language formulation is more generous.

4. The security and future well-being of the nation require action. This is most often invoked behind child welfare legislation. It has a modern sound of seventeenth and eighteenth century mercantilist doctrine, where doing things for children is done not so much in their interest as in the interest of the state.

5. In some cases, more generous and compassionate rationales are advanced alongside material ends. Although legislation on behalf of the mentally ill and the juvenile delinquent often looks to future employability, the arguments also include compassionate concern about the condition of these groups in state mental hospitals. For the delinquent there has emerged recognition that the causes of delinquent behavior are not necessarily found in the individual but many also lie in the opportunities which society has denied them. By implication at least society must share with the individual in handling the consequences of neglect.

6. Compassionate argument for the aged and children is usually matched with work objectives, or it is premised on doctrines of reciprocity: the aged have 'paid their dues': the AFDC mother is entitled to preferential help if she will do community service work for others (e.g., care for children of working mothers); and children will repay their help in their adulthood.

7. The concept of individuals having enforceable rights to social aid is only sporadically suggested, most clearly in developmental disability legislation. The able-bodied poor have no "right" to above-poverty welfare, only a right to be treated as all others of this class in access to what is enacted. But the seriously disabled are given a *legal* right to certain educational and health services.

SUMMARY

Opinion polls, social science and legislative history all enrich and enlarge understanding about the alternating attractiveness of altruistic and selfish behavior in human relationships, at least as expressed in collective public actions. They do not help us resolve the dilemmas of contemporary welfare but they do confirm the existence of a solid substratum of emotion and convention upon which welfare policy for the future can rely. This substratum does not give much encouragement to hope that a great leap forward in publicly financed welfare will have broad public support now or in the near future. However, the nature of the task is made clearer for those who seek to improve the public expression of caring for others which contemporary society seems to require.

The solid foundation for support, on this evidence, consists of these elements:

1. A continuing commitment to see that the clearly helpless are given some protection: children, the very disabled, the aged.
2. A continued conviction that work, the willingness to work, or the hope for improved capacity to work in the future lies at the basis of willingness to help others who are dependent and able-bodied, or potentially able-bodied.
3. In face-to-face societies, selfishness and generosity can flourish, but these attitudes do not define a single basic quality in human relationships. One or the other may be inculcated in early education.
4. In more complex societies selfishness and generosity are in competition and generosity is likely to be calculated on the basis of some form of exchange or reciprocity, mediated through work or other value society.
5. A door has been opened, slightly, for a right to care and for raising the quality of life for all. This opening seems to be contingent on, or linked with, some benefit for the giver as well as for the beneficiary; benefit in the form of economic or other gain for society from which all will benefit, or in the form of behavior valued by doner and donee alike.

If these elements are confirmed, then a continuity can be seen between contemporary emotion and thought on the subject of caring for others and the thinking which characterized earlier societies in the Western world. What remains unresolved is whether the changed conditions of the modern world, when compared with the past, will in time require or produce a quite different form of caring for others or a change in public sentiment which will be either more or less generous and expansive than in the past.

PHILOSOPHICAL
APPROACHES TO
HELPING THE STRANGER

We have thus far considered some of the historic approaches to helping the stranger, the changes in social organization which have placed traditional views in jeopardy and some citizen and social science data (opinions more accurately) about helping others. These sources may be interesting but do not resolve the current differences about social responsibility in the twentieth century context. However, a few anchor points have emerged and become accepted. Only a few vulnerable groups have been recipients of care and concern by their more favored compatriots. The able-bodied have usually been considered less worthy of concern in every epoch. The motivations have alternated between fear of divine retribution, self-regarding protection of class-privileged status, promotion of national wealth and well-being, religious or secular love of others. The means for expressing concern, regardless of motivation, was for a long time either personal charity, reliance on mediating social institutions such as a church, or sometimes government or local government. Usually each age has combined several motives and means, with one or another dominating the rest.

Since none of this answers clearly whether the history fits modern, urban, mobile, depersonalized society, are there new formulations which can be added to or substituted for the old ones?

Past religious beliefs, or concepts of status and hierarchy, outlined class rights and obligations and served as a guide to individual and group behavior. With the "decay" of these well-ordered bases for behavior more general, secular efforts have been made to define ethical concepts about obligation, legal rights, desert, and justice. Contemporary philosophers, scholars and critics have tried to define a contemporary intellectual basis for the next generation of social programs, giving lesser or greater emphasis to helping the stranger. They have considered the moral bases for answering old questions about altruism and selfishness, about the nature of interpersonal relationships and community cohesion. This chapter reviews a few of these efforts.[1]

A Confusion of Choices: Lacking Guidelines about General Well-Being

Philosophy wrestles with moral principles, complexity, disillusion and malaise. The modern world gives rise to enormous growth in the expectations which individuals have about life and a highly individualized society reinforces this by its idealization of self-fulfillment as a first criterion of behavior. When reality does not match escalating expectations, dissatisfaction sets in. Individuals resent taxation and obligation when they perceive their conditions of life to be less gratifying than they have been led to believe they should be. Confidence in government erodes as its ability to deliver a "good life" appears limited. But even in an era of the individual, the individual's gratification depends on a hidden hand of interdependence. Special interests with differing degrees of authority and influence, have come to confuse concepts of general community well-being. The competition of many interest groups increases demands upon laws or the public purse. Each group is satisfied only if it satisfies its wants without clarity about the general welfare. The awakening to the collective cost of the cumulative wants of all interest groups has been rude. Lacking alternative principles or framework, the idea has spread that it is impossible for all groups to be satisfied collectively, so it appears easier for individuals or interest groups to look after themselves. In that competition those who have greater power secure disproportionate shares of the general pool of resources and the dissatisfaction increases.

   The field of social policy and social welfare has entered that period of change outlined by Thomas Kuhn in *The Structure of Scientific Revolu-*

---

[1] Several authors have discussed these questions in the context of American social work and welfare. Among them are: John Morgan, ed., *Welfare & Wisdom,* Toronto, University of Toronto Press, 1966; Herbert Bisno, *The Philosophy of Social Work,* Washington, Public Affairs Press, 1952; Arnold Howard, *Social Welfare Values, Means & Ends,* New York, Random House, 1969; Nathan Cohen, *Social Work in the American Tradition,* New York, Dryden Press, 1958; Jane Addams, *Democracy and Social Ethics,* New York, Macmillan, 1902; Charles Levy, *Social Worth Ethics,* New York, Human Sciences Press, 1976.

tions. Old paradigms which explain the world about us run up against a growing recognition that too many phenomena are unexplained, contradictions are not resolved by the traditional formulae. Suddenly old formulae are no longer acceptable; a new one is in the course of making (Kuhn, 1970). In the nineteenth century Matthew Arnold said much the same:

> Modern times find themselves with an immense system of institutions, established facts, accredited dogmas, customs, rules which have come to them from times not modern. In this system their life has to be carried forward (even) if they have a sense that this system is not of their own creation, that it is by no means corresponds exactly with the wants of the actual life, that, for them, it is customary not rational. The modern spirit is now awake almost everywhere. . . . to remove this want of correspondence is beginning to be settled by the endeavor of the most persons of good sense. (M. Arnold, quoted by Kazin, 1981, p. 25)

The nineteenth and twentieth century explanations of basic change help us understand the current disarray in those formulae which in the past defined the liberal or welfare state. Bertrand Russell once defined the accepted twentieth century liberal faith as consisting of three main elements: enunciating the aim of improving the quality of individual and social existence; attributing failures in human well-being as much to environment as to personal deficiency; and recognition that our economy produces sufficient tax surplus to make possible what has since come to be called a social instrument for improvement of individual and social existence (Russell, 1927). To realize how far we have drifted from firm widespread consensus about this tripartite foundation for a liberal program for the welfare state we have only to consider the current renewal of emphasis upon personal and individual achievement rather than collective responsibility and the current conviction that a social increment in the economy is no longer either available or one which electors are prepared to furnish.

Old ethical systems are also considered irrelevant, inconsistent and ineffective as tools for consensus in policymaking. Policymakers can choose among several postures with which to reconcile technical and moral judgments: a religious view which is hostile to social policy by government; that of practical utilitarians who measure everything in terms of costs and benefits although the criteria for assigning costs or benefits are not concisely articulated; that of the narcissists with limited sense of moral obligation; and that of such contemporary philosophers as Rawls and Nozick. Each of these has strong advocates, so how to choose? The old view that morality derives from the fear of sanctions by either civil or superordinate authority have been eroded because there is less fear of either the judicial system, government or of God.

Put another way, one result of individualism and freedom is serious doubt whether moral standards developed for governing the relationships between individuals who know each other are transferable to guide behavior or collective actions of large numbers of persons who do not know each other. Even within a family framework, old standards have either eroded or been replaced by many alternatives in the conviction that old firm guides to obligation could be mechanisms for tyranny. In the larger policy arena conflict between realization of self or conformity to community includes the fear that reliance upon community mechanisms inevitably leads to limitations on self-realization.

This trend has been nourished by the contradiction between the promises advanced in the last 100 years and the shortfall in realizing them. We have had the promise of peace as a result of political action and the result has been a succession of increasingly devastating wars. We have been taught to believe that science and technology will bring us a world of plenty, and, while plenty has been increased, the scale of poverty and deprivation whether due to unreal expectations or maldistribution have not been reduced enough to match our expectations. Conflict and instability are blamed on rapid scientific change. The perceived rupture between promise and reality was illustrated by one dramatic incident in Zurich, Switzerland in 1981. In that summer a militant minority of youth resorted to violent attacks upon local police and government in order to force their special demands. But this was no violent outburst by the underprivileged; it was by relatively well-to-do youth from well-to-do families in a well-to-do society, all protesting a municipal decision to expend some funds upon redoing an opera house and doing less to provide a new youth center. This excuse may have been a proxy for other dissatisfactions with the social order for which the protesters held the state responsible. Similar outbreaks seemed to have occurred in Amsterdam and Berlin as well.

This constitutes one arena which philosophers have entered. They join the search for new formulations, new paradigms, with which to view the present confusions.

DIALOGUE IN MORAL PHILOSOPHY

Certain terms and concepts recur in discussion by present day moral philosophers in their search for ethical anchoring for welfare obligation. They often have a technical meaning but the same terms are also used in popular discussion. Each of these is analyzed by moral philosophers and reduced to its most precise subelements in a search for universal rules or laws which can then be said to govern human relationships. Some of these concepts are:

needs and wants
rights, obligation and justice
happiness
self and self-interest
means and ends relationship
reciprocity
just desert
autonomy
fairness
social order

A limited sampling of dialogue about the meaning of such terms is summarized below. The term *philosophy* is used here quite broadly to encompass the thinking of professional philosophers and of those in a variety of nonphilosophical fields (e.g., economics, management, education, law and science), who seek to develop moral or ethical ideas which can be fitted to technical and scientific knowledge. One moral issue is how to rebuild an acceptable basis for caring for the stranger in a society which is constantly being reordered. The discussion is often couched in terms of interpersonal relationships, but our purpose is to concentrate on concepts which apply to collective efforts by some on behalf of others who may not be known personally. In doing so we need to be alert to the modern world's urge to consider people as ends in themselves, rather than as means to achieve the ends of others—of a higher class or the nation-state. Part of the confusion arises because collectivist states attempt to so merge the individual into the collective whole of the nation that a distinction between self and other becomes difficult to maintain.

Entrepreneurialism (Capitalism) and Marxism

Any discussion of philosophical concepts needs to recognize the two dominant influences on modern political, economic and social thought of the past 150 years: the intellectual and political confrontation between Marxism and Capitalism. While neither is directly concerned with a narrow view of social welfare, each has a distinctive understanding about the preferred ways to a social society, which inevitably influence the kind of social welfare arrangements which develop. Table 12.1 outlines very schematically the main themes of each thought system as they bear on current welfare thinking. The evolution of welfare programs into contemporary welfare state models in capitalist or marketplace societies has come about as a result of a tug of war between these two approaches. "Pure" marketplace thinking, systematized so thoroughly in nineteenth century writing, opposed each new proposal for a social welfare program and then

TABLE 12.1   A Comparison of Major Concepts Affecting Social Welfare Policy in
Capitalist and Socialist Societies

WELFARE STATE	*SOCIALISM*
The production and control of most of the goods and services of society are in the hands of individuals or of private groups. Various limits can be placed on private choice, but these limits do not rule out the major choice-taking rule of private persons.	Most if not all goods and services are either produced or controlled by government, acting on behalf of all citizens. Control can take many forms: state ownership, centralized control or decentralized participation in decision, control in assignment of jobs or free movement.
Goverment intervenes occasionally to correct major market inequities or to arrange a few services for which market will not work in the interest of the state.	Democratic Socialism embraces central or decentralized public ownership of the means of production with some worker participation in production decision or with marketplace supply and demand.
The aim of society is the well-being of all, but the scope of government is limited by conviction, widely held, that flaws in the private system are minor and correctable without major system change.	Private activities are a minor area of service or production, usually manageable by a very small enterprise, not affecting many people; or they grow up as an "underground" economy about which little is known and which can be ignored.
Many social and human needs arise out of conditions other than work, and these require attention by organized groups, with or without government help.	The aim of society is the well-being of all, achievable only by a major redesign of the whole system of economic and social relations.
The family and informal support systems are the basic protection against noneconomic needs.	With a major change in society, most current social problems will slowly disappear if economic security is assured on an equal basis for all. New ones may arise in the future—to be met as conditions require.
	The family and informal support systems are the basic protection of noneconomic needs; with the exception of medical care and education.

reluctantly accepted each when it became clear that the acceptance was useful to keep the society intact and did not alter the other basic relationships. Usually such proposals were initiated, or at least supported, as interim measures by socialist critics. Despite the fears of conservative opponents this support did not lead to any increase in popular acceptance of socialist thinking, at least not in the U.S., nor has the adoption of socialist supported programs led to more than a welfare state modification of the basic capitalist structure of economic and political relationships. See, for example: the 40-hour week, anti-child labor laws, Social Security, Workmen's Compensation and health insurance.

The welfare state, with a few exceptions, treats social programs as residual—as minor elements—while the bulk of human existence continues to be governed by individual acts of interest groups and of individuals. The market exists not only for economic, but for social and interpersonal exchange as well. The state intervenes occasionally on the assumption that most affairs are still well-handled by a self-correcting structure of independent courts or citizens. Differences in conditions above a minimum floor are justified as encouraging independence, initiative and creativity.

But persistent inequities in entrepreneurial societies gave rise to socialist alternatives, which rely on a major reordering of the relationships between classes in society. This introduced in the strongest possible manner the rights of *all* persons to more equal shares in national income, to more security and well-being. To this was added a belief in increased equality in conditions among all classes.

The major difference between socialist and welfare state approaches to welfare lies in the extent of governmental responsibility. At the extreme, Socialism gives central government major, if not complete, control over all major decisions affecting well-being. Furthermore, such a system claims to replace class differentiation with equality in work, careers, education, medical care and incentives. In the welfare state, private influence and control dominate major decision making because most economic and social organizations remain in nongovernmental hands. A third alternative, democratic socialism, argues for public ownership but free market operations within a publicly owned system. Although democratic socialism has often been proposed, no nation has yet attempted to put it into effect—nor have its proponents clarified how such a hybrid would work differently from a model welfare state.

Within this conflict between capitalist and socialist thinking, moral philosophy has sought to deal with less grand political aspects of social welfare thought by concentrating on the meaning of certain concepts which will be used regardless of the political/economic structures of a given state. It is to these we next turn.

Selfishness, Equality and Justice

Some philosophers attempt to modernize ways of framing moral standards within a framework of logic and reason. John Rawls (1971) has proposed a philosopher's variation on the legal concepts of *justice* which is rationalist in reconciling self-interest and equality. It might be called *modified egalitarianism*. He argues that people, if given the opportunity under fair conditions, would identify principles for resource distribution which benefit themselves while also being fair to others. People could act as if they were in fact benevolent under certain assumptions (although activated by self-interest as well): individuals are in an original position in society with mutual disinterests as to their positions; they are asked to make rules behind a veil of ignorance—that is if they did not know in advance where they would be located in society. Then they would create rules for a social order of maximum fairness and justice for all because these rules would also benefit them. Rawls concludes that individuals would choose a society in which status, income and wealth were distributed equally *unless* an unequal distribution was found to be in everyone's advantage. If I tried to visualize a future society and did not know where I would be located in it and ended up being in the worst position as to possession of resources, I would want to have that condition improved or corrected by some redistribution. However, being reasonable, if it can be shown to me that some inequality is necessary for me to have an improvement in my position, I would be equally willing to accept an unequal distribution. If it is convincingly explained why some members of the society must have more resources in order to assure the production of the goods upon which my own well-being depends, then I can accept the difference in position. While motivation in real life is varied, Rawls argues from such analysis that people can be moved by a sense of justice to recognize the claims of others.

Rawls further concludes from such analysis that just and moral arrangements in society are those which positively favor those who are worse off while not depriving individuals of commonly held liberties. Government policies are accepted as giving preferential treatment to the most disadvantaged. Preferential treatment is accepted for those who are well-off provided that this can be shown in turn to have a subsequent benefit for the least advantaged. Assuming the theory works, in many ways the qualification on the principle of equality would justify both tax incentives for the wealthy on the trickle-down theory and affirmative action laws regarding discrimination.

One of the early twentieth century secular rationalists, Bertrand Russell, introduced a more simple and modest analysis arguing that, while *altruism is essentially selfish,* reason can produce a good society for all. Russell proposes that behavior of reasoning individuals can be evaluated by the results which they can expect from their acts, and that these need not be measured by a priori morality. Russell lays down the following tenets:

1. The existence of an instinctive feeling of happiness: one may not have an instinct to work but reasoning people recognize that some effort is prudently necessary to secure the goods which are essential for well-being and therefore necessary for happiness and joy in living. The prudent person is prepared to exercise that amount of work effort necessary to secure those goods.

2. Lessened conflict or friendly feeling: the absence of conflict is a necessary condition for happiness. Differences and inequalities exist between groups, but they seek conditions in which conflict is, if not completely absent, at least reduced.

3. Knowledge and its search: science in the search for knowledge is crucial to achieve an altruistic result because we have learned that information can be harmful unless it is subject to constant scientific and critical testing. We may have the knowledge or capacity to increase the production of goods, but in using this knowledge we produce goods which are frequently not necessary or useful, which make war more destructive or which substitute trivializing goods and amusements for others which might have more value.

In an age of uncertainty and doubt, we are now aware how important it is to *continuously search* for truth, knowledge, and wisdom which constitutes the best path for a reasoning person to follow in a search for happiness. For him this is a more useful path to follow than trying to impose a priori moral rules (Russell, 1927).

Justice in Difference or in Equality

Robert Nozick has revived traditional theories about the *marketplace* as opposed to the governmental interventions postulated by modern utilitarians or equalitarians. Nozick reasons that in the ideal world justice would be done for all when everyone who owns or holds anything acquired in a legitimate way is entitled to retain those holdings. No person or group (and this includes a collective state or government) is entitled to control resources nor to decide how they shall be allocated. Instead, each person should acquire and be secure in retaining that which he or she acquires from others either in exchange or as a gift. Equitable relationships evolve because individuals will exchange directly with each other the things which each wants from the other, thereby, avoiding all of the intrusions into liberty and privacy which legally enforced governmental redistribution entail. Nozick believes that there is, basic in human nature, a readiness to be altruistic on a voluntary basis (see the views of sociobiologists noted below) since those who are better-off under these arrangements are likely to have ample means. They will have the capacity to be benevolent and generally will be so. In his view, the most talented, energetic or acquisitive individuals want to be highly rewarded and also highly regarded by others, so that the needy will be taken care of by personal benevolence which can be encouraged. The total volume of goods available overall will be increased (Nozick, 1974).

Conrad Johnson considers the whole question of difference, *equity and fairness in a more relativistic framework*. He argues that concepts about equity are not universally generalizable—they are dependent upon the reference group which the analyst has in mind. There are certain concepts about what is equitable within a family, what is fair to divide among children in a family, which may be quite different from what the family considers to be fair distribution to others outside the family. Concepts of equity in a community are more varied and differ from concepts of equity within the family. For a community to exist at all it is necessary for its members to tolerate the differences which their members have (C. Johnson, 1981, p. 125). Extremes can be handled by the exclusion of persons who are too deviant from the standards of a majority, but in the end those who remain within a stable community tolerate each other within some boundary of controversy. What is considered equitable for a nation-state differs from views about equity held in a primary community. A national standard is probably less individualizing than standards in a primary community (Johnson, 1981). Such differences must be taken into account in policy formation.

If one accepts the principle that definitions of equity vary by the referent group, one still needs to seek principles or criteria which referents are likely to use. Are they then universal principles? In the end Johnson relies upon "common sense" perhaps on a case-by-case basis in trying to choose between the contrasting claims of merit and need. Answers will vary according to different social and economic conditions, therefore, the weight given to merit or to want will be determined differently. There are conditions in which it is necessary to encourage creativity in individuals, in a community or in a nation. There also are times when it is necessary to subordinate individual freedom in order to save life. These times vary and can only be ascertained by pragmatic common sense. But common sense needs to understand the association between merit and want in human affairs.

Another approach identifies key domains in life: socializing, economic and political. Equality and terms of fairness vary in each domain. Hochschild (1981) suggests that most citizens may prefer differentiation, or "inequality," in the economic domain; but in the political domain people prefer equality, especially as regards political rights. She recognizes that economic inequality encroaches on political and social domains so that clear differentiation is not possible. Her approach suggests that arguments about equality alone fail to take into account the natural human tendency to be discriminating about the relationships in different areas of human association. The areas of sharp conflict are, in reality, affected by areas where there is substantial agreement among different classes.

Walzer (1983) carries this idea further and postulates "complex equality." He denies that equality overall is a reasonable or possible goal. Instead he argues that customary conventions of people assign different kinds of opportunity, and resources to different areas of life—each governed by its own ideas about what is fair or just. Thus, necessities of life are accepted as distributable on the basis of need—each society fixing its own definition of need. Punishment should be distributed according to what a person deserves, advanced education according to talent, work according to the needs of an enterprise or an employer. Citizenship is assigned according to tradition in a community. And differences in wealth can be accepted as being fair when skill and luck, separately or in combination, produce these differences.

Walzer recognizes that these spheres are not watertight; influence leaks from one to another. Thus great wealth can come to dominate the political process or it alters access to opportunity or education. Production decisions made only by owners can distort conditions which result in other spheres. Some redistributive means are called for to prevent these distortions which militate against individual group or national well-being. One such mechanism, according to Walzer is government intervention in the economic sphere to preserve political equality. Another is more democracy in the workplace; or cooperative enterprises in other major spheres. He calls for much more attention to the potentials in cooperative activities to resolve dilemmas of complexity (Walzer, 1983; Axelrod, 1984).

Equality and Difference: Merit and Want

One issue which needs fuller attention is whether or not group preferences are subject to any constraint at all. This is often handled by addressing the relationship between merit and want or need. Those who fare well may do so by virtue of hard work, earned effort or great wisdom. Are they then entitled to keep all the rewards of this merit, even if the result is so much control over the goods of the world that others starve, or go needy? If a majority are well-off, presumably by merit, then their capacity to overlook the needy can be very great.

The preferences of majorities or of powerful persons have to be constrained at some point in order to avoid authoritarianism, injury or exploitation of minorities. One protective device is equal protection of the law for all in society within which differences in resource allocation can be accepted as not being necessarily inequitable as long as an ethical rationale for the difference exists; or if all regardless of resource, are treated equally in certain basic matters—taxation, freedom to hold one's possessions, etc. The difficulty remains in deciding what areas of life are to be treated as "equal" in law. A good rationale for equality or difference is one which is accepted by all in the community. It is not clear, however, whether this means all "rational" people or all who operate in their choice-taking behind the Rawls' veil (do not know their place in the society that the individual is trying to establish) or a dominating majority.

Such a relativistic approach does require some balance between protecting merit and avoiding too much need in order to keep stability and coherence in the society, the family or the community. This is perennially controversial; a variety of choices can be posited but the coherence and stability of the group—the reference group—must also be sustained by some means which override the great variety of piecemeal, ad hoc and pragmatic decisions which are made by smaller entities. In the family reference circle the contradictory decisions which might be made by parents or by the children needs to be subordinated at some point to an overriding reconcilation to preserve the integrity of the family. Similarly, a point is reached where the preferences of varieties of contending subgroups need to be reconciled beneath some overriding authority or consensus in order to maintain any coherent society. But such discussion of merit and want only poses the dilemma; it does not provide an ethically satisfying resolution.

Justice, Just Desert and Rights

The concept of justice is resorted to as an ethical resolution of conflict between merit and want. What is justice? That which is just. But some critics of the legal concept of "right" note that the right has to be a claim against someone. It is noted that the poor, the handicapped, and others disadvantaged are not necessarily suffering from an *injustice* that can be rectified by a legal concept; that no individual is at fault, but that rather there is an arbitrary distribution in nature which leads to the outcomes (Acton, 1971). Hayek (1976) and others have argued that most troubles and difficulty are not a result of anyone's plan or any society's plan but still "we cry out against the injustice when a succession of calamities befalls one family while another steadfastly prospers, when meritorious effort is frustrated by some unforeseeable accident. . . ." We may protest against such a fate but find it hard to blame anyone for the occurrence. Similarly, "our complaints about the outcomes of the market as unjust do not usually assert that some one individual has been unjust: there is no answer to the question of who has been unjust, except in Marxist identification of culpable classes. 'Society' has become the new deity to which we complain and clamor for redress if it does not fulfill the expectations it has created" (Hayek, 1976). *Justice,* in the terms used here, means holding individuals accountable for injuries done to others.

While there is some force to these arguments, it is also true that modern society creates rules, institutions and regulations which channel and funnel the distribution and retention of resources; it is accountable in the collective sense for the outcomes of these rules and regulations, even though individuals cannot be held accountable for them.

Others, however, argue that the concept of justice is not a suitable one for a relief of need because the exact meaning of the term *justice* covers distribution according to merit or desert and not according to need. An injustice is done if an individual merits or deserves a certain outcome and does not secure it. If one is concerned with need not merit then justice is not a satisfactory solution, since it is hard to argue for legal relief of need because one "deserves" it.

Some, such as Titmus (1974), try to combine a variety of moral or ethical views of human relationships and to equate the combination with justice: to each according to his need; to each according to his work. But to some extent these views, although comprehensive, are logically contradictory. Some philosophers argue that worth, merit and need are not compatible or at least are better treated separately.

To cope with this conceptual difficulty, some analysts advance several theories about rights which do not yet constitute widely accepted general ethical theory of justice: the competing principles of merit, desert, worth, entitlement, and need. All have some utility but their application depends upon a point of view in a particular social context. Justice becomes then an ad hoc practical decision taken by a given collectivity at a given time to deal with a specific difficulty.

Another line of approach tries to avoid this relativism by positing social rights rather than justice: are social and economic rights distinguishable from each other and can these in turn be distinguished from older human rights such as the right not to be killed or to be enslaved. Certain rights such as that to life and liberty do not clearly embody claims upon resources which have to be redistributed but rather operate to restrain certain inhuman behaviors akin to the negative confessions of Pharaonic Egypt.

The extension of a concept of rights to the social realm confronts at least two dilemmas which need to be dealt with. The first is access to resources in order to meet the socioeconomic rights which are postulated. The range and level of rights to be realized depends upon the resources available and these will differ from place to place. The situation in India, where the right to food for life is modified by the amount of food which the government of India can manage to produce and distribute, is different from that in the U.S. There is a certain relativism determined by the capital and current resources of a nation or community, implicit in thinking about how social rights are to be defined or bounded.

Concepts of Need: Basic Needs and Rights

Another line of reasoning tries to resolve uncertainty about the content of social rights by identifying *needs* which include both physical survival and personal autonomy. Each social system must see that some needs are satisfied for all members of society and direct resources to these ends rather than to other good but not as basic ends (Plant, 1980, pp. 37–51).

To move beyond this broad generalization requires examination of the term *need* and its possible meanings. The concept of *need* must differentiate between want and desire. The latter could be identified by the expressions of each individual in a society, but the concept of *need* implies a measure or standard which can be more or less objectively determined.

Historically, needs identification has been based upon a measure which someone other than the needy individual has established. Needs thus defined usually have an imprint of stigma. Stigma attaches to implied or explicit dependence upon decisions made by someone else. It can be an inherited revulsion from the status of slavery or it can be a rejection of the constraint upon autonomy which the dependence seems to imply.

If stigma is to be avoided, needs could theoretically be transmuted into rights—the right to have a need satisfied and sanctioned in a society. Much of the past thinking about need and welfare has relied upon generosity of the giver with varying views about how the stigma of receiving can be reduced or expunged. Reciprocity, or exchange between giver and receiver is another way to reduce stigma. Such exchange can be in the form of service, or deference either to an individual giver or to a society. The attempt to establish needs as rights creates a contest between equally valued rights; need based rights and the rights of those whose resources are attached to relieve need. If one is satisfied with benevolence and gratuitous behavior, then a person with means can be moved by moral sanction to help another in ways which are not demeaning. This is not a legally enforceable right of the needy person, except perhaps in the eyes of God with enforcement of the right in some afterlife. On the other hand, to postulate an enforceable, legal right requires a sanction or force to back up a transfer from one to the other. In other words, a gift is not a right and the concept of *right* involves the clash of two or more rights.

Philosophers discuss at some length the relationship between needs and wants, arguing that the uses which a particular gift or object is put bears some relationship to how society differentiates want from need. The poor person who is starving and who "wants" food may also be said to "need" food by an objective measure since survival rather than murder is an unchallengeable premise of human organization. In this event, the want and the need have a similar meaning. But if we talk about more than minimum food, then level of housing comfort or clothing variety or habit-forming drugs may be wants which are not necessarily needs sanctioned by a societally objective measure, although they may be needs for some individuals.

In order to escape the swampland of semantic elaboration, philosophy seeks to ascertain whether or not there are some goals, purposes, functions and states of life which it can be said all persons want and which can also be identified as being needs for all practical purposes. In other words, are there basic human needs? Social organization requires some moral code and persons living under that code are assumed to have the capacity and the power to act within that morality. Following from this, the capacities which individuals require to live within that moral code constitute their basic needs. Human beings must live whatever is a normal life span. To survive requires some level of nutrition and thus access to food can be said to constitute such a neutral "basic" need. Similarly, it can be argued that the surviving individual needs sufficient health and physical vitality, as well as psychological vigor, to have autonomy needful to perform as a member in this society. If one believes that individuals do not have to be autonomous actors but only robot-like executors of some externally imposed code, this argument might not prevail. But if the capacity of the individual to choose and to act independently is seen as necessary, then whatever is required for the individual to be relatively autonomous can become a measure of need. This autonomy may vary from the most primitive rural society to that of a most complex industrial society, but at least a start is made in trying to identify the components of autonomy—is it freedom of movement, is it an automobile in urban society, is it sufficient food, shelter and clothing to be able to interact with neighbors and colleagues?

This narrowing definition of *need* can be carried further. There are basic and general needs. If basic needs are taken to mean provision of food and shelter, one establishes a link with a long historic evolution of caring for the stranger—throughout history we find that such needs of the impotent poor are widely and well-accepted. In one sense the concept of *basic need* links to our beliefs about the individual and freedom. We argue that if persons are to be treated as ends in themselves, their social arrangements must assure their autonomy. Autonomous individuals are produced who are capable of making decisions and acting independently on their own. With this end in mind, certainly food and shelter are basic requisites.

Most of our difficulty about transferring these philosophical concepts into reality derives from the character of present society, its ways of distributing scarce resources among persons and classes which are bound together mainly by imperceptible and impersonal threads of association rather than close interpersonal relationships. Food to survive is clearly a basic need but when there is a great deal of affluence coupled with our understanding about the science of nutrition, we can readily elevate the standard of need relief at least to the level of guaranteeing a healthy survival rather than bare survival. To this may be added freedom from arbitrary interference, avoidable ill health and deep ignorance, all of which can objectively be seen to reduce personal autonomy, therefore, diminishing the person as the end of any action. This still assumes that the dimensions of the person as an end in himself or herself can be summarized in the individual capable of standing on his or her own two feet, able to make decisions, judgments, and to take actions with relative autonomy. For this purpose survival through nutrition, shelter, and freedom from arbitrary interference are essential. As we have noted above, the amount of resources available in a particular social pool may vary according to specific circumstances but the obligation to provide for some basic minimum needs is not a relative matter.

This resolution, however, does not take into account many of the other kinds of needs which special groups have come to argue for. Such other claimed needs are more in the nature of wants and desires. No obligation is imposed on other individuals or on society collectively to meet such needs, or wants because the results of meeting them, measured by autonomy, is uncertain. Also the social as well as personal cost of diverting limited available resources from other types of life-saving actions (e.g., other basic needs) may be so great that one cannot justify an imposed obligation in either social or personal terms. An example is a claimed requirement that everyone have certain kinds of transportation available even if the cost of that transportation becomes so great that less is available for basic food and shelter for everyone.

A reasonable approach to such dilemmas is offered by Springborg. She concludes that objective needs cannot be located; what is needed is a social, not mechanical, mechanism to mediate between conflicting needs. Needs are not alone objective but are intertwined with other symbolic clues about meaning. Thus, exploitation may exist and be defined, but unhappiness cannot be—as seen by evidence that increasing consumption has not reduced discontent (Springborg, 1981).

Obligation to Others

A discussion of rights, needs and justice must also consider how far people are obligated to act to care for others. It is well and good to say people *should* care, but *must* they? Are they obligated to? And what is obligation? Can it be legally enforced by some on others? It is unclear how much positive obligation one has to do something altruistically or unilaterally to ensure the well-being of another; what obligations have individuals to each other?

Is the obligation individual, or is it an obligation of many persons acting collectively to provide for the needs of some within that collectivity? The oldest argument is that the obligation to help another is essentially negative, not to directly injure another; and that the only positive obligations, to act to help, are those which we have imposed upon ourselves voluntarily.

The most clear-cut uncontestable right is the right not to be killed or maimed; that is we are obligated not to kill another. Nozick discusses this from the point of view of an *enforceable duty*—that which one individual can legally be forced to do for another. Thus, "no moral balancing act can take place among us; there is no moral outweighing one of our lives by others so as to lead to a greater overall social good. There is no justified sacrifice of some of us for others . . . to use a person in this way does not sufficiently respect and take account of the fact that he is a separate person and his is the only life he has" (Nozick, 1974). Following from this is the early liberal view that an individual may be compelled by law to respect the rights of others—that is not to harm them—but he may not be compelled to benefit them at his own expense.

But this remains a negative concept of helping. To consider the subject in positive terms some philosophers draw a distinction between perfect and imperfect obligation (Fishkin, 1982). The performance of a perfect obligation is legally owed by one individual to another. An imperfect obligation is one which an individual ought to perform for another as a matter of ethical decency, but has no legal obligation to perform. We are led to ask whether certain obligations are so deeply entrenched in common thinking that what is owed by one to another is transformed into a claim. The obligation not to kill has become the right not to be killed by another. In the modern economic world the obligation—perfect or imperfect—to help a starving soul may have become so entrenched that no individual can allow anyone to starve to death when the means are available to avoid it. However, such an obligation, as a right, does not tell us much about the level at which the debt owed is to be discharged. For example, at what level of nutrition can it be said there is an enforceable obligation for me to feed you? At the level of minimum nutritional survival and, if so, by what culture standard? Or, at the level of maximum health protection? Or at the level of sumptuous banqueting? While this seems hairsplitting, a clear, widely accepted answer is essential if the obligation is to be enforced.

The question of obligation also involves a distinction between obligation and ultra-obligation. Can I be forced to contribute to the support of every deprived person in the world or does my obligation only run to sustain an individual, or to those in my immediate family or my immediate community or my state? To relieve distress everywhere in the world as an obligation on me is at best an imperfect obligation, something I probably should do, but it is also difficult to trace either its extent or enforcement, so the generous idea does not translate into public policy.

A further difficulty arises in identifying the individuals who have explicit obligations to fulfill the social rights of others. It is possible to argue that the state has an obligation but who in the state, made up of elected officials plus 250 million citizens, are to be held accountable? We can get around this difficulty by struggling to secure consensus from voters which is enacted in law which then becomes an obligation of an elected official to carry out. In the end the concept of *obligation* must proceed through a long chain of acts in which social institutions are devised and sanctioned and then equipped with personnel and laws for enforcement to meet social needs, a chain of relationships quite different from that concerned with personal obligation between individuals. In this long chain, who is to be held accountable for performance? If it is the 250 million citizens acting as a collectivity, how are they held accountable?

A collective responsibility can be called upon when group solidarity is sustained by a broad and deep community of interest which binds a group to common ends and in a common lot. Rawls also argues that a natural duty exists for individuals to support just institutions. Where they do not exist we have a duty to assist in the establishment of just arrangements and institutions. In practical terms this argues for collective obligation to be responsible, but performance is left to institutions created by the long process noted above, and accountability for creating just institutions is ambiguous.

How much of welfare then is a matter of charity or of generosity but not of obligation? Along this path of reasoning those in need may have a moral claim to another person's charity. But the latter has no general obligation to help all. The alternate view is that the holding of wealth is truly a matter of strict obligation and that those who hold resources can be expected or be required to respond to those who have need based upon some general moral claim. But by what criteria and how? Such terms as *rights, justice* or *need* are argued about at some length but clear answers to the question of which provides the best moral foundation depends upon which of these two paths is followed and adhered to in a particular society.

Obligation and Reciprocity

The question of reciprocity arises in relation to obligation and rights because human beings worry about whether the relationship between individuals is one of equality or of subordination and superiority. The belief that there is an obligation to give or a right to receive something without any reciprocal act has little historic foundation. Even non-capitalist societies argue for the satisfaction of need "to each according to his need, from each according to his ability," a principle of implied reciprocity, although the form of reciprocity may be different in a socialist than in a marketplace economy. Is there now an obligation without reciprocity? Has obligation no bounds? If not, what is the modern form of reciprocity?

Whether we consider welfare to be charity or humanity, we also need to consider whether the reciprocal obligations are voluntary or legally enforceable and whether they run to particular persons or classes known to the giver. In homogeneous societies where most persons are likely to know each other or to know classes toward whom benevolence is exercised, the answers about moral behavior are embedded in concepts of personal interrelationships where reciprocity is visible. However, in large complex societies (great empires of modern superpowers) most people are anonymous except within small circles of association. The enactment of welfare provisions requires the distribution of benefits on the basis of some moral foundation, for persons who are unknown to the givers. The concept that all citizens of the U.S. "know" each other represents a very tenuous bond for purposes of moral enforcement of beneficence. Certainly it is quite different from the kinds of "knowing" possible between members of a family or a small rural community.

Old concepts of obligation and reciprocity between giver and receiver begin to fail when applied to large nation-states. The modern welfare state is an example of an institutionalized collective obligation and altruism for the meeting of certain needs. It has been widely justified as necessary in order to maintain the integument of a coherent and stable community in society. However, since the historical foundation from which this conception emerged is that of correlative rights and obligation, it is difficult to see how the recipients of welfare services in the modern state can be seen to reciprocate directly in any way for their "gifts." Once the meeting of particular needs is reduced to law, thus sanctioned by consensus, the recipients are not only to some extent relieved of stigma but also of the obligation to reciprocate. On several scores the link between the modern welfare state and old altruistic concepts about obligation is weakened. Perceptions that the dependent person is at least trying to help himself *may* have been part of the original concept of reciprocity. But it is difficult in the modern, more anonymous, urban and dispersed world of the twentieth century for those who are independent to see or know whether or not the dependent persons are trying to help themselves, or are lying back and 'accepting handouts'. In this time it is all too easy for the average person to assume that efforts at self-help have *not* taken place only because they are not visible. This can become a form of denial of an unpleasant truth about dependency. The stranger, the alien, has always been charged with undesirable traits, in part because of the very differences in culture which are interpreted as undesirable per se.

The subject is further complicated by the concept of ultra-obligation. Open-ended appeals to altruism and general principles of justice lead to questioning whether any limits can be placed upon generosity. Fishkin (1982) explores *limits of obligation* which are attached to any more general concept of altruistic behavior. Although he is writing in terms of individual behavior, certain concepts may be ultimately transferable to political action. Fishkin argues that there are three stages in moral obligation to do anything for others:

1. There is a *zone of moral indifference;* there are certain actions which do not as a matter of moral necessity either require action or justify denial.

2. There is a *zone of moral requirement* in which individuals are morally obligated to do something good or to refrain from performing acts which are universally definable as "wrong." This zone is easily acted upon under conditions calling for minimal altruism, that is, where a great deal can be achieved at very little cost to the doer or altruist, for example, to save the life of a human being by picking up a banana skin on the street.

3. There are *zones of supererogation* (or heroic acts).

The last of these is the most troublesome. These are areas in which human beings ought to act but ought not be blamed if they do not. The best example is whether all of us in the interests of being altruistic would be required to take heroic action which threatens our own existence. For Fiskin there is no moral basis for expecting individuals or societies to act at such an heroic level. We are expected to be kind and good to others in some circumstances, but our obligation changes as the scale of obligation changes. This scale is modified by the number of obligations we are expected to assume, by the number of recipients entitled to each obligatory act, and the number of altruists who are available to perform the acts. If you have a child and that child is threatened, you have a moral obligation to do everything possible to save your child—but is this so extensible that you have an obligation to act personally, or participate in acts, which seek to save all children everywhere.

The moral dilemma which questions of scale present are more sharply introduced by reference to the Katherine Genovese case in which a large number of persons in New York City were aware that a woman was slowly being killed in the street but no one acted. There was clearly an obligation to save a life but no one acted—whether because of a lack of sense of altruism for another human being, because of a belief that to intervene would be too heroic, or the belief that "somebody else will act."

The relief of famine in the Southern Hemisphere represents another example. If a neighbor or someone in front of us is dying for lack of food and we have sufficient food, we are likely to operate under a widely accepted moral injunction to contribute something to save that life. How far does one proceed with that obligation? Are we obligated to continue to give from our available means until each of us is reduced to the level of the starving in the African Sahel? This becomes a zone of moral indifference or supererogation. Our actions could make the world better but are we obligated to act individually or collectively? And at what point does selfishness take over so that our choice about the kind of life we want to live becomes more important to us than the amount of suffering we could prevent (Narveson, 1962)? Such dilemmas are not yet resolved by any general moral rules. We are guided by extensive moral relativism and variety.

Such questions force us to return to issues of collective responsibility. Moral strictures about altruism can move one of us to save an individual, but if a million persons are involved in making a collective decision, is the obligation of any one individual diminished because the obligation is now distributed in a collectivity? If we are all equally reasonable, we might conclude that each of us will act "justly." But, in reality, individuals are influenced by whether they think their personal act will make a difference in the expected outcome. If 250 million Americans are involved in making the decision to share their resources to save thousands in Africa, is my personal obligation diluted to one part in 250 million? Does my individual action make only a trivial difference; and, if trivial, will I act? Like-minded individuals can choose to act as they contribute to CARE but this is not the same as trying to get all citizens to act collectively through government.

Related to this dilemma is the question of an overload of obligations. In earlier times the appeals for help were limited to necessities: starvation, the crippled, and the manifestly impotent. But the list of appeals which now come to us for a variety of good causes, each of which may be justified in its own terms, forces us to reconsider whether each of us is required to act on all appeals. Is there a moral obligation to respond to all of them and, if not, on what basis are choices to be made? This overload of obligation which has evolved in recent times would appear to challenge the moral assumption upon which we have built our ethical concepts in the past. Either the basic nature of our individual moralities has to be modified or we may have to give up any beliefs that there is a general obligation to meet all needs in all cases. If there are no general obligations which are morally required, do we end up being pressured by zealots for special purposes which do not permit us any arena of choice or is there an enlarged zone of indifference in which perhaps I should but am not obligated to act?

Obligation: A Life Cycle View

Relativistic approaches do not satisfy the search for more universal principles which are not dependent upon intuition as a basis for human behavior and for political acts. Philosophical search for principles of just
distribution among persons or groups in society is often concerned with
ideal moral theory, with just principles general enough to provide a
framework for numerous specific acts of justice. What is basic and universal and what is adaptable and reversable within a general framework?
Much of the popular thinking involves reasonable resource distribution at
a particular snapshot in time. In reality reasonable resource access and
equity operates over an individual's lifetime. The question of equity for
the elderly provides an instructive example of justice over a lifetime, and
between generations (Daniels, 1981). It is reasonable to give the elderly
full access to medical care but what is an equitable distribution of medical
resources between the elderly and the young? Ten to eleven percent of the
population over 65 account for about 30 percent of the total medical bill—
is this a reasonable and fair distribution in relation to children and others? At the end point of one's life costly chronic illness warrants attention,
and a humane society would provide that attention. But, is that attention
and that care to be given regardless of what each person does throughout
his or her entire life to look after his or her own needs as well as relying
upon provision by society? Will we argue that it is just for me to be a
wastrel in my youth, but others are obliged to take care of me in old age
when I need medical care? An alternative philosophical approach would
argue that each person must make prudent provision throughout an entire lifetime to anticipate requirements in old age.

Transfer of resources between generations, represented by different
cohorts of human beings, requires that we re-examine the moral validity
of taking from youth to provide for the elderly as categories and vice
versa. Do the youth of one generation have an obligation to provide for all
the health needs of the elderly of another generation? How far does this
obligation extend? And is that obligation modified by the extent to which
the older generation has made prudent provision for itself. If we are not
able to think over lifetimes then there is a grave risk that the very fabric
of society and human existence will be destroyed as each generation acts
for itself without regard for those which precede and follow.

Since that is manifestly unacceptable, what are the principles which
guide public policymakers and what are the fundamental moral principles at stake as regards health for the elderly? What is the balance to be
struck between the responsibility I take for myself and the extent to
which I must rely upon the generosity of others to "see me through"? A
simple, practical application is possible if we ignore the intergenerational
moral complexities of the subject. Individuals as prudent savers can be

expected to take action looking ahead to their health needs in old age, but earnings in the younger years may not be sufficient to permit effective savings. However, does this excuse those who can from providing for their future? The best that can be said is that we are not yet able to disassociate personal responsibility for oneself from the altruistic or beneficent concern which we ask those who are better-off to show for those who are less well-off.

This dilemma is approached tangentially by the idea of *serial reciprocity*. A gift from one party or group is posited to create a sense of obligation in the other which is then satisfied by further gift-giving behavior—so producing a kind of reciprocity multiplier, in which the succession of gifts trigger latent feelings of benevolence in others. When it comes to the elderly, however, the concept of reciprocity and serialness may operate in reverse, for the aged recipient is less able to respond in kind because of the shortness of remaining lifespan. So if the multiplier effect is to induce behavior of the helping kind in others who perceive that their return may become visible for them at some future time, there must be a more generalized feeling of willingness to help generated in society of which they will become the beneficiaries in the future (Challis, n.d.).

Reciprocity: Moral Relations or Economic Exchange and Communality

The foregoing discussion would appear to involve some substantial component of reciprocity between individuals in some kind of social compact. Other lines of reasoning, however, seek to distinguish between social and economic policies on the basis that social acts seek to create moral relations which give individuals moral identities in relation to others while economic acts concentrate upon identities mediated through goods. In economic exchange there is usually a quid pro quo which, it is argued, is not necessarily the case in social transactions (Watson, 1980). In this line of reasoning social transactions and exchanges are unequal—the object of the exchange is the fulfillment of an obligation not the equal exchange of goods or things. What one party gives up is not necessarily what the other receives. Social welfare is concerned with social relationships and at the level of social policy it is concerned with cumulative relationships which constitute a coherent, stable and satisfying society of humans over time. It is not limited to immediate, direct bilateral exchange. The basic argument for this kind of unequal exchange can be found in an appeal to status, identity or community and it is the appeal to integration and community which is dominant (Boulding, 1973; Angell, 1958). Collective attention to the needs, however defined, or the wants of individuals will lead to their active identification with society or the community in which they are embedded. Economic relationships do not necessarily prevent alienation, therefore, attention to social relationships which extend and enlarge the kinship of human beings with each other becomes valuable. Although these sets of relationships do not depend solely or mainly on need and want satisfaction, many social policies claim to link alienation with absence of social support while provision aims to reintegrate all classes in society. Compensation for economic inequities or diswelfare, if adequately evolved, can ameliorate the effects of other economic policies. If reduction in alienation and extension of social integration and communal identity depend upon all individuals feeling that they have a place in their society, then all individuals are in the end responsible for all others. Attention to the interests of those who have been harmed is justified as a form of compensation. Whether this obligation is contractual in form to carry out moral obligations or whether it is self-enlightened behavior, is still unresolved.

SUMMARY

This brief canvass of some of the philosophical dialogue about rights, obligation, need and want and about moral philosophy seems to have made the task of answering the questions with which this book began all the more difficult.

Some philosophical constructs, for example, those of Rawls and Nozick, are based on differing assumptions about motive in human interaction. In the practical world of program or policy action, believers in the assumptions of one or the other draw on their work to justify their efforts. Neither reconciles conflicts between the assumptions which continue to divide citizens and welfare protagonists.

For those confronted with the practicality of daily decision making, the dialogue may seem to be a species of very fine hairsplitting. In defense it must be said that many of the terms and phrases which advocates as well as opponents of welfare state use have an ambiguity and generality about them. They are terms to which many different meanings can be attached, each being honest and justifiable, but not necessarily widely understood. The current efforts to deal with this ambiguity in language is a valuable first step in introducing more concrete and clear meaning into the words all of us use, and to increase the reasonableness of the debate about the future. The more all protagonists use words with commonly understood meanings the more issues can be joined, the more we understand each other fairly and the better is the chance to make a clear political choice in the worst case; or in the best case, to arrive at a sensible and acceptable resolution of contradictions which now cloud the argument.

These are some of the clarifications in current writing:

1. There is no a priori or absolute guide to the boundary between altruism and self. It is not useful to appeal for support for every cause on the grounds of generosity owed others. The boundary in policymaking is fixed by social agreements, and the appeal is debased if used too often and too loosely.

2. Program arguments based on need are likely to succeed best if the needs selected for attention are basic ones, limited to those life conditions necessary for survival or functioning of the autonomous citizen: nutrition, shelter, health, free movement and interaction with others.

3. Justice and equality are not the same. Justice requires that society formally identify specific rights for individuals or groups in terms which enable the holder of the right to enforce them by legal process against specific others who interfere with the exercise of the right. A value claimed as a right to legitimate what one owes another individual can remain an unenforceable claim. Rights to vote and not to starve are now assured within limits. A right to a job or to equality is not.

4. Beneficiaries can be said to deserve some action or help in two circumstances: when an enforceable right has been assigned as in 3. above; when the recipient has acted in ways which conform to ideas about reciprocity; through past work, rearing a child, helping others, etc. But this does not of itself assure benevolent action by individuals or the state. Something more, not clearly specified in the writing is necessary.

5. Obligation of society collectively, is a weak and insubstantial argument for it easily permits individuals within our society to avoid the obligation through arguing that "someone else, not I," am obligated. It is most effective when members of the collectivity agree on the objectives all share and when there is a strong community of interest. Since the general obligation in a democratic society requires affirmative consent by all, in the form of voting, it is most usefully appealed to when the social obligation is also one which most individuals in the society believe to be personal as well.

6. For public policy purposes, obligation used in advocacy is most effective when it is enforceable as in the case of justice. By definition such obligations are limited, and need to be differentiated from ideas of personal charity where the range of obligation is wider but also not enforceable.

It remains a future task to translate such bounding terms into practical social programs and policies.

In earlier times philosophers sought to deal with very similar questions, but they usually did so in societies where hierarchy, class relationships and an ordered ranking of status were either accepted as inevitable in nature or were imposed by force. Such order provided a framework within which the obligations which men owed each other could be fairly simply thought out. Then comprehensive philosophies were developed within accepted conventions about the social order. In today's world, this orderliness has been diminished. Conquest of some of the material limitations; relative growth in material goods for most, though not all, citizens of a nation; conviction about individual rights and individualism as a way of life all add up to an open world with many frontiers, many opportunities and many expectations. A new framework for altruism and obligation needs to be devised. Lacking that, old ones can be re-examined to see if they can still be made to serve. Moral or philosophical dialogue may seem as technical in its attempt to re-examine moral relationships as the physical and economic world has become technical and fragmented, but some semantic clarification has been achieved. At first glance the achievements may seem fragmented and partial and lacking a powerful synthesis. There are few powerfully appealing moral arguments which mobilize whole societies in any one direction. Many of the details seem to emphasize what cannot be done, not what should be done. But this is a part of the task to be completed before we will be ready for the next generation of thinking about welfare. Supporters of social welfare have to contribute to this hard logical thinking out in ways which will move the deepest impulses of ordinary citizens and also engage the attention of pragmatic policymakers.

13

A WELFARE AGENDA FOR THE END OF THE CENTURY
Recasting the Future on Foundations of the Past

The central tenets or premises of the welfare state, on which many national social programs are based, lie midway between those of an unrestrained free market of capitalism and a planned society controlled by government in all important respects. These principles or premises are the foundation for collective efforts in America to humanize the social and economic relationships among all members of the society without subjecting all to collective decision making. Put another way, they are efforts to balance personal freedom and collective obligation.

The pattern of this "middle way" changes as economic, cultural and social trends shift. For the U.S., the twentieth century brought a rapid succession of trend shifts which make it difficult to identify the solid foundations on which public support for social welfare programs can be maintained. The economic condition of most citizens improved in absolute and relative terms; social programs slowly became more extensive, universal and costly; and after a period when welfare helped redistribute national income, these effects were reversed.

In such times, it is easy to call for a new articulation of public or governmental responsibility for social needs; or to restate old principles for a welfare state in the hope that, by reiteration, those principles will reassert their power as an intellectual guide for social development. But, a successful effort is much more demanding. Much of the unease in arguments about welfare derives from the tendency for advocates to press for action toward the extremes of much more or much less government responsibility without having agreed upon a central foundation of public opinion about public obligation. In other words, there has not been articulated a value base about government social obligation which enjoys such wide support that all parties must use it as the starting point for future evolution of the welfare state idea (Freeman, 1983).

The challenge of the immediate future is to establish the core foundations and the basic programs for social responsibility on a more firm basis. This requires that advocates differentiate between what is essential as a foundation for governmental obligation, and what is desirable but not essential. The criteria for essentiality are not easily fixed and it is this to which believers in government responsibility must address their efforts—they need to agree among themselves on this essential base. Without such consensus, advocates are likely to dissipate their efforts by arguing among themselves more than they argue with the opponents of welfare.

There is common belief held by nonprofessional advocates of a political agenda that vigorous presentation of any set of ideas can lead a people and thus determine the choices of any governing system. Without demeaning the power of ideas, it is worth considering that ideas flourish best when there is an environment ready to receive them. The great men or great ideas interpretation of history is balanced by the equally persuasive interpretation that leaders lead because they sense and express the inchoate wishes and beliefs of faceless citizens. If this interpretation has validity, it may also explain the support which sustained the 1975–1984 efforts to radically revise American social welfare policy. Action to reverse the fifty-year growth in national governmental responsibility for social difficulties may be rooted in public beliefs rather than being an aberrant political episode.

The proposed agenda for social welfare seeks to combine these two interpretations, but it relies mainly on a conviction that, in the short run, that agenda is most likely to succeed which is rooted in the contemporary beliefs and perceptions of a majority of citizens.

The Function of Values, Traditions and Ethics

Some ambiguous but nonetheless potent forces join the recognizable realities of new social and economic pressures to shape the essential core for public responsibility. Given the traditions of the past, it is difficult to long ignore an ethical or value dimension which has to be incorporated in economic and political decisions. The tendency to self-realization and selfishness noted in Chapters 3 and 12 is a strong, but not exclusive, motivating force of the times. But, to reduce the destructive effects of self-centeredness requires some reaffirmation of ethical or moral obligations which individuals have to each other and to the social institutions which they create to express those obligations. The period of the 1980s is one in which those institutions are more denigrated than they have been for several generations.

However, it is not possible to assert with much confidence that any one of single ethical expression is the correct or preferred one. An ethical guide may precede the welfare program but an ethical base has to be restated. For the immediate future, it is important to seek some agreement about whether the inherited traditions of caring for some dependent others are to be expanded at all, and, if so, how far. For example, can the future build a deep conviction that the able-bodied adults without work opportunity are *entitled* to as secure social protection as the traditionally dependent classes? Or, do we want to assert that all people are entitled to care and help regardless of what they do, or fail to do, to "deserve" it? Or, must they deserve charity? Or, do we want to embrace an ethical doctrine of equality in condition for all people regardless of their contribution to the collective society? All of these views have been advanced historically, and today. But, a practical agenda for the future calls for some coalescing of opinion around one or the other.

Fairness of Reciprocity

In practical terms, a claim for ethical justice needs to be attached to practical economic and political steps for its realization. The traditions of helping others which still persist carry with them ideas about helplessness (e.g., children, aged and sick)—about which reciprocity and fairness were self-evident in small societies. Widows once considered helpless have been replaced by unwed mothers considered able to work. A modern view which uses a term like *fairness* is hard to operationalize in mass society where helper and helped seldom know each other, but fairness is still associated with beliefs about reciprocity, as it was historically. The future form of welfare can be enlarged, over the present, if it is rooted in these twin convictions: that people in organized societies not only need each other and depend on each other, but each needs to contribute to the general well-being within his or her capability. Both terms—*fairness* and *reciprocity*—are ambiguous, but advocates will need to settle the ambiguity for practical purposes by agreeing with each other about some definition. Reciprocity can mean work as hard as you can, or it can mean doing the best of which you are capable, or it can mean behaving in collectively sanctioned and approved ways. At one time, behaving well meant being grateful for charity; today, it may mean doing something useful to some others but not necessarily work at wages, or it can mean deserved reward for effort or behavior.

These slippery ideas are introduced because they seem inextricably tied to the more practical actions which have to be taken to reestablish and define the future direction for social programs in the U.S. There will be practical conflicts over economic distribution and there will be struggles for power and dominance among various group interests—conflicts which will engage most of our organized efforts. Success for those who believe in social obligation may well depend on their ability to also articulate ideas about fairness and reciprocity which build on the tradition of the past, which go beyond them, but not so far beyond that the support of average citizens is lost. The question to be agonized over is how to formulate positions on which most advocates can agree.

Dependency as Practical Ethics

A practical issue, debate over which can enlarge our ethical views about responsibility, is that of dependency. The view which citizens take about independence and dependence through life may replace the recent concern over poverty, or a change in their views about dependence may be a necessary prelude to a renewed attack on poverty. Small children are necessarily dependent on adults although the American culture of independent striving and personal achievement seems to be pushing independence of children into earlier and earlier years. But, as children enter adult life, the emphasis is almost entirely upon independent self-sufficiency and achievement. Then, to be dependent on others, except in some abstract economic transaction sense, is not only frowned upon but is considered demeaning. Social programs of the welfare state address unavoidable dependencies which arise in raising children, feeble old age, and illness. It is no accident that programs for the elderly occupy a central place in welfare: the state of growing old has long been accepted as a part of life processes, not because of personal inadequacy. If life begins with dependence on parents, old age can mean some growing dependence on family or on society, acceptable because inevitable. But, American culture has always taken an ambiguous stance regarding other dependency; little place has been left in daily affairs for most other dependents. Pity is left for them, but not full citizenship or full regard. Dependency is not viewed as a natural part of living, but as some aberration to be cured or shelved. Dependency is usually something to be "treated" as a disease, with optimistic faith in modern technology or science to achieve success. A youth-oriented, activist society tries to make some room for the inevitably dependent, but the effort is not wholehearted and results in more contradictions.

Dependency has another dimension: the authority of professionals and bureaucracy over individuals. Professional care, on which all depend at some time, gives control over decisions affecting life to professionals. Those who are economically and physically dependent on others lack the freedom to change caregivers, so they are even more dependent than most on decisions made by a bureaucracy, as well as by professionals. Medical care is the best example, but most services for the dependent are governed by decisions made by caretakers over the lives of those to be cared for, another example of the way in which dependency becomes demeaning in an activist society. How dependent should service users be on professionals? How much decision making can providers allow their clients?

Such moral dimensions of the problem involve open awareness of the inevitable hazards of birth, growing up and growing old. But, this awareness is not much debated at any level which will locate a respectable place for the dependent in the life of the society. Instead, the activist and competitive pressures of the times rely on the competition of interests and the pragmatic adoption of short-term solutions to long-standing social problems. The results have been generous in fiscal terms, but less generous in human relationship terms. Reduced to its most elementary level, the competitive character of American economic and social life produces change and material gain, but also leaves in limbo those who lose in the competition. Little attention is given to the central characteristic of a wholly, unrelieved, competitive society—for each winner there must be a loser. This reality is masked by doctrines of economic growth which point to increased productivity and wealth which *should* take care of losers. But, in the short run—and life itself is brief—the adjustment does not take place quickly enough for individual human beings. The national commitment to individual freedom, competitiveness and growth is not congenial to discussion about collective obligations to dependents; and government action continues to satisfy the needs of the independent better than those of dependents.

The recasting of a viable platform for governmental and collective responsibility for welfare will depend on how the electorate chooses to define the relationships between the dependent and the independent—a relationship which gives a respectable place for dependency, or for some cases of dependency at least, or a place of ignominy. Recent use of the phrase "the truly needy" begins the discussion, but the phrase itself is full of condescension, as if the condition of being needy is some residual aberration of some human beings rather than a condition for which place has to be given.

If we are to approach such matters intelligently, we need a constant reminder that most, but not all, of the dilemmas of dependency are of our own making. The number of young single mothers is a product of our open, freer culture with its constantly rising level of individual expectations. The same rise in expectations, a basic part of our culture, helps us understand why some low paying, insecure, despised service jobs are hard to fill with native labor and are filled by new immigrants whom our beliefs about freedom encourage to come. Some of minority youth employment is traceable to persisting racial prejudices. And the new class of able-bodied retired is a product of our new science. Altogether they present us with unprecedented problems which we seek to resolve within our historic values of freedom, concern for others and openness.

ELEMENTS FOR AN AGENDA

The challenges already noted suggest an agenda for the last fifth of the twentieth century which might establish basic government responsibility more firmly in terms acceptable to the citizens of the nation. It consists of four parts:

1. Agreeing to agree among advocates of any governmental responsibility;
2. selecting a basic core of government responsibility: Work and Income, plus a national health system;
3. redesigning social programs before expansion; and
4. creating an institutional capability for analysis, research and development (or diffusion).

A forward looking strategy involves a choice between at least two alternatives. We, that is, social or citizen activists, can limit our efforts to the very poorest and join a minority element in public thinking, in effect joining some party of the further left, hoping to change public attitudes, or awaiting some major economic catastrophe which will convert this minority into a majority. The alternative is to develop a program for the deprived which is consonant with the current attitudes of a large majority of citizens. The first of these suggests a very long-range outlook without much influence on current policy developments during the next decade. The second has the potential to influence current policy choices. The second works within the framework of cultural institutions and seeks to modify them. The first awaits a major transformation of social and political institutions. The following analysis is based on the second alternative.

Agenda 1: Agreeing to Agree

A new consensus among advocates may seem obvious, but it is also the most difficult to realize. The unresolved questions embedded in the current retreat from government welfare make it doubtful if any simple, direct, or quick resolution will be found without an extensive discussion and debate among advocates themselves, even more important than the debate between antagonists and supporters. Some welfare proposals have dealt with special categories of dependencies, the advocates for which are competing with others for some share of a welfare resource pie (the retarded versus the mentally ill, or children versus aged). The next period needs a consolidation of forces around a limited platform. It is not a time to advance many platforms, each claiming the loyalty of a small population, but no single one sufficiently broad in appeal or deep enough in its potential for future evolution to command widespread support. The period is one for exploration of new forms and new ideological centers for broad coalition around a core program. It may be frustrating but necessary to begin with some restatement of basic principles before the practical details of a political program are put into motion, but to begin with the details, lacking a wide enough base in principle or concept guarantees continuation of the present uncertainty.

A new consensus will be strongest if built on a few criteria. For one, the goals should reflect the beliefs of a majority of ordinary citizen-voters as much as they capture the wishes of active advocates. If they go beyond present acceptability, the added goals need to be sufficiently close to the beliefs of most citizens to be capable of acceptance. A basic and incremental program will inevitably have to start with the inherited views about public obligation and add on the new requirements of twentieth century society where they are most congruent with old beliefs.

A base from which to approach consensus might be found in the present Social Security system. It may require adjustments over time, but its basic integrity, a few basic principles, should be preserved at all costs. These include the non-means testing basis for benefits, the use of payroll, pay as you go, taxes, and coverage of the entire population for whatever benefits are authorized. An unstated corollary of such premises is that the benefit structure be contained by whatever level can be actuarially justified within the level of premiums or payroll taxes as authorized by a political process. Such premises have a firm foundation in public thought. If they are abandoned in search of a more generous or more redistributive system, then it is widely accepted that an anchor for public support is lost. This is not to suggest that other more redistributive programs are not necessary, only that they should grow out of and not in place of the present system of social security.

Securing a primary consensus will be exceptionally difficult, calling for statesmanship as well as leadership. The present fragmented character of organization among supporters of public responsibility for social well-being will be especially troublesome. Most of those who work in and for social welfare and who have even rudimentary organizations to work with are devoted to an array of specialized social services each with a narrow constituency. It is asking much that they turn away from their present primary interest in securing federal funding for rehabilitation, mental illness, etc., as the foundation for their specialized efforts and redirect their energies to the other more general issues such as work and income to which they have given lip service but not wholehearted effort.

This is a hard decision for the involved organizations to take for it violates a long-standing tradition of floating coalitions in which numerous supporting organizations nominally join forces behind one issue but in reality continue their major efforts along individual sectional lines at the same time. As a result, least effort goes toward a major objective, although the nominal listing of many organizations gives a spurious impression of major effort. The crucial dilemma is how to assure that the scant resources which such organizations have can be concentrated for a time upon a few issues—when their diverse memberships may not consider the selected priority issues to be theirs.

Much political coalition activity involves organizations which maintain their separate agendas and activities and allocate a minor fraction of their resources to the coalition effort. What is proposed here is a reversal of that procedure in order to increase the chances for success on one or two significant fronts at a time.

The effort to create a new consensus might succeed if it can capture the enthusiasm and energy of the numerous specialized groupings which now coexist. That enthusiasm can be generated if it becomes clear to all that the consensus embodies the best of past tradition and the demands of the twentieth century. What is at stake is the evolution in welfare thinking from a basically charitable foundation of the past to a universal right foundation for the future. The charitable foundation was one of concern for the clearly helpless and dependent. The universal right future is based on confidence that most disadvantaged people (not all) can manage their affairs reasonably well if they have reasonable means with which to live. The universal right future is not based on any belief that each and every human need gives its victim an absolute right to have the need taken care of by specialized care and service efforts financed and defined by government. But, a *few* universal rights are the basis for future evolution in welfare.

The next section outlines the case for work and income as the base for a universal rights based government obligation, but for Agenda 1, the task is for advocates to agree upon *any* course of action most likely to generate widest support for the most widely reaching programs.

In making a choice about strategy, advocates will need to weight most seriously the equation between ends and means, or aims and resources. It is at this level of strategy assessment that advocates need to be most hardheaded, and least emotional or self-deceiving about their strengths.

A number of myths about welfare strategy will need to be re-evaluated in the course of any serious new consensus and coalition building:

1. That the voting public is responsive to an open-ended and indefinitely expanding role for national government in welfare. A close analysis of opinion polls (Chapter 11) indicates how risky it would be to assume that because respondents to opinion polls seem to support many specialized activities that this translates into comparable support for indefinite growth in public responsibility. Public support is not a zero sum game, but neither is it infinitely expandable. There are limits to both economic growth and to public willingness to tax itself. Judgment is necessary about the best foundation for available public support. The assertion by advocates that *some* need exists does not inevitably translate into governmental support.

2. That there are available sufficient tax funds for all wants, if only funds were redirected, say from military to welfare purposes. Of course, redirection of tax funds would ease the welfare difficulties of the 1980s, but it is not only untrue that public dollars are part of a zero sum budget but neither are they fully fungible. Medical or military dollars are not automatically transferable to welfare. In simpler terms, the amount of tax dollars which an electorate will make available for welfare can be changed, either up or down, but the voter decision about how much to be taxed for welfare will be determined by the collective beliefs about welfare which voters hold, not by their readiness to give up one public good for another, when each is highly valued by a large part of the electorate. As outlined in Chapters 4–11, the beliefs about welfare are, as of today, less open-ended then advocates have believed to be the case. For such reasons, advocates, in reaching consensus will need to weigh what is empirically known about voter support, rather than making assumptions about support based on the wishes or wants of the advocates.

3. That past coalition building strategies for welfare will suffice in the future. In the past, the means and resources of advocacy groups have generally been not only modest, but minuscule when related to the large ends which have been sought. Modest resources have not been linked or leveraged to either larger financial or manpower resources, or to large citizen membership organizations. The final outcome of coalition agreement and consensus building will be most satisfying when it is based on a realistic matching of aims or purposes with resources mobilized for their realization. As will be argued next, the income and work focus seems to offer better opportunity to achieve

large aims with linkage to larger resources and support than any of the other alternatives.

Agenda 2—Choosing a Core—Work or Income Plus National Health

The first task for a consensus-seeking coalition is to find agreement on what constitutes a minimum but significant core for national social responsibility. There will be many candidates. It is here suggested that the core consist of national responsibility for work and income plus a national health system ahead of anything else.

In choosing what core program to support, questions of principle and metapolicy need to be settled. Once that task is completed, a few key technical issues become paramount, which are worth noting here. A key technical issue, once policy is adopted, is whether to design programs based on earnings or on insurance principles. Each has advantages and drawbacks and, since no ideal solution is evident, awkward technical decisions will have to be made. The choices are quite different from those proposed by the Reagan administration between 1980 and 1984, which argued for direct public investment in economic development rather than welfare as a path to economic strength via human development. Insurance- and earnings-related programs result in differences in provision among population groups; neither is egalitarian unless one uses the phrase "social" insurance to mean programs which are based on resource redistribution and not on actuarial principles of economic insurance measures. They also differ in the effect on employment practices and in the degree of consumer choice. While such matters lie outside the scope of this work they will continue to be the object of serious technical and political debate while new national policies are being reshaped.

Work at fair wages or some universal income security program for all citizens have been an accepted foundation for thinking about social welfare for a long time. Only upon some such foundation has it been possible to advance other social programs like health care, home help for the severely disabled, child day care and so on, all of which are premised on a belief in the autonomy of society's most vulnerable as well as for the able-bodied. Unfortunately, America's system for income maintenance is poorly understood, complex to administer, and insecurely rooted in public acceptance (with the possible exception of retirement provision). This uncertainty is compounded by the emergence of a body of adult able-bodied workers for whom work is not steadily available as a result of the major structural changes in the economy which continue to take place and which produce discontinuities between labor force demand and supply. These persist for long transitional periods of time, making the promise of work and economic growth in the distant future unsatisfactory.

Both work and income have received attention by government in recent decades but satisfactory results have not yet been achieved. Work, the preferred end for most citizens, eludes many, and income provision is uncertain. The extent of government responsibility for both is still contested, and advocates have not agreed on which approach, among many proposed, offers the best prospect for effective policy. Until agreement is reached on work and income obligation of government, the entire concept of government obligation for the vulnerable wavers between the charitable and the punitive. The needy are stigmatized as either helpless and incompetent, or as needing the prod of hunger to look after themselves. The search for better policy has also been obscured by the rhetoric of debate which makes it seem as if supporters of welfare want equal income shares for all, whereas the argument is really about reducing or increasing, not abolishing, the gap between incomes of those who have and those who do not.

The practical reasons for the salience of this issue are not limited to any abstract conviction about the saving virtues of work as a religious imperative. In the American tradition, the independence which comes from having earned one's means of livelihood is most valued. Whether sensible or not, this does represent what the electorate uses first as its criterion of full membership in society. It is the touchstone of reciprocity and fairness. This view was not only historically determined, when men and women over the millennia had no alternative to labor. People are also most free, most autonomous, when they are not dependent on someone else for choices and decisions which govern the lives of each. And, that independence comes first when each individual earns the means to acquire necessities or luxuries to choose what and where and how to use them. When the means are provided gratuitously by others, even at the distance which modern welfare places between giver and beneficiary, the recipient is never wholly free or self-confident. It is also arguable that such a "dependent" individual also has his or her own self-respect and self-confidence diminished and eroded. The issue is not only one for the individual. The foundations of a democratic society rest upon assumptions that citizens are autonomous actors in society. Unfortunately, the conditions for autonomy in modern society are not automatically self-realizing.

Others may argue that autonomy and self-respect are not dependent on earning or on work, and that such ideas are old fashioned, but it is hard to deny the force of reciprocity. A recipient of income from another is likely to feel more equal if some return is given to the giver, if not in work then in some other form of service or gift, or contribution to the social well-being. Work and earning can have different forms, but their basic relationship remains. Such concepts of reciprocity were first articulated in ancient Greece where poets, artists and dramatists were seen as valued contributors to society; although they were not considered to be "at work," they "earned" their respect. For such reasons, relief, or guaranteed welfare, is not a substitute for income earned by some socially valued activity and the resulting sense of achievement. This view is supported by the eagerness with which relief recipients seek work when opportunities are realistically available. It is also supported by the reactions of relief recipients about the degradation they feel as relief recipients.

In a narrower sense, many of the nonfinancial social problems which the public wants attended to and which social agencies seek to alleviate can only be adequately dealt with if socially, mentally or physically troubled persons have economic security and opportunity to lead independent lives. Treating physical or mental disability or emotional distress when the individual is suffering from unrelieved economic insecurity or deprivation is usually a losing effort (Bremner, 1956).

The evidence about a close association among socially useful activity, economic status and social psychological illness is not definitive, but is widespread and suggestive that valued work has therapeutic value in itself. During World War II, hundreds of thousands of adults who were previously out of work were suddenly in demand as youth were drafted into military service. Not only did the volume of dependency decline, but the salience of many sociopsychological problems began to recede or were redefined. Other studies reveal that the rate of mental hospital admissions and the demand for mental health services rises during economic depressions and recedes during booming economic periods (Bremner, 1956). This is not to argue that social problems are only economic in origin, but to note that some part of many sociopsychological difficulties are either diminished in intensity, or are shaped by lack of opportunity to fit into the dominant culture of the times which values work as a vital part of group citizenship.

The salience of work is also seen in the success of efforts to develop work opportunities for the retarded, the physically and mentally disabled, and the elderly, an outcome desired by the disabled themselves.

This foundation of work as a basis for social policy is weakened by blind spots in public thinking. One is how to value motherhood and family. The blind spot is most evident in the reactions to single parents with small children who are economically dependent on others. The public seems to simultaneously want them to be out working so they will not have to depend on welfare payments, and also to be at home to "earn" respect as nurturing parents. If work is assured for all, should single parents of small children have to "earn" their support by work outside the home, or can their "work" within the home be considered of such social importance that it satisfies the desire for reciprocity necessary to justify support by others? In many ways these parents could be viewed the same as other able-bodied adults unable to find work, if a reasonable income program supplements a work program.

Another blind spot is the attitude about human nature and the willingness to work. It is assumed by some that the poor will work only if forced by hunger. The evidence is overwhelmingly in the other direction when every announcement of work brings out a flood of applicants. But, the best test for this view would be a wider availability of work at reasonable income.

Some critics of social intervention argue that social benefits only keep the poor from working (Murray, 1984), and that withdrawing benefits will be a sharp incentive for the dependent able-bodied to find work, or to work harder. A contrary view is supported by substantial economic analysis. Lampman (1984, pp. 141–144) found that at best there may be an aggregate reduction in hours worked by those in the labor pool of about 6 percent. A large part of the reduction is offset by investment in health and education which increases productivity in the long run as well as improves the quality of life for all. The reduction is also offset by a widespread natural human tendency to reduce working hours slightly as income rises in order to enjoy a higher standard of life.

Approaches to Work and to Income Assurance: Dilemmas of Past Programs

If the salience of work-derived income is accepted, the question remains of what to do and how to proceed? The last decades have witnessed numerous governmental efforts, so what should or can be done differently? Or, do we only need more of what we have tried? Advocates are not yet agreed about the answer.

Public Service Employment. Numerous federal and state initiatives have been undertaken since the pioneer works programs of the 1930s. These programs employed a total of 15,582,000 workers between 1932 and 1942, mainly on public investment projects such as construction of highways, public buildings, water and sewer facilities and recreational facilities. In 1941, they accounted for 36 percent of the nonself-employed workforce, and cost about half of the defense expenditure for 1942 (Kesselman, 1978).

In 1971, an Emergency Employment Act was passed to: improve work chances for groups such as Vietnam veterans and older workers; to reduce barriers to work in private and civil service workplaces; to seek transfer of one-half of these workers to regular and permanent public or private sector jobs. About 185,000 workers were hired at the program peak, or about one in twenty-five of the unemployed. Fifty-four percent of the people hired secured more permanent work and 26 percent were not employed after the end of the project.

Other efforts were generated under Title X of the Public Works and Economic Development Act. A 1974 Job Opportunities program was authorized under this Title which employed over 100,000 persons at an average cost of $13,881 per person per year (Evans, 1984).

The major approaches now available are: government stimulation of employment in the private sector; subsidy of special work efforts by private employers; public service employment; training and relocation; and work for welfare recipients only (Joint Economic Committee, 1974).

Experience with such programs has highlighted the limitations of each approach as much as it has revealed the controversies among various interest groups.

Job Subsidy and Job Creation Programs. Such programs are costly ($10,000 to $25,000 for each job); and less than half of the jobs represent new job creation. Although used in England, Japan and West Germany, as well as in the U.S., they may displace other employees whose wage is not partly subsidized; they can lead to reducing wage levels; the turnover of workers is high and, therefore, inefficient, increasing the costs of producing goods; they may become inflationary if pursued on a large scale; and, become very costly if made large enough to perceptibly reduce unemployment levels (Garfinkle, 1978; Department of Labor, 1979; CBO, 1982).

In Japan and Western Europe, between 60 and 85 percent of subsidized jobs involve displacement, not additional jobs. In the U.S. such displacement has ranged between 15 and 65 percent (Haveman, 1982). Attempts to target programs to those who have no work or cannot find work on their own have not been especially successful to date and have been administratively costly.

The sum of past experience is large, but does not satisfactorily answer the objections of poor targeting, cost, effectiveness. For example, the 1972 Public Service Employment program reduced total unemployment by only 0.2 percent. There are great difficulties in deciding how to target public employment programs. Shall they be only for workers displaced from dying industries? Or, for those who had worked in such industries ten years or more? Or, for youthful new job seekers? Not every displaced worker will be long out of a job; many quickly find work themselves. Is it really useful to subsidize public jobs when some proportion of workers soon find jobs in the private sector? How to discriminate between these and others who fail to find new work? (Borus, 1980).

There are also substantial budgetary costs involved. One estimate (Ball, 1981) estimates that one billion dollars in public works construction would support 24,000 jobs, one-half directly in construction and the rest in related work. But, in 1984, several million people were out of work. To offset this, the Department of Labor has estimated that as many as three million jobs, one-half for low-skill workers, can be created by a public service employment program.

Training and retraining is a popular approach, and one premised on the assumption that, once trained, jobs are there for the filling by trainees. If we omit vocational training for youth as part of basic education, and consider retraining for youth not in school and for adults displaced from former jobs, then both government and industry have tried various approaches. A few large corporations undergoing technological transformation have undertaken to retrain at least part of the labor force for new tasks. Others have offered to move workers and their families to new plants in new parts of the country. Such efforts do not characterize most industries, and are limited to those few which are large in scale, strongly organized by a trade union, use scarce skilled workers, or are financially secure enough to absorb the costs.

Publicly supported retraining programs are a basic part of the Department of Labor's mandate. The results of these programs are mixed. They do retrain workers and some do find new jobs. However, some studies have noted that many more workers who would be eligible for such training seem to find work on their own, often more rapidly and at better pay than those who opt to take time out for retraining (Borus, 1980). As with public service employment, the question of targeting such programs is serious, for the answer determines whether public funds are used to retrain workers unnecessarily, or whether they are used only for a minority of workers who cannot make the transition between jobs on their own. A variation on conventional retraining methods is suggested by "individual training accounts." These could be set up in any industry and paid into by both employer and employee. In case of unemployment the fund can be drawn on by the employee to learn new skills and to pay for relocation to a new area. It is limited in that it would reach only workers in larger, better organized industries and would work only if alternative work were available in a reasonable time (Hormats, 1984). If unused, the account reverts to the employees' retirement account.

Basic Vocational Training Programs. These programs are a part of the Department of Labor and Department of Education mandate to attend to the needs of the economy. Major training programs include: Vocational Education, Manpower Development and Training legislation. They have had some impact, but have not dealt with the lack of work opportunity which still exists. They have usually been narrow in focus, concerned with work in a locality, short term in nature, dealing with the lowest work levels, assuming a strong labor demand. They often fail to meet the requirements for continuous technical learning in a scientifically changing economy; for a national framework where work opportunity moves fluidly around the country.

Youth programs for either work or training have been tried intermittently since the Civilian Conservation Corp (CCC) and the National

Youth Administration (NYA) of the 1930s. These were not much in evidence between World War II and the 1970s, but later numerous programs were tried: Youth Conservation Corps, Neighborhood Youth Corps, Youth Employment and Demonstration Projects. While all of them had a training component, analysis of results suggest that lack of job opportunity was as much or more a criterion than training itself (Sherraden, 1980; Ginzberg, 1979).

Recent analyses indicate that in a period when the economy is improving, as in the early 1980s, a well-designed training and job placement program may be more effective than public employment programs. In part this is explained by the fact that the next decade is expected to be one with a relatively smaller cohort of youth entering the labor market, thus creating a situation with less "overcrowding" of the workplace. Poor and minority teenagers can be expected to benefit if aided by better education, better focused training, and job placement activities (Rivlin, 1984; Gueron, 1984).

Much the same conclusion can be drawn for young mothers who wish to work provided their children are cared for; and for the able-bodied elderly who wish to remain economically active. For the latter, new forms for economic and social activity can be considered and are being tested in small-scale demonstrations: cooperatives, mutual aid, reduced work and pay schemes as workers near retirement, reducing work time but stretching work life in the later years, and many others (Cahn, 1984; Morris, 1985).

Welfare Work

A number of efforts have been made to prepare welfare recipients for early work. Given that most recipients, other than those receiving Aid for Dependent Children, are disabled or aged, such programs have concentrated on single parent families where the parent is a woman with small children and no mate or spouse to share income production. Various approaches have been tried, such as work incentives and Work-Fare (required work for welfare). Some have been punitive, requiring relief recipients to work hours necessary to make up for their relief payments. Some variations have been declared unconstitutional although voluntary work for relief programs have been upheld. More sophisticated efforts have combined several elements: an able-bodied relief recipient must apply for work, he or she is evaluated and either must, or is encouraged to, enter into some work training program. Training can be a combination of on-the-job experience and education. Such programs seek to locate jobs or to facilitate job location by relief recipients. They have not been notably successful thus far (Sanger, 1984; Department of Labor, 1978). However, those which are based on voluntary participation with training work best in giving gratifying experience to many people which may in time lead to work (Ford Foundation letter, 1984). Most of the jobs thus provided have been low skill at low wage, and incentives have been inadequate, compounded by poor administration.

There remain critical ethical questions about pressure to force young mothers to work when there are small children at home, especially when day care services are not readily available. There are also serious obstacles in that work may be temporary, during which relief security is lost, and regained with so much delay and difficulty that the real income position of recipients is worse than before. Also, even steady work at low wages often leads to a loss of such benefits as food stamps, medical care, and housing supplements, so that the net position is worsened. To offset this, many young people find the job experience one which truly makes them more confident in going out to find work, when there is work to be had (Sanger, 1984; Ford, 1984).

On balance, one must conclude that the national government and private industry have tried to tackle the problems of unemployment, during periods of high and low employment. The efforts have not been adequate for the task in a shifting economy but they provide an experience base out of which more effective programs might be shaped if the obligation to act by government is secured. Advocates will want to concentrate rather than disperse their efforts to find a preferred solution to the work option (Bluestone, 1984).

The Income Alternative

Even if work for all is assured, some groups will still lack income. Their needs have been met in one way or another through all of recorded history, and the present is no exception. In fact, present programs have enlarged the definitions of need beyond the traditional sick and aged to include some of the able-bodied. The core agenda for the future calls for ways to restructure and redesign income programs for these groups.

Income security involves attention to five overlapping and not clearly separable groups: the able-bodied unemployed in the workforce, those never in the workforce, those with severe handicap or illness which removes them at least temporarily from the workforce, the retired with low benefits due to low lifetime earnings, and the retired with other sources of income. These groups are differentiated by different legal statuses regarding their entitlements. Some have paid into contributory insurance funds (the regularly employed temporarily out of work, the retired); others have earned benefits without cash contributions to a fund (veterans); others have never had an opportunity to acquire legal entitlement through contribution or service (the severely handicapped, and those who never worked because of lack of opportunity or will or ability). Each group is treated differently in present arrangements, producing an impenetrable maze of rules and regulations and eligibilities. The intent of the complex varieties is to treat each group according to a different conception of entitlement or desert, but the criteria for deservedness are ambiguous and often unfair.

The nation has dealt with the problem through several categorical programs: AFDC, SSI, Workmen's Compensation, Veterans' Benefits, Food Stamps. Each of these is intended to meet the needs of different populations and each involves complex administrative and monitoring procedures, large staffs, hard to rationalize eligibility procedures and widely differing standards. They have proven costly in administration and unsatisfactory as to results. If we except veterans and the work injury program, the two main elements of income support lie in AFDC for the able-bodied and SSI for those presumed to be permanently out of the labor force. The first is full of inequity in treatment among the different states and heavily stigmatizing. The latter is somewhat more generous and treats all alike anywhere in the country.

In recent years, advocates have pressed for enlarging public responsibility in new areas and for increasing expenditures in each category in order to reduce the gaps which separate the poor from the better-off—a major redistribution of national income. This objective has been obscured by some of the argument which leads opponents to suspect that advocates seek an equalization of incomes, not just a reduction in the gap. A standard is still lacking about the basic income entitlement which is so related to earned income that wide acceptance is possible. The level to which the well-to-do think the poor are entitled as a matter of right remains to be identified.

The most vexing design problem involves the provision of basic income for the able-bodied, usually through AFDC or local General Relief, unable to find work even after the work programs are introduced. It has eluded resolution for many reasons: how to give security without major income redistribution between working and nonworking populations; how to void the "poverty (or welfare) trap" in the transition between income provision and earned income; and, what support level is consensually acceptable. If the level of guaranteed income support for the unemployed is high, then very large numbers of fully employed workers become eligible for supplementation of earnings and since their numbers exceed those of the unemployed, costs escalate so high that irresistible opposition is activated. And, if benefits are cut off when very low wages are earned (say at a bare subsistence rather than at an economy level), then the poor are worse-off when working, thus, other opposition arises so that no consensus has been reached. The last major effort at welfare reform was attempted by the Nixon administration, when a version of a negative income tax was proposed. It failed in part because supporters of the idea were divided over the level of income to be assured.

A major obstacle to solving this problem lies in deeply rooted views about reciprocity, the balance between rights and obligations. On one hand there are clearly identified groups without income through no fault of their own. On the other hand there are less well-defined groups which resist work that is low in pay, status or security. The attitude about the latter is often used to resist any income support programs, without recognizing that our culture is pervaded by education and belief that individuals are entitled to the best that life has to offer. Certain job categories do not fit into this national model. So we are left with the ideal, but also some belief that individuals in need do not fit into the model because they will not try. The disparity between an idealized middle class American lifestyle and economic reality of the poor is thus blurred by arguments over who has earned the right—a modern version of the old Greek view about reciprocity. The evidence is seen in the resistance of native Americans to performing such tasks as stoop farm labor, crop picking, staffing restaurants, serving as attendants in nursing homes and hospitals. Many of these jobs involve dirty and taxing labor, they are poorly and erratically paid, and are not well regarded by most citizens. They do not at all fit into the vision of life which the national ideal holds out for all citizens who work.

There are other contributing obstacles—the racial minority make-up of part of the poor population to mention one—but the major trouble lies in the variety of poor people whose needs must be addressed but whose conditions vary so much that no single simple administrative approach seems to work. There is also the fear, held by some, that a too generous income guarantee will lead many able-bodied people to leave the workforce to live in presumed comfort without work. The rather ambiguous evidence of major negative income-tax experiments conducted in the last decade do indicate that there is a slight decrease in employment rates, but most of this was accounted for by wives or single mothers who had left part-time, low paid work when family income was secured (Pechman, 1975; C. Brown, 1980; Kershaw, 1976). While the concern about labor force erosion due to relief is real, it is also paradoxical in a period when all evidence suggests a surplus of labor, not a shortage. Such labor shortages as exist are mainly in skilled work for which the unemployed are generally ill equipped.

Since there has been no "perfect" income solution yet devised, the agenda needs to open debate on second-best alternatives which can rally sufficient popular support to pass a legislature. In other words, aiming for the best need not drive out an effort to achieve the less ideal good. Such debate has to deal with persistent contradictions in the wishes of advocates. In the past, one of the ideal solutions envisaged an individual focused relief system to meet the multiple and diverse needs of all people in all possible conditions. This required large staffing, extensive bureaucratic monitoring, control, and complex management procedures. This has been rejected since 1960 as both costly and intrusive.

American ambiguity, even schizophrenia, about helping the able-bodied poor is nowhere more evident than in the maze of procedures and routines imposed by legislation and by regulation designed to control expenditure and reduce fraud. The controls are subject to annual revision because of the continuous tug-of-war between those who seek to reduce programs and those who seek to improve them. A recent well-documented case study of the consequences of this situation found that relief entitlement and eligibility for poor, part-time working mothers had to be recalculated fourteen times in thirty two months. Each change involved a minimum of two hours of form filling and checking for each case plus an unspecified amount of central computer and administrative or supervisory time. This came to about half of each staff member's total work time. In addition the recipients sustained income loss when they had to report periodically in person (no time off for that) and risked losing their jobs because of their absence (Joe, 1985). With 3.8 million AFDC recipients (of whom about 500,000 work) these administering complexities become obstacles in themselves. No acceptable resolution of this dilemma has yet been found and any to be devised will require compromises by both protagonists and antagonists.

One alternative is to fix a national minimum floor of income which all persons should be assured of receiving if in or out of work, or unable to work, i.e., a negative income tax. Low income workers would receive supplements if earnings are below the minimum. Individuals out of work could be free to supplement their guaranteed income with private part-time earnings without suffering a dollar-for-dollar loss of public income, at least until total income climbs above the economy budget level. When welfare advocates considered past efforts—the Nixon welfare reform and a negative income tax—they could not accept a rather low national floor for entitlement to start with, in exchange for a secure national system which would replace abolition of poverty or income equalization as a national objective. Opponents of welfare could not give up or trade off their opposition to supporting able-bodied adults and especially single women with small children. It is worth searching for some compromise in which conservative opponents and liberal supporters each give up something to achieve a more secure foundation for income assurance.

Another less comprehensive alternative would be to concentrate on the needs of children. A uniform children's allowance or a family allowance has long been advocated whereby a standard sum is paid *all* families with minor children, the fact of having children being sufficient justification for the program. One rationale for such allowances is that it corrects inequities which result from wage policies based on the worker not on family needs. This could replace AFDC but be awarded to all families: those with higher earnings would have this payment subject to income tax retrieval so that those paying tax would not benefit unfairly. A less palatable approach would be to pay the allowance only to poor and working poor families (with children) alike, a variation of present AFDC (Handel, 1982).

Since all of this has been proposed before, it is here suggested that the agenda requires a new strategic and tactical approach which will reassess what level of generosity can be made acceptable to enough people to ensure passage—a revised welfare reform package. A variation of the negative income tax approach has been proposed by the Institute for Fiscal Studies in England, which proposes a system of benefit credits which entitled individuals would receive in proportion to their other income: 100 percent if no income, proportionally less as other income rises or falls (Dilnot, 1984). The issue is whether universal certainty of income is worth the price of a lower level income floor to trigger government action. Such trade-offs are the core of compromise to get action in a consensual society.

If we broaden reform efforts to erase the invidious distinction between the so-called able-bodied and other traditionally "helpless" groups, then the contradictions to be addressed multiply. But, the possible results in a universal income program might be worth the difficulties.

A national income program for all—able-bodied and physically or mentally incapacitated and socially disadvantaged alike—makes a kind of appeal for simplicity. But, it does skirt the fact that such diverse groups do have different needs. Aside from that, the various interest groups, the legal history and the advantages of current protection are embodied in large federal programs such as Supplementary Security Income, AFDC, Unemployment Insurance, Veterans Benefits and Food Stamps. Can they, or should they, all be treated alike? And, if yes, at whose level of support, e.g., veterans are treated much better, in relative terms, than others. The range of unresolved issues is still formidable. Supporters of each category will have to reconcile their own differences in order to mobilize sufficient influence to overcome the opposition of those who have always been unsympathetic to social programs. Most of the conceivable remedies have already been proposed, without wide agreement, and new ones are lacking. Issues in need of resolution are:

1. Equal treatment and adequacy in benefits. Should the condition of the worse-off among citizens be slightly improved, or should their conditions be brought up to the average level of all others in society? Or, somewhere in between? And, should poor people in similar circumstances be treated alike? In other words, is the objective to be fair, by some measure not yet agreed upon, or shall it be equality? Equality in treatment of all citizens by government as to an income floor is both desirable and achievable, at least for those in comparable circumstances. But, does this extend to equality of income for those who work full time, and at what level? Or, to all who work and all who do not or cannot work? And, at what level? There has been little call for absolute equality but there has been great ambiguity in the effort to reduce income disparities.

The following suggests the disparities which have evolved in the ad hoc, specialized approach of the past, disparities which are hard to fully justify in logic or in humanity:

TABLE 13.1   Average Monthly Benefit Payments in Some Federal Maintenance Programs in 1981

Families under Aid to Families and Children	$282.00	(range $89.00 to $416.00) per month
Supplementary Security Income for Aged	146.00	
Supplementary Security Income for Disabled	229.00	
Unemployment Benefits ($107 per week)	560.00	
Miner Families, Black Lung Disease:		
Miner with family	442.00	
Widow and family	315.00	
Social Security, Retired	386.00	
Social Security, Disabled	413.00	
Social Security, Widows	349.00	

SOURCE: *Statistical Abstract of the U.S., 1984, Washington, D.C., Department of Commerce.*

Only the inherited prejudices about work, earning, race or marital status justifies the basic income differentials between aged, disabled, unemployed males and unmarried mothers. Such inequalities could be remedied by a common base income standard for all federally funded income programs. But agreement about a level which is widely acceptable is not in sight. A compromise between equal treatment and high benefit levels seems necessary.

2. Equity in treatment. Equity is not the same as adequacy or equality for it requires some measure of just desert or fairness for all, in like circumstances, the helper and the helped (see Chapter 12). For welfare, a classic example is the differential in treatment accorded AFDC family recipients in the various states where monthly income can be as low as $89 a month (plus Food Stamps) in Mississippi, or as high as $416 in California although the subsistence needs of recipients do not differ (Statistical Abstract, 1984). Reorganization to alter this situation can take the form of a federally standardized and regulated program,

much like that of Supplementary Security Income for the aged and disabled. It should be relatively easy to rally supporters to the claim that all dependent adults (and their minor children) are entitled to a minimum income and that this level should be the same everywhere. However, supporters still need to resolve several serious differences among themselves before a unified demand for reform is raised.

3. Income redistribution versus ameliorating distress is an issue which separates more radical from more moderate advocates. Each relief program involves some redistribution, but the key issue is whether an income program is intended to radically alter the income distribution pattern which results from the working of the basic economic system. Although there is a natural desire to find simple and comprehensive solutions, it is more realistic and promising to separate the two. The main function for social welfare is to press for an acceptable, decent and humane base for existence for all citizens.

This objective so stated obscures two difficulties which need to be overcome. The present stage of American public belief will not accept a welfare income base which exceeds the income which a full-time employed low income worker can earn. The issue is to find agreement about the size of the gap between the two. The welfare base cannot yet compete with the level fixed by the workplace. In like fashion, welfare is not yet acceptable as a way to raise the level of low income workers whose earned income is below the poverty level which public opinion has thus far set. This supplementation does occur in some extreme cases where welfare is sometimes used to supplement labor market income: full-time unskilled workers with large families and the seasonally employed. But, welfare is an unlikely instrument to remedy more widespread flaws in the workplace through labor rate subsidy. If the workplace pattern is unjust, economic workplace remedies seem more suitable, e.g., labor organization, minimum wage laws. Although welfare can contribute its testimony about the consequences of workplace inequity, such as poverty with full-time low wage work, it is not equipped to devise relevant economic remedies, except for the few extreme cases noted.

What welfare can do is concentrate on the most acceptable and humane program for those who are in and out of the labor market. At this level can the advocates come to some agreement about a minimum common standard of income for all citizens who lack the means to support themselves which is linked to but still can be below the level of full-time earned income?

One approach could evolve along the following lines:

1. a standard flat but low assured income base for all dependent adults, able-bodied or not;
2. a separate children's allowance for each child;

3. an aid attendance allowance for the extra personal care required by the physically and mentally disabled and provided by another adult and determined necessary by medical screening.

This has a certain logical consistency, but it also involves technical, administrative and political difficulty as does any attempt to rationalize the existing categorical system of many programs.

After considering all the difficulties which impede a meaningful redesign of income programs, a final alternative remains—to accept the categorical approach of today with all its administrative costs, complexities and inequities. It can be argued, not unreasonably, that competition among special interest groups is the best way in which Americans can raise the total level of public concern for the disadvantaged, even if at the price of high cost and inequity. If this is to be the conclusion, then it would be wise to avoid muddying the advocacy waters by also trying to wipe out differences among categories or to rationalize relationships among them in the hope of saving money through coordination.

Other Core Programs: National Health?

Once the provision of work, or income security lacking work, has been solidly established, the question arises—should other services become the natural obligation of the national government which governs so much of economic behavior? If one accepts the argument for limited federal obligation in the current phase of American maturity, the one additional subject for a national obligation may be health although other human needs, such as housing or child care might compete with it. The major gap in the American system of social obligation is a reasonable arrangement to meet the hazards of illness and disease, hazards to which all are subject; the costs of which are very high for the sick; and the solution for which relies on a powerful set of professions and economic interests upon whose participation in a solution is essential. These groups include physicians, nurses, and the drug industry. In extreme cases, inattention to serious health risks reduces individuals to poverty and dependency.

The present halfway measures taken by government—Medicare and Medicaid—have proven to be costly and unsatisfying. They introduce financial support into an otherwise unreconstructed health delivery system where choice about what is to be delivered and the pricing of that delivery is left to multiple private forces which are not competitive. That system is built around the most costly forms of medical care—hospitals— and is built around illness rather than health development. It depends on decisions made by physicians who are governed by professional plus economic motives. Despite these flaws, there is wide public acceptance of medical care as a necessity, of the drive for new technology, and of some form of insurance protection. It is only lately that the flaws in the current system have become so visible as to force public attention toward a change: extraordinary increases in the rate of expenditure; the explosion in medical technology; the neglect of health services in the community as compared to the institution; and the impenetrable complexity of present financing and insurance procedures (Starr, 1982).

Several social difficulties could be minimized if a more rationalized health system were to evolve, with better distribution of health care and more equitable financing. The threat of impoverishment and insecurity for the working and middle classes would be reduced if such a health care system could be devised at a controlled cost. The difficulties encountered by many social protection programs—for the aged, the young physically handicapped, the drug and alcohol addicted and the delinquent would be reduced if all citizens had comparable access to whatever medicine has to contribute.

A further strong argument for a universal national approach to this subject is financial. The central place which medical and health care holds in American policy and thinking has encouraged a rapid growth in public expenditures for health, a much more rapid and proportionate increase than in any other human sector service. Such costs now total about 10 percent of the gross national product and are still growing more rapidly than any other sector of the economy. This not only makes it more and more difficult to secure funds for other human needs, but it also places health and medical services in a strategic position when it comes to defining the approach to all other needs.

As the health dollar squeezes the rest of welfare financing more and more, social programs are drawn into close relationships with that medical system—care of aged, treatment of children's health, drug and alcohol addiction, mental illness, child abuse and occupational disability. Basic economic institutions, such as hospitals, nursing homes, the drug industry, and the health institutions and insurance companies, already have a major stake in the welfare sector.

Such considerations call for some resolution of the provision of health care, an issue which has been battled over politically at least since 1929. Public or professional action to establish public responsibility is more promising in the health field for it touches on the incomes and lives of all citizens, not only a deprived few; it is also an area of public interest sanctioned by the respect accorded the healing professions. There is a 60-year history of effort to draw upon. For the next few years, it should be possible for those interested in federal social responsibility to adopt a joint strategy which focuses on this issue, assigning subordinate effort to the many other less established welfare interests.

Agreement about a comprehensive national approach to health service delivery can be sought along with agreements about work and income, but compromises are necessary by advocates on a few central issues: the balance between hospital and in-community or at-home medical care; the balance of effort between cure and prevention, or between high technology support and community health; the use of insurance or general revenue financing; the extent of physician or public control in allocation decision making; limitation on medical system freedom to charge without control (i.e., fee for service, individual practice versus group or managed health care in some combination); and, some control over the speed of technological change in medical care.

If the case is accepted for health provision as a core choice for national responsibility on some universal basis, the realizing of the case also requires some painful choices among equally desirable ends which advocates need to settle. An idealized amalgam of the main desires of advocates would look like this: the scheme should make health services available to all, at a moderate cost, with free consumer choice of providers and with incentives for scientific advance and growth in the health system, and both freedom and remuneration for its professionals and staffs—without excessive gain by either personnel or institutions. Such an ideal has serious built-in contradictions. It is not too difficult to construct a plan which is universal and which sustains free choice and the provider system; but, such a system is likely to be very costly and the providers gain disproportionately fast in comparison with the rest of the population. If cost is contained, free choice is probably going to be impaired, and medical provider freedom will also be circumscribed. So, the task is to find the best compromise among these desirable ends: freedom, low cost, universality and scientific progress.

One of the aims of any widely acceptable compromise will be limitation on health system income and control over the direction and pace of growth. This can result from a system of insurance in which benefits are determined by what consumers or insurers are willing or able to pay, with inequities in access and coverage. Or, it can result from capping the total invested by government and consumers combined, leaving the system to adjust its services as it can. Access to care, and control over growth and direction will be controversial. The compromise may have to be in who makes the decisions or in how decision making is shared.

In the current national environment, hopes for a national health system patterned after the English Health Service is unrealistic, but the tempo for moving more of medical care into some form of group, prepaid practice has accelerated. Health maintenance organizations and medical care contracted between insurance companies and preferred medical care providers (to secure a discount in payments) are far advanced, as is the growth of proprietary and investor-owned-for-profit medical agencies. A universal network of health maintenance organizations may be the way of the future, but those interested in a better health care system will still need to look closely to see if the promises of such organizations will be realized, lacking a national pattern of government or of consumer standards and financing. As HMOs grow in number, they may begin to behave as private physicians and hospitals do today, in which case the problems will remain: high cost, uneven coverage, inequity in access. Mass HMOs will still be forced to make or to save money, and trim services accordingly unless some external framework for service and cost is set. Such groups can be directed by physician interests acted out collectively rather than in private offices. Such collective decisions can be in self- or in public interest.

The National Association for Public Health Policy has advanced a broad agenda consisting of these elements:

1. investment in prevention programs where changes in lifestyle can reduce illness;
2. federal financing of comprehensive health care for the entire population in place of the present programs for the poor and aged;
3. Physician payments *only* through group prepaid practices (HMOs), community health centers or independent medical practice associations; prospective payment to both public and private hospitals in lieu of cost reimbursement;
4. federal grants for capital construction;
5. differential financial incentives for health care in rural or underserved regions;
6. regional planning for education;
7. administration through health departments;
8. federal–state joint development of health care uniform standards.
(National Association for Public Health Policy, 1984)

This platform assumes that there will be an increase in federal health care expenditure.

One approach to enormously complicated relationships would be to develop the means for making the core of the health system (e.g., medical professions, institutions, drug companies) responsible and accountable for a wider range of outcomes than the narrow acute care formulae now provide for. For example, to lead the health system to link directly community health and care, primary care, long-term care (with social supports as needed), prevention, and acute hospital and medical care; and do all this within whatever funds are provided whether through insurance, government or private payments. This would tilt medical care away from the bias to use its resources for acute, crisis, in-hospital care (Sheps, 1983).

Modest steps in such a direction were being taken in 1984. The pressures to contain hospital costs is forcing some medical care out of hospitals back into the community. Some of the response takes place under proprietary auspices; in others, some hospitals have begun to broaden their responsibility to encompass out-patient, at-home, nursing home, home nursing, and long-term social support care services, as well as in-hospital treatment. In a more experimental mode, the idea of a social HMO is being tested in four sites through backing of the federal government and several foundations. In this experiment (thus far limited to the elderly), patients enroll for more comprehensive benefits than are normally pro-vided, combining hospital, nursing home, home care, and social support services, as well as preventive health and ambulatory medical care. Fi-nancing is on a capitation basis, with a fixed sum paid in advance and based on the scope of benefits contracted for in an insurance, not a welfare, model (Morris, 1976; Callahan, 1981). In a more traditional mode, several communities, among them the city of Boston, Blue Cross/Blue Shield of Massachusetts, and the State of Massachusetts are experimenting with enrollment of the poor in managed health programs operating out of neighborhood health centers.

Because of the efforts to contain medical costs, the field of health care has entered a period of much turmoil and change which can either produce a new system or create enough chaos that government will have to take leadership in creating a new approach in the next decade. The opportunity is certainly present for a coalescing of interests by compro-mise behind a new pattern for national responsibility which can differ from those proposed in the past.

Agenda 3: Redesigning Social Programs before Expansion

In practical political terms, some secondary activities will have to be carried on while primary interests are being coalesced and a new plat-form is being worked on. Many social services, other than those already discussed, could regain credibility and security if their services were re-designed. While less crucial to the future than income reform, the re-design of other social service programs could further public confidence in welfare as a basic institution. Social welfare personnel have devoted much more attention to these many less universal services, but usually on a case, not system or structural level.

A lower priority has been assigned by the author to these "other" services, but not because they are unworthy of attention. These other welfare activities address the needs of beneficiaries who are more or less helpless. A decent and humane society finds ways to help the helpless. What is at issue is how best should the American society approach *this* human need, and is national government the only or major guarantor of action? In a period when the relations between national government and all other parties to the social order—state and local government, voluntary organization, philanthropy and industry—are being reviewed, the responsibility for the miscellany of personal social services is an especially promising area for re-examination. A solidly rooted national program of income assurance provides the foundation for organizing other welfare, and that solid foundation has yet to be constructed in an effective and acceptable structure. The residual service programs also command wide popular sympathy which can be drawn upon to reconstruct the division of responsibility between government and voluntary or private action. The outcome may be a new form of social contract among the parties, including families of the stricken, or it may be more agreement about the growth of national responsibility. The outcome will be hastened if advocates give attention now to some of the troubling aspects of service organization outlined in the next section.

Those other social programs represent a small part of federal expenditure: child welfare, mental illness, developmental disability, rehabilitation, substance abuse (drugs and alcohol), family life, etc. But, they do involve a disproportionate amount of effort by professional personnel and affect the lives of many citizens. The following identifies some of the areas in which reorganization or basic improvement would be useful, but about which a sufficiently broad agreement has not yet been reached to assure major change. Public acceptance of such social programs will be more readily achieved if the technical difficulties are resolved before there is any major effort to further increase federal commitments for very specialized activities, which are not universal in their reach.

Centralization or Decentralization: Coordination and Integration of Services. Where there exist many specialized services, coordination among them becomes important as human social needs are not easily segmented. Independent service agencies resist those coordinating proposals which infringe on their freedom of action, but coordination which does not alter relationships among agencies is also meaningless. Efforts to break out of this dilemma encounter differences among social welfare advocates which are as great as the differences between them and the opponents of any government responsibility. To cite one national example, the argument for smoothing out state differences in treatment of AFDC families usually requires a uniform national income standard, which carries with it an extension of federal power. However, to reduce the federal role through decentralizing opens up the door to even greater diversity among the states in the way similar classes of people are treated. Decentralization and equity seem to oppose each other, and both are valued by advocates. It would be salutary if advocates could agree more than they do now about the advantages and disadvantages of a federally controlled program—or of centralization at any level—and then accept the price of that control. Or, alternatively, to assess the advantages and disadvantages of decentralization with its greater reliance on the states as "laboratories for experimentation." This approach brings program decisions closer to where people live, but it assures more diversity in treatment. And, it demands much more intensive supporter mobilization state by state which may strain the resources of most advocacy groups.

Decentralization of large service agencies may also need attention. Present service agencies depend for the most part on centralized control of both financing and services—whether either or both can be decentralized remains untested. Some experiences in industry seem to succeed but marketplace forces have provided an external framework for choices that are made. The major welfare markets lack such a disciplining control and clients seldom have control over their own assets in buying services. Service providers are also unfamiliar with work patterns in which their daily decisions might be affected by marketplace influences, so that bureaucratic procedures have evolved to mediate the exchange relationship between providers and consumers. Some efforts in public welfare have shown small but promising gains in this direction but the evidence is not yet available on which to base any major decentralization design (Orlans, 1982).

At the level of local organization, there is also a continuous search for better methods for coordinating the work of diverse local service programs. Unfortunately, local coordination is as elusive as decentralization. Social agencies persist, serving different populations with widely differing needs, which leads to specialization in care and fragmentation of eligibility standards for entitlement.

Marginal improvements can be sought by agency agreements over two approaches. One is the simplification of application procedures for services and standardized assessment procedures, so that applicants can know the rules of each program from which they seek help, and so that agencies can more readily accept referrals from each other. This calls for a better articulated client movement among many agencies plus a common application form so that frustrating visits and reapplications can be reduced for people in trouble. In effect, the aim should be to structure services so that each agency welcomes applicants from others rather than trying to discourage them by procedural obstacles.

The second approach is to increase the use of the case manager principle, developed recently in health agencies for long-term patients. Case managers specialize in helping applicants through the maze of agencies and procedures on the premise that if the maze cannot be simplified, professional guides through it can be provided. Case managers need not control the applicants so much as act as specialists to size up what combination of agencies might possibly help an applicant with his or her presenting problem and then help the applicant negotiate the maze. This approach has worked but is administratively costly. In reality, every service agency tends to hire its own case managers. But, they often act as gatekeepers to control access to their own agency. There are few examples where a communitywide case manager system has authority to affect admission to independent agencies; instead, each agency maintains its barriers.

Administrative Reorganization: Who is in Control. Many dissatisfactions result from the complexity of welfare procedures. The public has difficulty in understanding these procedures, and operating confusions result. In theory, good administration should be able to settle such matters, but most social welfare programs, and especially those which depend on federal or state subsidy, are burdened by two elements of control: professional and administrative. At one level, professional welfare workers (as is true for medicine and nursing) believe they can manage their work best if unencumbered with too much red tape. On the other hand, it is widely believed that some management and fiscal control is necessary in any organization which handles public or private funds to control professional expenditure or to guard against fraud. In the past 20 years, most social programs have seen top level control shift from welfare trained personnel to accountants and fiscal or business management trained administrators with little prior knowledge of the welfare service they administer. The result has been to tilt agencies from service (with efficiency) to efficiency (and less priority to service).

However, a new, more professional cadre may be in the making—a new blend of social worker and administrator. The future will be more secure if the components of this new staff are defined; and if they can be concerted in a career-stable manpower cadre which can count on a career ladder to run a welfare service enterprise (as a service) efficiently— rather than to run a business in which service is secondary.

Bureaucracy and Simplified Procedures. Organization in welfare is compounded by the reliance on detailed, procedural rules and regulations and on a heavy flow of justifying paper reporting which, in turn, is subject to constant post-auditing. In income maintenance agencies, where this trend is most pronounced, the regulations which staff must observe may fill hundreds of pages of manuals, the contents of which are constantly being changed. This trend has spread to nonfinancial services where agencies depend on several third party incomes. Despite the growth of computers and of management information systems, there has also been a reduction in the ratio of staff to total load so that the service systems are still cluttered with confusion and uncertainty and unhappiness among all parties.

Part of the explanation for this accumulation of procedural detail may be found in the distrust which surrounds so much of welfare. Some voters are convinced that no one associated with welfare can be both honest and efficient; officials at different levels of government share some of these views; and the persistent suspicion about people who must depend on others for help leads to the creation of numerous checks and counterchecks to remove the taint of fraud or deceit.

Computers and management information systems have been hailed as the remedy. But, these systems depend upon difficult to achieve accuracy of explicit and detailed information fed into the process. The capacity to retrieve the vast amounts of such information requires an added level of manpower to analyze and report findings in staff usable form which introduces a new source of potential error. To date, the new technology has permitted centralized staff to acquire valuable insight into a system's working, but has not yet proven capable of reducing the complexity of system operations for front line use by those who directly deliver help.

Another major obstacle to bureaucratic simplification lies in the rapid staff turnover and low state of career esteem to which much of major social welfare has fallen. The major public welfare agencies, the largest employers, are usually considered way stations for young people while they seek their major career lines. The result is a rapid turnover in front line staff, leaving relatively few who are satisfied to remain and give some continuity to programs. To make any important operation work with unskilled staff in constant turnover requires extensive supervision at many levels, and the accumulation of complex procedural manuals which break down the functions into their simplest units. But, middle and top management also turn over rapidly in state agencies. The situation makes for the most extensive bureaucracy, which relies on breaking procedures down into repetitive, small decision units more suitable for processing things than for people (Morris, 1976).

Extensive professional supervision is sometimes offered as a solution to the poor fit between routine operations, management, and human behavior. Supervision has its own complex of difficulties but above all, a great increase in supervising personnel is seen as an unacceptably high level of administrative cost and as proof of inefficient management.

Reorganization and simplification of structure should be possible, though difficult. Reduction of bureaucratic procedures may be less difficult. Sustained attention to such issues at the level of service delivery can improve confidence while larger issues of the scope of national responsibility are being sorted out.

The Challenge of Welfare for Profit. If we think of redesigning a social service system rather than changing a specific service like child protection, then the field needs to deal with the emergence of proprietary social welfare and fashion the relationships between it and more conventional nonprofit and public activity. It is only possible here to outline the issues that will be involved in redesigning a system which contains the full range of providers. In the areas of day care for children, child welfare, nursing homes, home health care, home social support services, medical care (hospitals), mental health, personal counseling, to name a few, service providers now include: profit-making corporations, nonprofit voluntary agencies with a community base, nonprofit agencies without a community structure, governmental agencies, and services provided by industrial or commercial employers for their employees. The proprietary agencies are better named as investor owned (they have stockholders who expect an ultimate return for their investment) and some of these providers are financed by stock issues on a national basis listed on a national stock exchange.

The ensuing competition has several potential consequences. The profit agencies may serve those who can afford to pay leaving the poor for the nonprofit sector. This would involve a major change in financing the nonprofit sector since many of these agencies depend on fees from clients which might be lost. On the other hand, the financial resources for capital investment of the profit sector are enhanced by their superior management capacity to make economic management decisions without major regard for community group pressures. The nonprofit sector could conceivably be forced to behave more and more like the proprietaries in order to survive economically. Still another consequence is that in the new competition, all types of agencies will compete against each other for governmental reimbursement wherever a government benefit is involved. Since government has begun a trend to purchase services for which it is responsible from nongovernmental agencies—that is to contract out its public obligation to private providers—the division of services will come under new kinds of scrutiny: will the governmental criterion be the cheapest service or the best, and how will the best or the cheapest be measured. The least costly service may be the most efficient but it may also be the shoddiest and the assertion that the nonprofit sector is always the best is not sustained by present evidence.

The current competition is forcing the kind of restructuring of services which occurred, on a smaller scale, at the turn of the century when children's agencies and agencies for the aged began to specialize and break up into institutional and noninstitutional services—both under voluntary nonprofit auspices. Although much smaller in scale than the present competition among more diverse providers, the conflict persisted for some decades before a reasonable accommodation was found.

Agenda 4: A Research and Development Capacity

The sketchy review of some of the troublesome contradictions which plague many efforts to advance or to solidify social welfare programs provides the basis for the final agenda item. Advocate effort in the next few years could profitably be directed to these contradictions in a systematic fashion in an attempt to discover ways of resolving them. Trial and error experimentation is useful but not sufficient. More systematic analysis and testing is called for. In many ways, this large area of national activity—social welfare—still functions at an eighteenth century apprentice level, with hardly any significant application of modern research and development technology. Except for minimal professional education for frontline service delivery, there is no powerful intellectual infrastructure to carry out the self-criticism, analyses and testing which the contradictions call for. There are valuable national and regional organizations and a few government or university research centers, but most of them are poorly financed and overcommitted to the daily problems of maintaining a large and complex welfare system under daily emergency conditions. Support has not yet emerged for a network of research and development centers (R and D) similar to those which have made such useful contributions to the evolution of modern society in the physical sciences, medicine, military capability and business.

During the next few years, some portion of welfare effort will need to be devoted to developing comparable analytic centers and to confronting the kinds of dilemmas noted above. Such centers can grow around or out of major national welfare service associations, out of major universities or out of professional associations. To succeed, such associations may have to decide how much of their meager resources they are willing to set aside for long-term purposes, rather than devoting so much to the promotion of current short-term objectives without ever confronting the internal contradictions which continue to make the ends of social welfare so uncertain.

The kind of R and D capability which is necessary has three major components: a policy oriented research and data analysis staff; collection, updating and maintenance of a data base focused on the R and D objectives, which can synthesize data collected by government, research data of other centers accessed on a sharing basis, and original data gathered directly by the welfare R and D centers; and, a network of links between several research analysis-type centers and consumers of findings. The last of these is perhaps most important. The standard pattern of the past has been to communicate research results via publication or within one community. This is valuable for research and academic personnel, and may slowly filter into use by developers of policy or of programs. But the process of use and idea diffusion is slow, unpredictable and wasteful. What modern R and D technology has shown in so many fields is the potential in more actively connecting information with organization use structures or networks which are interested in putting into practice and into use the implications of evidence. Business develops its market this way; science has extended its influence this way; and conservative political movements opposed to government welfare have also extended their influence in policy making by similar developmental means.

Social welfare has several handicaps as it attempts to adopt these methods of research and of linked development. Its base constituency is fragmented and not motivated by a common impulse which governs business or political ideology. Welfare is still sometimes conceived of as a layman's spare time activity or as the realm of minor functionaries carrying out distasteful tasks of social rescue through welfare. Instead, as we have seen, welfare has become an important factor in modern economic, political and social development. What is called for is readiness to act in technical and strategic ways commensurate with these roles.

Dreams of the Future

The limited platform suggested previously is not the outer boundary of welfare conceptions, but it represents the essential foundation building which must be completed if social programs are to be secure, or if America is to become something other than a grudging and reluctant welfare state. Broader concepts of social justice, other actions by government to create a more equitable and cohesive society can be dreamed of and planned for, but they are unlikely to be realized unless the foundation is securely in place. But, the welfare agenda outcome will also be shaped, in time, by the beliefs which citizens have about the kind of society they anticipate in the coming decades. Three main models of the future have emerged:

1. *A world of boundless abundance* provided by the existing economic and social order. This model applies equally to capitalist and socialist societies. It envisages a world in which maximizing economic growth is possible, without destroying basic resources, that work for all will result naturally, that basic political and economic structures do not need to be altered, and that minor dependencies which persist can be taken care of by modest diversions from personal and public incomes through family, charity or public provision for the helpless.

2. *A world of leisure and creativity* without dependence on any forced labor. New productivity forces, in this model, will cut the link between work and income; work will take on a new form, without compulsion. The Athenian world would become general in which 10 percent of the population which then have leisure to pursue intellectual and artistic interests will now become 100 percent, but without the Athenian 90 percent of the population who had to work with their hands and were either slaves or poor craftsmen.

3. *A third or middle road accepts the constancy of change* in economic and social relationships, *but accepts a continuing tension* between differing interests without removing the tensions or by removing some of the

interests. The tension persists within a stable consensus seeking order which does not lapse into anomie and lethargy, nor into class conflict and polarization. (Cornes, 1984)

The main agenda issues could be addressed in each of these models of the future, but the way the issues are answered for political and policy action purposes will differ. The first and second scenarios call for little welfare action, for they presuppose that economic growth will abolish both poverty and dependency. That is only slightly oversimplified for even in such a future some people will be sick or unable to work. But, for the most part, such life hazards are assumed manageable by savings or insurance with which any need can be met. They call for the creation of wholly new patterns of living and of self-realization. While the hazards of illness and injury are still present, these views place much more confidence in the promise of scientific advance to deal with most of such conditions. Welfare needs or wants are seen as at best a minor residual flaw in an otherwise benign world of self-realization.

For those who are concerned with the realities of human existence in today's world, those who look for answers in such futurism can only seem to be dreamers and escapists, but the attractiveness of escape from trouble is undeniable.

The proposed agenda is set in the context of the third, or middle, course which most closely approximates the world we now live in and the world as it is likely to be for some generations to come. This approach is realistic—visions of cataclysmic changes which will remake society in the span of one lifetime are not supported by any historical evidence. Great upheavals which destroy the foundations of a society in one generation recreate a new order after the passage of decades or generations. In the interim, changes in the attitudes and behaviors of people change quite slowly. The time frame for this agenda is only the next two decades. It calls advocates to the practical and the basic work necessary to enrich a tradition of caring for others and to modernize and reshape social support programs of government in their lifetime in the U.S.

APPENDIX

SUMMARY OF SELECTED LEGISLATION AND RATIONALES ADVANCED TO SUPPORT ENACTMENTS[1]

1. *The Federal Housing Act of 1937* provided for federal funds to construct low income housing for families of moderate means. A major rationale advanced was that of providing employment for some of the then 15 million unemployed, many of whom were in the construction or related industries. Legislation also called for federal intervention "to alleviate present and recurring unemployment *and* to remedy the unsafe and unsanitary dwellings for families of low income that are injurious to the health, safety and morals of the citizens of the land." Then Secretary of the Interior, Harold Ickes, argued: "We need to improve the moral condition and do away with the vicious surroundings which turn out more criminals than we need." Mixed motives seem to have been invoked, to give jobs to some, and to improve housing for others.

---

[1] The material on the following pages is based on a reading of the official legislative history of the legislation—the hearings and testimony which preceded final adoption. Graduate students who prepared the material for a seminar at Brandeis University were: C. Brill, S. Elliott, V. Hoffman, D. Hubbard, L. O'Leary, F. Marx, B. Mathews, C. Ponty, R. Pulice, R. Stein, S. Wisensale, and K. King.

2. *The Community Mental Health Centers legislation of 1963* substituted federal funds and regulations for, or supplemented, state programs which previously had dominated the field of mental health care. One of the major supporters, the Joint Commission on Mental Health and Illness, reported in 1960 that there had been a serious lag in the treatment of the mentally ill which reflects a fundamental pattern of social rejection in this society. The continued existence of large isolated state hospitals, mainly custodial and punitive, were seen as continuing evidence of this social rejection. Not only a humane society but a cohesive one which rehabilitates rather than stores its mentally ill requires national action which can only come from the national government. John F. Kennedy, then President, supporting the legislation argued that the mentally ill and the retarded had long been neglected and that the nation is obligated to live up to its own standards or "compassion and dignity *and to achieve the maximum use of its manpower*" (emphasis added). In the Senate debate May 27, 1963, Senator McGovern argued "no bill before Congress appeals more to our humanitarian sympathies or to our approval of intelligent social action." And Senator Ribicoff, former Secretary of H.E.W., argued that the cost in dollars was less significant than the loss of precious human talent which could not be measured. Senator Humphrey, then Majority Leader, argued that the legislation is aimed at one of the most persistent and tragic evils of our nation. "It is estimated that one American in ten will spend some portion of his life in a mental institution. This situation should be intolerable in so wealthy and powerful a nation."

3. *The Child Health Act of 1967* provided for screening and rescreening of children plus both funds and regulations to assure that appropriate medical care be provided to children needing medical attention. The rationale, while occasionally couched in terms of compassion for children, was primarily concerned with the older mercantilist doctrine that a healthy, able-bodied adult population is required for the good of society. "If future generations are to become good self-supporting citizens able to assume the responsibilities and burdens of democratic rule they had to be protected as children." (In other words, a safeguarding of their lot was considered essential to society.) Lyndon Johnson, President in 1967, urging enactment argued: "Our goal must be clear, to give every child the chance to fulfill his promise." This was an advance over previous justification for it identifies children's opportunities to fulfill their personal promise for the future rather than society's. But in view of the accompanying discussion about economically independent and healthy life in adulthood one is entitled to wonder whether "the chance to fulfill his promise" is a generous way of saying that each person has an opportunity of working when he or she grows up.

4. *Supplementary Security Income legislation (1972)* consolidated previously separate programs of income maintenance for the "surely deserving"—the aged, the chronically disabled and the blind. Although the final level of income support provided was not especially generous, the legislation is noteworthy for its taking a small step in the direction of treating income for this population as somewhat less demeaning even though still means tested. This modest generosity was justified on the grounds that it tended to provide "the most adequate support we can afford for those whom we do not expect to work" (Senator Russell Long, Chairman of the Senate Finance Committee, 1971). Without probing deeply into the justification for federal support, there was ready acceptance of the idea that for this population the federal government had an obligation, but one to be met only marginally. The debate did not concern itself with the merits of the relief programs for these populations, which had earlier been introduced in the Social Security legislation, but was primarily concerned with administrative improvements to save costs. The debate included an intriguing clue that even for this dependent, helpless and deserving population, those who provided something useful for society would be treated somewhat better than those who did not. The final version of the bill excluded from eligibility determination income which a beneficiary might receive for services given as a foster parent—such earnings he could keep without having them deducted from his supplementary income. In the hearings the testimony of the then Governor Gilligan of Ohio received much attention because a modest number of AFDC heads of households were put to work assisting the elderly in simple household tasks as an argument for being somewhat more generous for AFDC households. The final report of the bill argued: "A sympathetic understanding of the needs of the helpless and the conviction that all those who are capable of participating in the economy of this country should have the opportunity and responsibility to do so." Welfare even for this population was not a right in itself.

5. *Title XX, Amendments to the Social Security Act (1974).* This provided for the consolidation of a variety of federally funded social service support programs into a single legislative package. These social services had slowly been added to federal programs in the course of the years with a variety of antecedent rationales. The current legislation was justified in large part on the following premises: that government has an obligation to assist society's most vulnerable people to obtain the highest possible level of independent living of which they are capable; further that the reduction of dependency also represents a saving of public funds otherwise required for institutional maintenance support. The priority for public social services should be on those people with low incomes and that as

an individual's status improves he or she should contribute more to the cost of services through the payment of fees (Mott, 1976). The debate over this legislation was mainly concerned with the objectives for the services and how they should be best controlled. The legislation was loosely drawn with very broad objectives (to encourage self-support, or self-care, or lacking that, to ensure community-based care and institutional care only as a last resort). Some federal responsibility was assumed without question. But many practical issues confused the understanding about the legislative motivation. There was a continuing struggle between the states and the federal government as to accountability for achieving the objectives which are so loosely drawn to relieve distress, to get people to work, etc.; the services which were to be included were vaguely defined and presented almost impossible tasks of measurement across the many states; the question of entitlement as between persons who are clearly unable to work at all and those who are able to work but only at low incomes was impossible to resolve with confidence. But above all, the motive of saving tax dollars was inextricably mixed with calls to help people out of misery.

6. *The Juvenile Justice Delinquency Prevention Act of 1974.* The rationale of this legislation was an especially complicated mixture. There was underlying concern that delinquency among juveniles was increasing and that the safety of society required that there be some improvement in the ways in which they were being attended to. But why the federal government? Substantial evidence was advanced indicating deficiencies in the treatment and care of juvenile delinquents in local and state jurisdictions. These difficulties included: an overuse of secure institutions in which juveniles were placed with hardened criminals; substantial injustices inflicted upon youth in that noncriminal and minor delinquencies often led to long periods of detention and incarceration disproportionate to the harm done by the youth, the absence of almost any rehabilitative programs to reduce the growing incidence of delinquency; the frequency with which problem children, not necessarily delinquents, were incarcerated in ancient custodial institutions and subject to much abuse (nearly half of the nation's institutionalized juveniles were locked up not because they had committed a crime but because they had run away, were truant or were not wanted at home).

The final program was justified in part to protect society, in part because of compassion for problem youth who were not criminal but were treated as criminals, a recognition that punitive treatment did not provide rehabilitation or opportunity to enter into a productive adult role in later life. The combination of rationales suggested that youth in trouble with the law were not totally responsible for their behaviors and for their difficulties; that while they should be held responsible in part, it was necessary that special opportunities be given to them in order to compensate for difficulties over which they had no control. It is quite likely, although not clearly expressed in the legislative history, that some of these reforms were stimulated by a recognition that a disproportionate number of youth delinquents were black or members of other minorities whose social and life situation was of such disadvantage that they could not be held wholly culpable. The apparent inability of most states to meet these difficulties was sufficient justification for the federal government to intervene on the grounds of assuring equitable treatment everywhere in the U.S. for all individuals in a like situation.

7. *The Developmentally Disabled Assistance and Bill of Rights Act of 1975* asserted: "Persons with developmental disabilities have a right to appropriate treatment, services, rehabilitation and they should be designed to maximize developmental potential of the person and be provided in a setting that is least restrictive of the person's personal liberty." This legislation gave to each individual "a right" although the definition of appropriate treatment and rehabilitation and what constituted maximum development potential opened the way for substantial redefinition in the future. The seriously disabled child is one of a small group which throughout history has been considered an appropriate object of our philanthropic or charitable attention although usually on the basis of compassion rather than rights. Perhaps it is the very helplessness of this population which has led to the introduction of a clear "right" for these children, a right which has not been extended to many others who are beneficiaries of social programs.

8. *The Child Welfare Act of 1980* provided funds and federal regulation to alter the pattern by which children removed from their home care and placed in foster care were ultimately to be cared for. In the written and oral testimony before the Subcommittee on Public Assistance of the Senate Finance Committee in 1979 (the Hearings Report, Sept. 24, 1979) the following rationale was advanced: "The fact that there are 500,000 children in foster care represents a moral claim which impels the Congress and the people of the United States to act on their behalf in the name of human decency." This argument for simple decency drew on descriptions of the sad plight of many of the children in foster care, conditions which were offered as leading a moral person to conclude that something must be done. More selfish elements beneath such motives peep out in the equal argument that handicapped children, if helped, will become functionally—that is economically—independent as adults. Other arguments advanced seem less relevant for our purposes: that poor design in previous state administered but federally funded programs would be preventive of difficulty in the future and would thus lead to savings at some

future time. However, a spokesman for the Child Welfare League of America advanced a mercantilist argument supporting this legislation by noting that in the '60s there was a declining number of young children in the American society and that young people have become a major but declining resource in the nation for whom something needed to be done in order to preserve that resource for the future.

REFERENCES

Abraham, Katherine. "Structural/Functional vs. Demand, Deficient Unemployment: Some New Evidence," February 1982, Massachusetts Institute of Technology and National Bureau of Economic Research, unpublished manuscript.

Abrams, Mark. "The Future in Great Britain: Images of the World in Year 2000." Cited by Paul Barker in *New Society,* November 29, 1979, p. 480.

Achenbaum, W. Andrew. "The Meaning of Risk, Rights and Responsibility in Aging America." In *Aging and Meaning.* Durham, NC: Duke University Press, publication forthcoming.

Acton, H. B. *The Morals of Markets.* London: Longman, 1971.

Addams, Jane. *Democracy and Social Ethics.* New York: Macmillan, 1902, p. 14.

Alcuin. "Letter to Ethelred." EHD, Vol. 1, pp. 775–776, in Hadden, A. W., F. M. Powike, and C. R. Cheney, eds. *Councils and Ecclesiastical Documents Relating to Great Britain and Ireland.* Oxford: Clarendon Press, 1871.

Allen, J., and B. Hanamond. *The Bleak Age.* London: Penguin Books, 1947, p. 52.

Almond, G. A., and S. Verba. *The Civic Culture.* Princeton: Princeton University Press, 1963. (Also: Boston: Little, Brown, 1965.) Cited by Paul Barker in *New Society,* November 29, 1979, p. 480.

Alt, James E. *The Politics of Economic Decline.* Cambridge: Cambridge University Press, 1979.

American Society for the Prevention of Pauperism. *Proceedings of the First Ten Years.* New York, 1824, p. 180–181.

American Tract Society. "Proceedings of the First Ten Years." New York, 1824, p. 11.

249

Angell, Robert. *Free Society and Moral Crisis.* Ann Arbor, MI: University of Michigan Press, 1958.

Aristotle. *The Rhetoric of Aristotle.* (Q. E. Sandys, ed.) Cambridge: Cambridge University Press, 1877. Reprinted Dubuque, IA: W. C. Brown, 1966.

Arnold, Matthew. Quoted by Alfred Kazin in *One of Us. The New York Review of Books,* November 5, 1981, p. 25.

Aspen Institute for Humanistic Studies and the Public Agenda Foundation. "Work and Human Values: an International Report on Jobs in the 1980s and 1990s." Aspen, CO.

Asser. *Life of King Alfred.* Oxford: Clarendon Press, 1904.

Astin, Alexander. "The American Freshman, a National Survey for Fall, 1979." Los Angeles, CA: American Council on Education, University of California, Los Angeles.

Attenborough, F. L., ed. *The Laws of the English Kings.* Cambridge: Cambridge University Press, 1922, p. 127.

Auclair, Philip A. "Public Attitudes Toward Social Welfare Expenditures." In *Social Work,* March–April, 1984, Vol. 29, No. 2, pp. 139–144.

Axelrod, Robert, and William D. Hamilton. "The Evaluation of Cooperation," in *Science,* Vol. II-11, March, 1981, p. 1390. Also: New York: Basic Books, 1984.

Bahmueller, C. F. *The National Charity Co.* Berkeley, CA: University of California Press, 1981.

Bailey, Roy, and M. Brake, eds. *Radical Social Work.* New York: Pantheon Books, 1975.

Ball, Robert. "Employment Created by Construction Expenditure." *Monthly Labor Review,* 104, Dec. 1981, p. 39.

Bane, Mary Jo, and David Elwood. "Slipping into and Out of Poverty." Working Paper 1199. Cambridge, MA: National Bureau of Economic Research, Sept., 1982. Also "Dynamics of Poverty" in *Focus,* 5-1, Summer, 1981, Madison, WI: Institute for Poverty Research.

Bawden, D. Lee, ed. *The Social Contract Revisited.* Washington, D.C.: Urban Institute Press, 1984.

Bede. *Bede's Ecclesiastical History of the English Nation.* (Don David Knowles, ed.) London: Everyman's Library; New York: Dutton, 1954, p. 91.

Ben Dor, Zvi. "The Israelite Bet-Ab from the Settlement to the End of the Monarchy." Unpublished dissertation. Jerusalem: Hebrew University of Israel, 1982.

Berlinguer, Enrico. "1929 and 1979." From *New York Times,* October 29, 1979.

Berthoud, R. "The Reform of Supplementary Benefits." London: Policy Studies Institute, 1984.

Bingham, Alfred M. *Insurgent America.* New York: W. W. Norton & Company, 1935.

Bluestone, Barry, B. Harrison, and L. Gorbach. *How to Create Jobs.* Washington, D.C.: Center for National Policy, 1984.

Blumberg, Paul. *Inequality in an Age of Decline.* Oxford: Oxford University Press, 1980.

Boaz, M. *op. cit.* Hands.

Bolkestein, H. *Wohltatigkeit und Armenpflege in Vörchristlichen Altertum.* Utrecht: A. Desthoek, 1939. From DeSchweinitz ms., cited below.

Bolkestein. *op. cit.* Hands. Also: *Economic Life in Greece's Golden Age.* Leiden: E. J. Brill, 1958.

Booth, Charles. *Life and Labor of the People of London, 1840–1916.* New York: AMS Press, 1970, Series 1-Poverty; Final Volume, Social Influences.

Borus, Michael. *"Assessing the Impact of Training Programs."* In Eli Ginzberg, *Employing the Unemployed.* New York: Basic Books, 1980.

Boswell, James. *The Life of Johnson.* New York: Oxford University Press, 1957.

Boulding, Kenneth. "The Boundaries of Social Policy," in *Social Work,* Vol. 12, No. 1, 1967.

_____ *The Economy of Love and Fear.* Belmont, CA: Wadsworth Press, 1973.

Breasted, Henry. *The Dawn of Conscience.* New York: Charles Scribner & Sons, 1934, pp. 123–125, 396.

Breckenridge, Sophonisba. *The Illinois Poor Law and Administration.* Chicago: University of Chicago Press, 1939.

Bremner, R. H. *From the Depths.* New York: New York University Press, 1956, Chapters 4 and 5.

Brenner, M. H. *Mental Illness and the Economy.* Cambridge, MA: Harvard University Press, 1973.

Brewer, Thomas. *Memoir of the Life and Times of John Carpenter.* London, 1856, p. 27.

Britannica, Encyclopedia. 11th ed. New York: Encyclopedia Britannica Publishing Company, 1911.

Brown, Charles. *Taxation and the Incentive to Work.* New York: Oxford University Press, 1980.

Brown, Peter, C. Johnson, and P. Vernier, eds. *Income Support.* Totowa, NJ: Rowman and Littlefield, 1981.

Bruce, M. *The Coming of the Welfare State.* London: B. T. Batsford, 1961, pp. 143–146.

Burns, Eveline. "Social Insurance and Evolution Toward What?" in *American Economic Review Supplement,* 34:1, pp. 199–211. Also: See *Social Service Review,* 49:2, 129–140.

Byers, Ted. *America's Almshouse Experience: Dependent Poverty: 1750–1920.* Waltham, MA: Unpublished manuscript provided by author.

Cahn, Edgar. "Surplus People." Unpublished manuscript. Coral Gables, FL, University of Florida Law School, 1984.

Callahan, James, and Stanley Wallack. *Reforming the Long-term Care System.* Lexington, MA: Lexington Books, 1981, pp. 185–218.

Carlyle, Thomas. *Chartism.* London, 1840, pp. 19–20.

Carus-Wilson, E. M. "An Industrial Revolution of the 13th Century," in *Essays on Economic History.* London: Edward Arnold Ltd., 1934, pp. 41–60.

Challis, D. J. "The Measurement of Outcome in Social Care of the Elderly." Canterbury Mimeo—Community Care Project, University of Kent at Canterbury, Paper 31–2.

Chill, E. "Religion and Mendacity in Seventeenth Century France," in *International Review of Social History,* 1962, pp. 400–425.

Cialdini, Robert. See Kenrick.

Cicero. *Re De Officio II.* See Cowell, F. R.

Cloward, Richard, and Frances Piven. *Regulating the Poor.* New York: Pantheon Books, 1971.

——— *The New Class War.* New York: Pantheon Books, 1982.

Cohen, Nathan, ed. *Social Work and Social Problems.* New York: National Association of Social Workers, 1964, p. 16.

Cole, C. W. *Colbert and a Century of French Mercantilism.* New York: Columbia University Press, 1939, Vol. 2, p. 464.

Colonial Laws of New York, 1664–1776. Albany, 1894, Vol. 1, Chapter 9, p. 131.

Colvez, A, and M. Blanchet. "Disability Trends in the U.S. Population 1966–76," in *American Journal of Public Health,* Vol. 71, No. 5, 1981, pp. 464–471.

Commissary Court of London. Guildhall Mss. 9177, Vol. 1, pp. 183, 227, 289, 362.

Commission, His Majesty's, *For Enquiring into the Administration and Practical Operation of the Poor Law,* 1834, p. 13.

Committee on Pauper Laws, Commonwealth of Massachusetts, Massachusetts General Court, 1821.

Commonwealth of Massachusetts. *Report of the Commissioners on the Pauper System.* Boston: General Court, 1835, pp. 39–45.

Congressional Budget Office (CBO). *Dislocated Workers.* Washington, D.C.: U.S. Government Printing Office, July 1982, p. 38.

Cook, Fay Lomax. *Who Should be Helped?* Beverly Hills, CA: Sage Publications, Inc., 1979.

Cornes, Paul. "The Future of Work for People with Disabilities." *Interchange.* New York: World Rehabilitation Fund, June 1984, No. 9.

Coulton, T. G. *The Medieval Village.* Cambridge, England: Cambridge University Press, 1925, pp. 118–119.

——— *Ten Medieval Studies.* Cambridge, MA: Cambridge University Press, 1930, pp. 156–157.

Cowell, F. R. *Cicero and the Roman Republic.* London: Pitman & Sons, 1948, Chapters 3 and 17. (Re: the Common People and the Status of the Poor.)

Creech, Margaret. *Three Centuries of Poor Law Administration: A Study of Legislation in Rhode Island.* Chicago: University of Chicago Press, 1936, pp. 284–286.

Croly, Herbert. *The Problems of American Life.* Cambridge, MA: Belknap Press, 1965.

Daniels, Norman. "Am I My Parents Keeper?" in Peter Brown, ed., *Income Support* (and the President's Commission for the Study of Ethical Problems in Medicine, Biomedical and Behavioral Research), Washington, D.C.: U.S. Government Printing Office, 1981.

Davis, Natalie Zerman. "Poor Relief, Humanism and Heresy," in *Society and Culture in Early Modern France.* Stanford, CA: Stanford University Press, 1975.

DeGrando, Joseph. *The Visitor of the Poor.* 2nd ed. Boston, 1833, p. 4.

Derthick, Martha. *Policy Making for Social Security.* Washington, D.C.: The Brookings Institution, 1979.

DeSchweinitz, Karl. Quoted in unpublished and incompleted manuscript *The Dilemma of Need.* At the Social Welfare Archives, University of Minnesota, Chapters 12, 14, 15, 17, 18, 21, 25, and 26. (Re: the executors of the testament of Richard Whittington enrolled 1423.) No source given.

DeTocqueville, Alexis. *Democracy in America*. New York: Alfred E. Knopf, 1980.

Dicey, A. V. *Relation Between Law and Public Opinion in England. 2nd ed. of 1914*. London: Macmillan and Company. Reprinted 1948.

Dill, Samuel. *Roman Society from Nero to Marcus Aurelius*. London and New York: Macmillan and Company, 1905, p. 530.

Dilnot, A. W., Kay, J. A., & Morris, C. N. *The Reform of Social Security*. London: Clarendon Press, 1984.

Disraeli, Benjamin. *Sybil: or the Two Nations*. London: Hugenden Edition, 1881, p. 76.

Dix, Dorothea L. "Memorial to the Legislature of Man 1843," in *Old South Leaflets*, Boston, Vol. 6, No. 148, p. 2.

Douglas, David C., general ed. *Ecclesiastical History of the English Nation*. Everyman's Library. London: Dent; New York: Dutton, 1954, Vol. 1, pp. 625–626, re: Bede-Letter to Egbert EHD, Vol. 1, 738.

Duby, Georges. *The Early Growth of the European Economy*. Translated by H. B. Clarke. Ithaca, NY: Cornell University Press, 1974.

Eberhard, Arnold. "Education for Altruism: The Society for Brothers in Paraguay," in Pitrim Sorokin, *Altruistic Love*. Boston: Beacon Press, 1950. See also: *Forms and Techniques of Altruistic and Spiritual Growth*. Boston: Beacon Press, 1954.

Economist. "The Spectre of Unemployment." June 9, 1984, pp. 43–44.

Economist. "Social Security," September 8, 1984, pp. 56–58. (Rowntree, Joseph, Trust Conference on Social Policy, Arms and Resources for the 1990s.)

Economist. April 23, 1983, p. 97. Citing Dr. David Weatherall, Nuffield Professor, Oxford University, in an article "Gazing into the Crystal Ball of Genetic Research."

Economist. March 24, 1984, p. 71.

Economist. June 9, 1984, p. 43.

Economist. June 16, 1984, p. 61.

Eden, Fredrick Morton. *The State of the Poor*. London, 1797, Vol. 1, pp. 58–59.

Elton, G. R. "An Early Tudor Poor Law." *The Economic History Review*, 2d Series, Vol. 1, No. 1, 1953, pp. 55–57.

Employment Research Associates. Extrapolated from "Military Spending: An Occupational Hazard." April 9, 1984. Lansing, MI.

Evans, Robert. "A Job Program." Unpublished manuscript. Waltham, MA: Brandeis University, March 29, 1984.

Feldstein, Martin. Statement on "Meet the Press" on NBC, November 21, 1982.

Fishkin, James S. *The Limits of Obligation*. New Haven, CT: Yale University Press, 1982.

Ford Foundation Letter, April 1, 1984. Citing experience of the Manpower Demonstration Research Corporation.

Freeman, Gary, and Paul Adams. "Ideology and Analysis in American Social Security Policy Making." *Journal of Social Policy,* January 1983, Vol. 12, Part 1, pp. 75–95.

Freud, Sigmund. *Civilization and Its Discontents*. New York: W. W. Norton, 1962, Chap. 3.

Fuchs, Victor R. *How We Live*. Cambridge, MA: Harvard University Press, 1983.

Furniss, E. S. *The Position of the Laborer in the System of Nationalism.* Boston: Houghton Mifflin, 1920, p. 118.

Galper, Michael. *The Politics of Social Work.* Englewood Cliffs, NJ: Prentice-Hall, 1975.

Garfinkle, Irving, and John Palmer, ed. "Issues, Evidence and Implications," in *Creating Jobs.* Washington, D.C.: Brookings Institution, 1978, p. 1.

Gee, Henry, and W. D. Hardy. *Documents Illustrative of English Church History.* London: Macmillan Company, 1921, p. 42.

Gergen, Kenneth, Martin Greenberg, and Richard Willis, eds. *Social Exchange: Advances in Theory and Research.* New York: Plenum, 1980.

Gilbert, Neil. *Capitalism and the Welfare State.* New Haven, CT: Yale University Press, 1983.

Ginzberg, Eli. *Good Jobs, Bad Jobs, No Jobs.* Cambridge, MA: Harvard University Press, 1979.

Glasser, Ira, Willard Gaylin, S. Marcus, and D. Rothman. *Doing Good: The Limits of Benevolence.* New York: Pantheon Books, 1978.

Goitein, J. D. *A Mediterranean Society: The Community,* Vol. II. Berkeley, CA: University of California Press, 1967.

Gouldner, A. W. "The Norm of Reciprocity." *American Sociological Review,* Vol. 25, No. 2, 1960.

Greenberg, Edward S. In *Journal of Politics,* November 1981, Vol. 43, No. 4, p. 64.

Griscom, John. *Memoirs of John Griscom.* New York, 1859, pp. 157–158.

Gueron, Judith. *Lessons from a Job Guarantee: The Youth Incentive Entitlement Pilot Projects.* New York: Manpower Demonstration Research Corporation, June 1984.

Hacker, Andrew. "Where Have the Jobs Gone?" *New York Review of Books,* June 30, 1983, pp. 27–31.

Hadden, A. W., F. M. Powicke, and C. R. Cheney. *Councils and Ecclesiastical Documents Relating to Great Britain and Ireland.* Oxford: Clarendon Press, 1871, Vol. 3, pp. 371–372.

Handel, Gerald. *Social Welfare in Western Society.* New York: Random House, 1982.

Hanham, Ruth H. "Aging in America: The White House Conference of 1981 in Retrospect." *American Journal of Public Health,* Vol. 73, No. 7, July 1983, p. 799.

Hands, A. R. *Charities and Social Aid in Greece and Rome.* London: Thames & Hudson, 1968.

Hands, A. R. *op. cit.* Quoting Farrington, Diaborus Siculus, Universal Historian, 1938, pp. 16–19 and Diaborus, V., pp. 35–38.

Hansard. 3rd Series, Vol. 23, Col. 1337.

Harrington, Michael. *The New American Poverty.* New York: Holt, Rinehart and Winston, 1984.

Harris, Louis. Survey reported in *New Society,* July 10, 1980, p. 73.

Hauser, H. *Thought and Political Action of Cardinal Richelieu.* Paris: Presses Universitaire, 1944, p. 145.

Hausman, Leonard. Testimony, House Budget Committee for Task Force on Entitlements, March 10, 1983.

Haveman, Robert, and John Palmer, eds. *Jobs for Disadvantaged Workers*. Washington, D.C.: Brookings Institution, 1982.

Hayek, F. *Law, Legislation and Liberty*. Vol. 2, The Mirage of Social Justice. London: Routledge & Kegan Paul, 1976.

Hillel. See Philip Blackman. *The Ethics of the Fathers*. Gateshead: Judaica Press Ltd., 1979.

Hochschild, Jennifer. *What's Fair?* Cambridge, MA: Harvard University Press, 1981.

Hoffman, Martin. "Is Altruism a Part of Human Nature?" *Journal of Personality and Social Psychology*, 1981, Vol. 40, No. 1, p. 121.

Hofstadter, Richard. *The Age of Reform*. New York: Vintage Books, 1955.

Homans, George. *The English Village in the 13th Century*. Cambridge, MA: Harvard University Press, 1942.

Hormats, Robert. "A Western Strategy for Jobs and Growth." *Trans-Atlantic Perspectives*, German Marshall Fund of the U.S., September 1984, No. 12, p. 11.

Howe, Irving. *A Margin of Hope*. New York: Harcourt Brace Jovanovich, 1982.

Hufton, Olwen. *Europe: Privilege and Protest, 1730–1789*. Ithaca, NY: Cornell University Press, 1980.

Humbert, R. M. Memorials of the Hospital of St. Cross and Alms House of Noble Poverty. Winchester, 1868, pp. 29–33, 37.

Jaffe, Natalie. "Attitudes Toward Public Welfare Programs and Recipients in the U.S." Institute of Public Sciences and Public Affairs, Duke University, 1977.

Job. Chapter 31, verses 16–23. Chapter 29, verses 12–17.

Joe, Tom. *A Dream Deferred: The Economic Status of Black Americans*. Washington, D.C.: Center for the Study of Social Policy, 1983.

Joe, Tom, and Lorna Potter. "The Welfare System: A Briar Patch for Anna Burns." *Public Welfare*, Vol. 43, No. 1, Winter 1985, p. 4.

Johnson, Conrad. In *Income Support*, ed. Peter Brown, *op. cit.*, 1981, p. 125.

Johnson, E. A. J. *Precedessors of Adam Smith*. New York: Prentice-Hall, 1937, p. 285.

Johnson, Samuel, as cited by Paul Theroux in *The Old Patagonian Express*. Boston: Houghton Mifflin, 1979.

Johnstone, Hilda. "Poor Relief for the Royal Household of 13th Century England." *Speculum*, Vol. 14, No. 2, April 1929, pp. 155–156.

Joint Commission on Mental Health and Illness. *Actions in Mental Health*. New York: Basic Books, 1961.

Joint Economic Committee of the Congress. *Studies in Public Welfare*. Paper 19 in Public Employment and Wage Subsidies. Washington, D.C.: U.S. Government Printing Office, December 30, 1974.

Jones, H. M. *Athenian Democracy*. Oxford: Basil Blackwell, 1957.

Jordan, Bill *Paupers*. London: Routledge & Kegan Paul, 1973.

Jordan, W. K. *Philanthropy in England 1480–1660*. London: George Allen & Unwin, 1959, pp. 246–263, 384.

Judge, Ken, Gillian Smith, and Peter Taylor-Gooby. "Public Opinion and the Privatization of Welfare." *Journal of Social Policy*, October 1983, Vol. 12, Part 4, pp. 467–489.

Kallen, David, and Dorothy Miller. "Public Attitudes Towards Welfare." *Social Work*, Vol. 16, No. 3, July, 1974.

Kenrick, Donald, D. Baumann, and R. B. Cialdini. "A Step in the Socialization of Altruism and Hedonism." *Journal of Personality and Social Psychology*, May 1979, Vol. 37, No. 5, pp. 747–755.

Kershaw, David. *The New Jersey Income Maintenance Experiment*. Vols. 1–3, Vol. 1, Labor Supply. New York: Academic Press, 1976.

Kesselman, Jonathan R. "Work Relief Programs in the Great Depression" in *Creating Jobs*, Palmer, J., *op. cit.*

Klebaner, Benjamin Joseph. *Poor Relief in America 1790–1860*. Doctoral Dissertation. New York: Columbia University, 1951, p. 103.

Kohlberg, Lawrence. *Essays in Moral Development*. Vol. 1, The Philosophy of Moral Development, Moral Stages and the Idea of Justice. New York: Harper & Row, 1981.

Konrad, George, and Ivan Szelenyi. *The Intellectual on the Road to Class Power*. New York: Harcourt Brace Jovanovich, 1984.

Krohn, Cornelius, J. W. Fretz, and R. Kreider. In Pitrim Sorokin, *Forms and Techniques of Altruistic and Spiritual Growth*. Boston: Beacon Press, 1954.

Kuhn, Thomas. *The Structure of Scientific Revolution*. Chicago: University of Chicago Press, 1970.

Kutza, Elizabeth. "Age as a Criterion for Focussing Public Programs." Mimeo, prepared for the Federal Council on Aging, Washington, D.C., December 15, 1980.

Kuznets, Simon. *Modern Economic Growth: Rate, Structure and Spread*. New Haven, CT: Yale University Press, 1966.

Labarge, Margaret Wade. *A Baronial Household of the 13th Century*. London: Eyre and Spottiswoode, 1965.

Labor, Department of. R & D Monograph No. 67, 1979, p. 171. *Assessing Large Scale Job Creations and Perspectives on Public Job Creations*. R & D Monograph No. 52, 1977. Washington, D.C.: U.S. Government Printing Office.

—— & Department of Health, Education, and Welfare. *WIN: 1968–1978: A Report at Ten Years, Ninth Annual Report to the Congress*. Washington, D.C.: U.S. Government Printing office, 1978.

Lampman, Robert L. *The Share of Top Wealth Holders in the National Wealth*. Princeton: Princeton University Press, 1962.

Lampman, Robert. *Social Welfare Spending: Accounting for Changes 1950–1978*. New York: Academic Press, 1984.

Langland, W. *A Vision of Piers the Ploughman*. Translated by K. M. Warren. London: Edward Arnold, 1913, p. 126.

—— Ibid, p. 127, Passus VII.

Lasch, Christopher. *The Culture of Narcissism*. New York: Norton, 1978.

Latourette, Kenneth Scott. *A History of Christianity*. New York: Harper & Row, 1953.

Lee, Charles E. "Public Poor Relief and the Massachusetts Community 1620–1715." *New England Quarterly*, Winter 1982 (Vol. 14), p. 564.

LeGrand, Julian. *The Strategy of Equality: Redistribution and the Social Services*. London: Allen & Unwin, 1982.

Leiby, James. *A History of Social Welfare and Social Work in the United States.* New York: Columbia University Press, 1978.

Leonard, E. M. *The Early History of English Poor Relief.* Cambridge: Cambridge University Press, 1900.

Levin, Meyer R. *Ending Unemployment: Alternatives for Public Policy.* Baltimore: University of Maryland Press, 1983.

Levine, Charles. "Cutting Back the Public Sector: The Hidden Hazards of Retrenchment." *Cutback Management in Criminal Justice.* Chevy Chase, MD: University Research Corporation, 1982, pp. 56–69.

Levy, Frank. *The Logic of Welfare Reform.* Washington, D.C.: Urban Institute, 1981.

Lewis, Charles, R. Fein, and D. Mechanic. *A Right to Health.* New York: John Wiley & Sons, 1976.

Little, Lester. *Religious Poverty and Profit, Economy in Medieval Europe.* Ithaca, NY: Cornell University Press, 1978.

Loch, C. F. *Charity and Social Life.* London: Macmillan, 1910. Reprinted as *3000 Years of Social Service* by Charity Organization Society. London, 1938, Chapters 9, 10, and 11.

Lubov, Roy. *The Progressives and the Slums.* Pittsburgh, PA: University of Pittsburgh Press, 1962.

Luther, Martin. *Works of Martin Luther.* Philadelphia: A. J. Holman & Company, The Castle Press, Vol. 2, 1931, p. 134.

Lyndwood, William. *Provincial Canons of Fourteen Archbishops of Canterbury.* First Edition, 1432, pp. 133–134. See Brian Tierney, *op. cit.;* and Karl DeSchweinitz, Chapter 9, *op. cit.*

Machiavelli, Niccolo. *The Prince.* London: Oxford University Press, Reprint 1952, pp. 44, 46, 72.

Maimonides. In Isadore Twersky, *Introduction to the Code of Maimonides.* New Haven, CT: Yale University Press, 1980, pp. 256–266.

Malthus, Thomas Robert. *An Essay on the Principle of Population.* 2nd ed. London, 1803, pp. 410–411, 413.

———— *First Essay on Population 1798.* Reprinted Royal Economic Society. London: Macmillan and Company, 1926, p. 83.

Mandevil, Bernard. "An Essay on Charity and Charity Schools," in *The Fable of the Bees.* ed. F. B. Kaye, Oxford: Clarendon Press, 1924, Vol. 1, p. 287.

Marshall, T. H. *Social Policy.* London: Hutchinson University Library, 1965.

Mathews, Fredrick D. *The English Works of Wycliff.* EETS original Series 74, London, 1880, p. 234.

McLoughlin, William. *Modern Revivalism.* New York: Arnold Press, 1959.

———— *Revivals, Awakenings and Reform.* Chicago: University of Chicago Press, 1978.

Mecke, Wayne. *The First Urban Christians: The Social World of the Apostle Paul.* New Haven, CT: Yale University Press, 1983.

Mencher, Samuel. *Poor Law to Poverty Program.* Pittsburgh: University of Pittsburgh Press, 1967.

Mill, John Stuart. In *Justice & Equality,* edited by Hugo Bedaw. Englewood Cliffs, NJ: Prentice-Hall, 1971.

Miller, William Lee. *Welfare Values in America: A Review of Attitudes Toward Welfare and Welfare Policies in the Light of American History and Culture.* Institute of Policy, Science & Public Affairs, Duke University, Spring 1977.

Mitchell, Arnold. "An Approach to Measuring the Quality of Life Concept." Washington, D.C.: The Environmental Protection Agency, 1973, pp. 11–17.

Moneypenny, William F. *The Life of Benjamin Disraeli.* New York: Macmillan Company, 1910, Vol. 1, p. 374.

Montefiore, Claude. *A Rabbinic Anthology.* New York: Meridian Books, 1960.

More, Sir Thomas. *Utopia.* Edited by Robert M. Adams. New York: W. W. Norton, 1975.

Morris, Richard, ed. *The Prick of Conscience.* Berlin: The Philological Society, 1863, p. 94.

Morris, Robert. "Alternative Forms of Care for the Disabled." In *Developmental Disabilities: Psychological and Social Implications.* New York: Alan Liss, 1976.

———— "Diffusion of Innovation." Mimeo unpublished report of a study to the National Science Foundation, Washington, D.C., at Waltham, Brandeis University, Levinson Policy Institute, 1976.

———— "The Elderly as Surplus People: Is There a Role for Higher Education?" *The Gerontologist.* Washington, D.C.: The Gerontological Society of America, forthcoming, Fall 1985.

———— *Social Policy of the American Welfare State.* New York: Longman Inc., 1984.

Morrison, Robert. "A Note on Visions." In *Daedalus,* Winter Edition, 1980.

Mosteller, Frederick. "Innovation and Evaluation." In *Science,* Vol. 211, February 27, 1981.

Mott, Paul. *The Development of Title XX: Meeting Human Needs: The Social and Political History of Title XX.* Washington, D.C.: National Conference on Social Welfare, 1976.

Munro, D. C. *Translations and Reprints from Original Sources of European History.* New York: Longmans Green, 1923, Vol. 6, No. 5, pp. 16–17, 19.

Murray, Charles. *Losing Ground: American Social Policy, 1950–1980.* New York: Basic Books, 1984.

Myrdal, Gunnar. *The American Dilemma.* New York: Harper & Row, 1962.

Narveson, Jan. "Aesthetics, Charity, Utility & Distributive Justice." In *The Monast* 56, 1962, pp. 527–551.

Nash, Gary B. "Poverty & Poor Relief in Pre-Revolutionary Philadelphia." *William & Mary Quarterly,* January 1976, pp. 9–10.

———— "Urban Wealth & Poverty in Pre-Revolutionary America." *Journal of Interdisciplinary Science,* Vol. 1, No. 4, Spring 1976, pp. 556, 559–560.

National Association for Public Health Policy. "A National Health Program for the United States." South Burlington, VT, 1984.

New York Times. Sunday, August 26, 1979. Report of a 1976 study sponsored by the California Division of the American Cancer Society.

New York Times. "Increase in Government Confidence Appears in Post-Election Attitude Poll." *New York Times,* November 19, 1984, p. 1.

Newacheck, Paul, P. Budetti, and P. McManus. "Trends in Childhood Disability."

American Journal of Public Health, March 1984, Vol. 74, No. 3, pp. 232–236.

Nicene and Post-Nicene Fathers, A Select Library of. *St. Ambrose on the Duties of the Clergy.* (De Officiis), 2d Series, Vol. 10, pp. 54–55; Book 2, Chapters 15–16. P. Schaff, ed. Select Library of Nicene and Post-Nicene Fathers. New York: Scribner, 1900. Photolithoprinted 1956.

_____ *St. John Chrysostom.* Homilies in Timothy Homily XI, p. 443; and Homily on the Statutes to the people at Antioch, Vol. 13, p. 443, New York, 1894. See P. Schaff, ed. Christian Literature Company, quotations as excerpted by DeSchweinitz, *op. cit.,* Part III, Chapter 1.

_____ *St. Gregory, the Book of Pastoral Rules,* 2d series, Vol. 12, p. 45.

Nichols, Sir George. *A History of the English Poor Law.* London, 1898, Vol. 2, p. 466.

Nisbet, Robert. "The New Despotism." In *Commentary,* June 1975. Also see *Social Change and History.* New York: Oxford University Press, 1969.

Nozick, Robert. *Anarchy, State and Utopia.* New York: Basic Books, 1974.

Oaks, Whitney. *Basic Writings of St. Augustine.* New York: Random House, 1948, Vol. 2, p. 604.

Odyssey of Homer, ed. E. V. Riev. London: Penguin Classics, 1946.

O'Malley, Padraig. "Lost: The Public's Confidence." In *Boston Globe,* November 1, 1981, op-ed page.

O'Meara, Kathleen. *Frederic Ozanam, His Life and Works.* Edinburgh, 1876, p. 103.

Orlans, Harold, ed. *Human Services Co-ordination.* New York: Pica Press, 1982.

Owen, David. *A Future That Will Work.* New York: Viking Penguin, 1984.

Pease, Otis. *The Progressive Years.* New York: George Braziller, 1962.

Pechman, Joseph, and M. P. Timpane. *Work Incentives and Income Guarantees: The N.J. Negative Income Tax Experiment.* Washington, D.C.: Brookings Institution, 1975.

Pemberton, Alec. "Marxism & Social Policy." In *Journal of Social Policy.* Cambridge: Cambridge University Press, Vol. 12, Part 3, pp. 289–307, July 1983.

Plant, Raymond, Harry Lesser, and Peter Taylor-Gooby. *Political Philosophy of Social Welfare.* London and Boston: Routledge & Kegan Paul, 1980, Chapter 3, pp. 37–51.

Porter, Curt, and Arnold Johnson, eds. *National Party Platforms.* Urbana, IL: University of Illinois Press, 1956, pp. 189–190.

Prentice, William Kelly. *The Ancient Greeks.* Princeton: Princeton University Press, 1940.

President's Commission for the Study of Ethical Problems in Medical Care. Washington, D.C.: U.S. Government Printing Office, 1983.

Pritchard, James B., ed. *Ancient Near East Texts.* Princeton: Princeton University Press, 1955, pp. 4–13, 34, 409.

Pullan, B. "Catholicism and the Poor in Early Modern Europe." *Transactions of the Royal Historical Society,* 26, 5th Series, 1976, pp. 15–34.

Pusey, P. E. Homilies of St. John Chrysostom in *Fathers of the Holy Catholic Church Anterior to the Division,* Homily XI, London: Oxford, 1854, pp. 144–149.

Radke-Yarrow, Marion, and C. Vahn Wexler. Paper delivered at the Biennial meeting of the Society for Research in Child Development, New Orleans, 1977. See also Martin Hoffman, "Is Altruism a Part of Human Nature?" *Journal of personality and Social Psychology,* 1981, Vol. 40, No. 1, p. 121.

Raffaele, Tim. "Morality & Making Policy." *New York Times,* op-ed page, May 22, 1981.

Rawls, John. *A Theory of Justice.* Cambridge, MA: Harvard University Press, 1971.

Reagan, Ronald. Acceptance Speech, Republican Presidential Nomination at Detroit, 1980.

Rein, Mildred. *Dilemmas of Welfare Policy: Why Work Strategies Haven't Worked.* New York: Praeger Publishers, 1982.

Report on the Poor Law Commissioners. First Annual Report, London, 1835, pp. 43, 62, 96–97, 190.

———— Report on the Continuance of the Poor Law. London, 1840, pp. 45–46.

Rice, Dorothy P., and Jacob Feldman. "Living Longer in the U.S.: Demographic Changes and Health Needs of the Elderly." In *Milbank Memorial Fund Quarterly,* Summer 1983, Vol. 61, No. 3, pp. 362–396.

Riev, E. V. *The Odyssey of Homer.* London: Penguin Classics, 1946.

Riis, Jacob A. *How the Other Half Lives,* Sam B. Warner, Jr., ed. Cambridge, MA: Belknap Press, 1970. Also: *The Battle of the Slum.* New York: Macmillan, 1902.

Rimlinger, Gaston. *Welfare Policy & Industrialization in Europe, America, and Russia.* New York: Wiley, 1971.

Rivlin, Alice. "Helping the Poor" in *Economic Choices 1984,* Rivlin, ed. Washington, D.C.: The Brookings Institution, 1984.

Robertson, A. J. *The Laws of the Kings of England from Edward to Henry I.* Cambridge: Cambridge University Press, 1925, p. 121.

Rosenhau, D. L., P. Solvay, and K. Hargis. "The Joys of Helping" in *Journal of Personality and Social Psychology,* May 1981, Vol. 40, pp. 899–905.

Rotha, Mary Clay. *The Medieval Hospitals of England.* London: Methuen and Company, 1909, p. 24.

Rothman, David. *Discovery of Asylum.* Boston: Little, Brown, 1971.

———— *Doing Good: The Limits of Benevolence.* New York: Pantheon Books, 1978.

Russell, Bertrand. "On Moral Standards and Social Well Being." In *Collected Papers.* New York: Modern Library, 1927, p. 265.

Salisbury, John of. *Policraticus.* Stateman's Book of John Salisbury. Trans. by John Dickenson. New York: Knopf, 1927, p. 244.

Salter, Frank R. *Some Early Tracts on Poor Relief.* London: Methuen and Company, 1926, pp. 97–103.

Sanger, Mary Bryna. "Generating Employment for AFDC Mothers." In *Social Service Review,* March 1984, Vol. 38, No. 1, pp. 28–47.

Sarna, Nahum. *Understanding Genesis.* New York: Schocken Books, 1966, p. 158.

Schaff, P., ed. See Select Library of Nicene and Post-Nicene Fathers.

Schaller. *Une Aspecte de Nouveau Courrant Sociale.* Neuchatel: Edition de la Boconniere, 1850, p. 41.

Schiltz, M. E. *Public Attitudes to Social Security 1935 to 1965.* Washington, D.C.: U.S. Government Printing Office, 1970.

Schlesinger, Arthur M. *The Politics of Upheaval.* Boston: Houghton Mifflin, 1960.

Schneider, David. *The History of Public Welfare in New York State.* Chicago: University of Chicago Press, 1938.

Schorr, Alvin. "Social Policy and the Poor: Divided Allies." In *Public Welfare,* 1980, p. 37.

Schwanse, Peter. "European Experience." In R. H. Haveman, *Jobs for Disadvantaged Workers.* Washington, D.C.: Brookings Institution, 1982.

Senate of the State of New York. Journal of 47th Session, January 1824, pp. 95–108, Appendix A, pp. 1–154.

Senior, Nassau. In *Edinburgh Review,* October 1841, Reprinted in *Historical and Political Essays,* London, 1865.

Sennett, Richard. *Authority.* New York: Knopf, 1980.

Sheps, Cecil, and Irving Lewis. *The Sick Citadel.* Cambridge, MA: Oelgeschlager, Gunn and Hain, 1983.

Sherraden, Michael. "Youth Employment & Education: Federal Programs from the New Deal through the 1970s." In *Children & Youth Services Review,* 1980, Vol. 2, pp. 17–39. Also: *National Service.* New York: Pergamon Press, 1982.

——— "Chronic Unemployment: A Social Work Perspective." Unpublished manuscript. St. Louis, MO: Washington University, August 1983. Also: "Employment Policy and Labor Market Reality." Unpublished manuscript, delivered at the 110th Annual Forum, National Conference on Social Welfare, Houston, May 1983.

Shimoda, Harvo. "Employment Effects of Incremental Employment Subsidies." *Japan Labor Bulletin,* February 1981, pp. 5–8.

Shonfield, Andrew. *Modern Capitalism.* New York and London: Oxford University Press, 1965, Chapter XIII, pp. 298–329.

Shurtleff, Nathaniel, ed. *Records of the Governor and Company of the Massachusetts Bay, Boston.* 1854. Vol. 4, p. 365.

Silk, Leonard. "The Economic System." *New York Times,* August 8, 1984, p. 2. Citing work by Clopper Almon, University of Maryland.

Society for the Prevention of Pauperism. In the City of New York. *1st Annual Report of the Managers.* New York, 1818, pp. 12–24.

Sorokin, Pitrim. *Forms and Techniques of Altruistic and Spiritual Growth.* Boston: Beacon Press, 1954.

Spence, Harry Lewis. "Creating an Underclass." *Boston Globe,* April 11, 1981, p. 10.

Spencer, Herbert. *Social Statics.* New York, 1886, p. 342.

Spengler, J. J. "French Population Since 1800." *Journal of Political Economy,* Vol. XLIV, October 1936, p. 585.

Springborg, Patricia. *The Problem of Human Needs and the Critique of Civilization.* London: Allen & Unwin, 1981.

Starr, Paul. *The Social Transformation of American Medicine.* New York: Basic Books, 1982.

Statistical Abstract of the United States. U.S. Department of Commerce, 1974, p. 28.

Statistical Abstract of the United States, 1982–1983. Washington, D.C.: U.S. Government Printing Office. Tables 417, 554, 732: In 1982, the average AFDC family grant was $288 a month; the highest was $371 in New York for an annual income of $4,452. In that year, the poverty level for a female headed family of three was $6,386. For the total population, 9.6% lived below the poverty level.

Statistical Abstract of the United States; Bureau of the Census. Washington, D.C.: U.S. Government Printing Office, 1984. These disparities also reflect difference in state economic resources, but not accurately. In the 20 years since 1960, southern states once poor, like Louisiana and Texas, became well off and northern states, once wealthy, have suffered economic losses.

Statutes at Large of Pennsylvania. Vol. 8, Chapter DCXXV, pp. 76–96.

Steiner, Gilbert. *The State of Welfare.* Washington, D.C.: Brookings Institution, 1971, pp. 239–240.

Stephens, W. R. W. *St. Chrysostom.* London, 1872, p. 238.

Stevenson, Olive. *Claimant or Client.* London: Allen & Unwin, 1973.

Taylor-Gooby, Peter. "Public Attitudes to Welfare." *London Social Science Research Council Newsletter* 50, November 1, 1983, p. 151.

Thompson, E. P. *The Making of the English Working Class.* Harmondsworth, England: Penguin Books, 1968.

Thurow, Lester. *The Zero-Sum Society.* New York: Basic Books, 1980. Also: *Dangerous Currents.* New York: Random House, 1983.

——— "A Fading Middle Class." *Boston Globe,* August 28, 1984, p. 56.

Tierney, Brian. *Medieval Poor Law.* Berkeley, CA: University of California Press, 1959, Chapter 1.

Titmus, Richard. *Social Policy.* London: Allen & Unwin, 1974.

Townsend, Joseph. "A Dissertation on the Poor Laws by a Well Wisher to Mankind." London: Commercial Pamphlets, 1886, Vol. 7, pp. 400–449.

Tuckerman, Joseph. *The Principles and Results of the Minority at Large in Boston.* Boston, 1838, pp. 85, 88.

Twersky, Isador. *Introduction to the Code of Maimonides.* New Haven, CT: Yale University Press, 1980.

Ulhorn, Gerhart, Abbot of Locum. *Christian Charity in the Ancient Church.* New York: Charles Scribner & Sons, 1883.

United States Census. *Current Population Reports: Consumers Income.* P. 60, No. 105, pp. 61–177.

Vincent, E. R. P. Translation of Niccolo Machiavelli, *The Prince.* London: Oxford University Press, 1935, p. 48.

Vives, Juan Luis. *Concerning the Relief of the Poor.* Translated by Margaret Sherwood. New York: New York School of Philanthropy (Now Columbia University School of Social Work), 1917, p. 6.

Von Wright, G. H. "The Good of Man." In *Talking About Welfare.* Noel Timms and David Watson, eds. London and Boston: International Library of Welfare and Philosophy, Routledge & Kegan Paul, 1976.

Wall Street Journal. "Machines Blamed in Europe Joblessness." *Wall Street Journal,* November 19, 1984, p. 1.

Walzer, Michael. *Spheres of Justice: A Defense of Pluralism and Equality.* New York: Basic Books, 1983.

Watson, David. *Caring for Strangers*. New York and London: Routledge & Kegan Paul, 1980.

Webb, E. A. *Translation of the Book of the Foundation of the Church of St. Bartholomew*. London: Humphrey Milford, Oxford University Press, 1923, pp. 7–8.

Wildavsky, Aaron. "Richer is Better." *The Public Interest,* No. 60, Summer 1980.

Wilensky, Harold. *The Welfare State and Equality*. Berkeley, CA: University of California Press, 1975. Also: *Industrial Society and Social Welfare* (with Charles Lebaux). New York: The Free Press, 1965.

Will, George. The Godkin Lecture, John F. Kennedy School of Government, Harvard University, 1979.

Wills, Gary. *Inventing America*. New York: Vintage Books, 1979.

Wilson, Dorothy. "The Swedish Dream Grows Tired." *New Society,* December 6, 1979, p. 544. Citing *Current Economic Trends,* December 1977, p. 290.

Wilson, E. O. *Sociobiology*. Cambridge, MA: Harvard University Press, 1975, Chapter 5.

Wilson, John A. *The Burden of Egypt*. Chicago: University of Chicago Press, 1951, p. 48.

Witte, Edwin. *Development of the Social Security Act*. Madison, WI: University of Wisconsin Press, 1962.

Wulfstin. Sermon of the Wulf to the English. EDH Vol. 1, p. 586. See Hadden, A. W., *op. cit.*

INDEX